D1529198

# GIFTS FOR GOOD CHILDREN

For my own good children
Alice, Polly and Beatrice

'FOR A GOOD GIRL'. A creamware alphabet mug,
printed and painted, and with a copper lustre rim,
circa 1800.
*Private Collection.*

# GIFTS FOR GOOD CHILDREN

# THE HISTORY OF CHILDREN'S CHINA

## PART 1

## 1790~1890

NOËL RILEY

Published by

RICHARD DENNIS
The Old Chapel, Shepton Beauchamp,
Ilminster, Somerset TA19 0LE.

Photography by
Michael Stannard Photographic Studio
John Morley Photography
Colin Jeffrey Associates
Paul Taylor Photography

Print & Origination
Flaydemouse, Yeovil, Somerset.

Production
Wendy Wort

Published in 1991 by
Richard Dennis
The Old Chapel, Shepton Beauchamp,
Ilminster, Somerset TA19 0LE, England.

© 1991 Noël Riley, Richard Dennis

ISBN 0 903685 29 9

A catalogue record for this book is available from the British Library

*front cover:*
Children's pottery mugs printed in monochrome on canary yellow grounds,
two with silver lustre borders, circa 1810.

*back cover:*
Children's plates with monochrome prints taken from *The School-boy* by
William Upton (Darton 1820). Probably James & Ralph Clews of Cobridge,
circa 1820 (see page 114). The plate (bottom left) 'HE RETURNS', is the
fourth recorded in this series with the implication that all six illustrations
from *The School-boy* were reproduced in this series of plates.

# ACKNOWLEDGEMENTS

Books like this only happen through the efforts and know-ledge of lots of people. In my attempt to draw together different threads of expertise I have enjoyed the enthusiasm, support and guidance of collectors, museum staff, librarians, dealers and fellow authors. The outstanding pleasure of my researches has been the opportunity to meet so many kind specialists, particularly in children's book illustration and in ceramics, who have given unstinting encouragement and in some cases much of their precious time to help me. I am particularly grateful to the following: Norman Blackburn, Donald and Rosalind Blagden, Tessa Chester, Lawrence Darton, Nick Dolan, Faith Eaton, Andrew Edmunds, Margaret Fuller, Geoffrey Godden, Robin Gurnett, Tim Holdaway, Lionel Lambourne, Griselda and John Lewis, Caroline Lister, Steven Moore, Iona Opie, Carol and Robert Pugh, Cathy Ross, George Rylands CH., Litt.D., Robert Scott, Ian Sharp, Peter Stockham of Images, and David Temperley.

Of the many others who have taken the trouble to decipher pages of murky photocopied images and to answer questions, or to ply me with valuable suggestions and contacts, the following deserve special thanks: Elizabeth Adams, Paul Atterbury, Michael Ball, Maureen Batkin, Clarice Blakey, John Blundall, Patricia Carter, Alwyn and Angela Cox, Marilyn Cranshaw, Peter Day, David Drakard, Rodney Engen, Hilary Evans and the staff of the Mary Evans Picture Library, Mr Fish of London Zoo, Rodney Hampson, Michael Heseltine of Sotheby's, D. W. Hopkin of the National Railway Museum, Clifford (Doggie) Hubbard, Sally Kevill-Davies, David Knott, Roger Lee, Terence Lockett, Jeremy Maas, John May, Anthony Oliver, the R.N.I.D., Holger Scheick, Mrs. Varty, Jonathan Voak, Pamela Williams, John Worthy and John Yule.

A big thank you goes to Audrey Atterbury, ever ready to dig out information on almost any subject, and a steady supplier of invaluable contacts; to Michael Stannard our long-suffering photographer, and to Wendy Wort, head of the production team, who can be relied upon to pull everything together with cheerful efficiency.

The heroism of my husband, Peter Owen, must not go unsung: he has provided the essential home back-up for innumerable excursions as well as cheerfully sharing his wife with 1384 plates and 256 mugs for over a year.

Finally, I am deeply grateful to Richard Dennis whose project this is: his unique blend of patience, generosity and reckless enthusiasm have been a constant encouragement.

A child's mug in use: an illustration from *The Prize*, March 1884. Courtesy of Peter Stockham, Images, The Staffs Bookshop, Lichfield.

# CONTENTS

## How to use this Book

We decided to divide our illustrations into subject areas according to the printed illustrations on the plates and mugs. The rarity of marks made factory divisions a non-starter, while categorising according to border patterns would have emphasised them at the expense of the transfer print which were our chief interest. We are well aware of the disadvantages of our decision. One is that sets, and even the fronts and backs of the same mugs, sometimes have had to be split; where this has happened I have provided cross-references as often as possible.

Another is the recurring difficulty of deciding on categories, as so many prints fall into more than one. The series of limerick illustrations from *Sixteen Wonderful Old Women* (page 180) for example, could have found a place with Children's Stories and Nursery Rhymes as well as among caricatures (where they are). Certain Occupations and Trades are also part of Country Life, and so are some of the Games and Pastimes. By no means all the animals are confined to Flora and Fauna; they also appear, at least in supporting roles, in almost every other chapter; Piety and Virtue permeate innumerable subjects throughout the book. The chapter headings therefore must be seen only as a way of breaking the illustrations into manageable groups and not as an attempt to categorise them definitively.

For the sake of clarity in the captions I have developed a descriptive formula for border mouldings, which I hope will make for easy recognition as well as helping to link commonly recurring patterns across chapter boundaries. The borders I have described as 'rose, tulip and aster', 'vitruvian scroll and alphabet', 'dog, fox and monkey' are typical examples. 'Blobbed daisy' or 'dimpled floret' borders might sound eccentric, but such descriptions should highlight the diversity of interpretation of the well-known daisy border.

In case my descriptions of edges are not self-evident, a wavy edge is an edge with equal curves all round it; an indented edge is one with sparse indentations; a rococo edge is one with a rhythmic pattern of indentations, and an erratic edge is one with irregular, uncontrolled, shaping. The 'same plate' means one with the same border and transfer print.

The illustrations of plates and mugs (on right-hand pages) are numbered from left to right, starting at the top of each page, and all examples are from Richard Dennis's collection unless stated otherwise. Reproductions of sources relating to the transfer prints are on left-hand pages, as near as possible to the appropriate captions. Numbers in the captions refer to figure numbers, except where page numbers are indicated. An asterisk beside a figure number indicates that this example or one closely similar is also shown in colour. The captions to the colour plates will be found on pages 92 and 105. Where a factory is mentioned more than once on the same page, I have given full details only the first time. Diameters of plates are measured across the top surface at the widest point, while for the mugs I have given the height and the diameter across the base. In all cases I have done my best to record inscriptions and identifying marks exactly as they appear.

# INTRODUCTION

Richard Dennis's formidable assembly of children's wares – 1400 plates and 250 mugs – offers a rare chance to study a popular but relatively uncharted area of ceramic history. Our objective has been to collate as much existing information as possible about children's plates and mugs, particularly with regard to their social background, and to discover the sources and inspiration for their printed designs. Merely cataloguing such an array has been a considerable labour and researching the design sources is clearly an almost limitless project. While we have unearthed little new information about the factories that produced children's wares, we have been relatively successful in finding source material for the prints: the score presently stands at over 200.

The recording and illustration of a large number of examples, not only from Richard Dennis's but from private collections as well, is designed to provide a useful basis for further research. Such a book as this is bound to raise as many questions as it answers, and perhaps that is as good a reason as any for publishing it.

The earliest documented child's mug is probably the tin-glazed example dated 1752 from the Fitzwilliam Museum that we illustrate here. Many of the 'trifles' of succeeding decades were probably given to children, and small mugs exist which may have been for children's use, but few, if any, are documented. China made specifically for children before the end of the 18th century has not survived in significant quantity, and it is unlikely that much was ever made. The early 19th century surge in book production for children coincided with suitable developments in the ceramics industry, and for the first time children came into their own as a marketing target. We have therefore chosen this period as a starting point for our study of children's wares.

Exactly what is, and what is not, a child's plate is a question we have constantly asked ourselves. Many children's plates have moulded borders, yet it is clear that not all moulded-bordered plates were designed exclusively for children. Commemorative mugs and plates were (and are) often given to children, but this does not make them specifically children's wares.

Probably the earliest known documented child's mug: a Liverpool delftware example painted in blue with a father holding his daughter's hand and inscribed 'MARY TURNER AGED 2 YEARS 14 DAYS SEPt. 2 1752. ● 5 ins. ht.
*Courtesy of the Fitzwilliam Museum, Cambridge.*

*Is this a children's plate? The rose, honeysuckle and swagged garland border painted in a predmoinantly iron red palette is common to many plates with more obviously child-oriented transfer-prints. The bare-breasted goddess in her chariot (probably Venus), pulled over the clouds by two doves has been traced to the *Ladies' Amusement* by Jean Pillement (1762). ● Mark: O impressed and ♉ painted ● 6 ins. diam.
Probably Baker, Bevans & Irwin, Glamorgan Pottery, Swansea 1813–1838.

Examples of miniature children's pottery used for play, first half 19th century. Diameter of plate with pony 3 ins.

We have come to the conclusion that there cannot be a cut and dried answer. While it would be reasonable to suggest that plates with moulded alphabet borders, transfer prints from children's book illustrations or mugs and plates with individual names inscribed on them were made especially for children, many more may have been aimed at a wider market that embraced both children and adults. Temperance movement subjects as well as commemoratives come into this category and so, probably, do the Robert Burns verses and many of the caricatures. Plates with freehand painting like the lustred houses on page 139 and those decorated with flowers and chinoiseries are likely to have been intended for general ornament.

Toy plates and cockles (for serving shellfish on market stalls) have found a place in this book, if only a small one, on the basis

A toy dinner service of creamware, decorated with manganese prints after Adam Buck; similar designs are to be found on larger children's wares of the 1815–1825 period. *Private Collection*

Two large jugs decorated all over with transfer prints, many of which are also to be seen on children's plates.

that their decoration is often the same or similar to that on larger children's wares.

Contemporary nomenclature is none too clear. An 1846 price list includes 8 in. 'Twifler plates', and 'Muffin plates' of 7 in., 6 in., 5 in., 4 in. and 3 in. The latter were probably children's plates and they varied in price according to size. 'Fancy shapes' that is, presumably, moulded borders such as alphabets or daisies, cost extra and so did printed or 'Common Painted' designs. For example a dozen printed or painted 5 in. plates would cost 2s. from the manufacturer, or 2d. each, while a dozen plain 'cream' 3 in. plates would be 6d., or ½d. each. As late as 1895 the Longton firm of H. Aynsley & Co. were advertising 'ABC, muffins and toyware' among their new wares (*Pottery Trade Gazette*, April 1895).

How far these wares were intended for actual use is another question. Moulded bordered plates must have had a limited practical function, especially among children, and we suggest that most of them were probably ornamental. The mugs on the other hand seem more likely to have been used, if only for 'best', and this may account for their relatively low survival rate.

All the plates and the majority of the mugs we have studied are of earthenware: we have excepted a handful of bone china mugs as representatives of the social habit of giving a mug inscribed with a child's name on its baptism. Such christening mugs were usually of more expensive materials – silver or porcelain – than the general run of named children's mugs.

Another type of christening or possibly Easter present, the inscribed pottery egg, is not included in this book, but it is worth mentioning that these relatively rare survivals, mainly products of the Tyneside and Wearside potteries, often have the same or similar transfer-printed pictures or inscriptions as plates and mugs. Examples showing N for Newsboy (622) and T for Train (574) from *The Mother's Picture Alphabet* have been recorded.

Jugs and other useful wares are also to be found decorated with many of the prints recorded here. Notable examples are large mid-19th century jugs covered in scrap-like transfers which include pictures from the Frolics of Youth series and animal subjects (see pages 49 and 191).

Few areas of ceramic study can be more varied or more confusing than the one under scrutiny here. Practically all the major potteries operating during the 19th century as well as a host of minor and often anonymous ones produced children's wares. We have identified products from more than 60 factories, but far more than this were undoubtedly making earthenwares for children at one time or another during the 19th century. Very few pieces are marked, and the same border patterns and engraved designs appear on plates made as far apart as Sunderland and Swansea or Burslem and Bovey Tracey. Buying, borrowing and even stealing of designs is evident, while copying went on indiscriminately.

What may seem surprising is the almost total absence of overlap with other areas of cheap 19th century ceramics, notably Staffordshire figures and blue and white transfer-printed earthen-

*Colour Plate 1*

X     XI     XII     XIII     XIV     XV     XVI     XVII     XVIII

*Colour Plate 2*

wares. Even when similar subjects have been chosen, such as sporting scenes, the producers of blue and white wares invariably used different source illustrations from those making moulded-bordered plates. Similarly, Staffordshire portrait figures of famous individuals such as John Wesley or the Duke of Wellington tend not to correspond with the images of them used on children's plates. Of the very few Staffordshire figure subjects that have been identified closely with transfer prints on plates, one (My Brother, 92, 93 and 94) has an unidentified source, and two others (The Defender and The Deliverer 1224 and 1225) represent souvenirs of the Great Exhibition. We have found only one plate whose print corresponds with that of a colour-printed pot lid (502).

Creamware mug with turned bands and a loop handle, inscribed 'Nursery'. • Mark: WEDGWOOD impressed • 2⅝ ins. ht.; 3⅝ ins. diam.
This is one of the few known items of early children's ware made by Wedgwood; it probably dates from circa 1800.

Another rare example of a marked piece from a major factory, in this case, Minton: a toy plate with erratic edge and unmoulded border decorated with green printed stylised flower patterns, and a green print of a child playing with a St. Bernard dog and two puppies. • Mark: BB (for Best Body) New Stone and the year mark for 1854 • 5 ins. diam.

## TECHNIQUES AND MATERIALS

Although we are dealing almost entirely with earthenwares, their quality of potting and decoration varied enormously. This is to be expected in a century span which starts in the period when decorated pottery was still a luxury available only to the wealthy and ends when developments in mass-production enabled cheap ceramics to find a place in the homes of the working classes.

The wares themselves reflect this. In the early part of our period, delicately potted creamwares and pearlwares, some with canary yellow glazes, were decorated with fine transfers of scenes in which the children were handsomely dressed and paraded expensive possessions such as ponies, rocking horses, watches and dolls, while servants are sometimes in evidence. The earliest mugs tend to have only one printed illustration, while after about 1830 most have a transfer on each side. Towards mid-century the amusements depicted become more universal: dressing up, playing with pets, and sports are among the favourite subjects on increasingly robust wares. During the second half of the century moulds may be far from crisp, transfers inaccurate and overpainting on them distinctly clumsy: these pieces were obviously produced in bulk for a constantly widening market.

The method of transferring a print from an engraved copper plate to the unglazed earthenware surface remained roughly the same throughout our period. Oil-bound colour was worked into the engraved lines on the heated copper plate and any excess colour was wiped off before a sheet of damp tissue paper was laid on it and it was put through a press. The resulting 'pull' was removed from the plate, again by gently heating it, and cut to the right shape before being applied to the ceramic surface and rubbed to make sure the colour adhered evenly. The piece would then be dipped in water to remove the tissue paper and fired at a low temperature to fix the colour. Finally it would be glazed and fired again.

While fine enamel painting or gilding occurs on a few of the porcelain mugs, and a small sampling of plates are decorated with freehand lustred designs, the vast majority are embellished with transfer prints in black and other colours. A great many have painting applied on top of the underglaze prints, clearly to add a splash of colour to what childish eyes might have found a monotonous picture in black, brown, green, purple or red. Splashes they often were, too; it is known that children were frequently employed to carry out this colouring work, just as they were in the production of picture books during the first half of the 19th century. Several children, each wielding a brush loaded with a different colour, probably added their dashes and blobs as the plates passed along the line. Blue transfer prints were hardly ever overpainted in this way.

Another method of jollying up the monochrome printed wares was to add colour to the moulded borders. Judging by the differences in quality of this type of decoration, some was done by competent adults (as in the Swansea examples) while much was also daubed in by child labour.

Children's plates provide some of the first successful examples of printing in colours: the firm of William Smith of Stockton-on-Tees evidently employed a colour printer of great competence at a time when Jesse Austin was still perfecting his technique at the factory of F. & R. Pratt of Fenton. Among the productions of this as yet anonymous craftsman were the series of Pastimes, printed in four colours and each conveniently impressed with Smith's pre-1848 mark (see page 68). This was not Smith's only claim to market pre-eminence: he seems to have led the field in the export of children's plates, especially to Germany and Holland, and in 1847 he became a partner in the Belgian firm of Cappellemans at Jemappes.

The kinds of all-purpose illustrations known as stock-blocks were probably as often kept by printers for the ceramics industry as by the suppliers of printed ephemera and packaging. The development of the electrotype in the middle of the 19th century allowed many copper plates to be produced from a single engraved wood block and this must have greatly encouraged the use of stock blocks for children's wares as well as multiplying the production of different images generally. The mugs and plates printed with two children holding a banner with a varying inscription is an obvious example (see page 249). In this case the wood block engraved with the two children would have a blank space in the middle for inserting different sayings, thus giving more flexibility to the subsequent copper-plate image.

## REVERSAL OF TRANSFERS

In some cases a transfer print on a plate or mug may appear reversed when compared with its original source or with examples from other factories. There are at least two possible explanations for this. First, the design may have been poached from a potter's collection of transfer pulls. These prints on tissue paper taken from the engraved copper plates were kept as records as well as being part of the normal transfer-printing process, and on them the image appeared reversed (if it was then applied to a ceramic surface it would be reversed again and therefore appear the 'right' way round). Occasionally a pottery decorator would move to a new factory, taking with him designs from his former employer in pull form. When re-engraved onto a copper plate this image would naturally be copied in its reversed form.

Secondly, engravers for books, when re-using an existing illustration, often copied the image as it appeared on the printed page, rather than on the copper plate or wood block: because printing is a reverse process this meant that the image would then appear in reverse in subsequent printings.

## PRODUCTION AND MARKETING

One of the reasons why so few children's wares are marked is that, at least from mid-century, most represented the cheapest end of the domestic ceramic market. On the whole they are not wares that the factories were particularly proud to produce or to acknowledge by marking, and the added expense of stamping was rarely deemed justifiable. In addition they may have had good reason, such as the infringement of copyright, to keep their wares anonymous. It is significant that the producers of some of the best quality pieces, such as Clews, Davenport and William Smith, were among the few in the habit of marking at least some of them.

While some factories are known to have employed their own engravers, most, particularly in Staffordshire, made use of copper plates supplied by specialist firms. Hanley and Shelton in the Potteries were traditional centres for engraver's studios. Pottery factories would also buy or exchange copper plates from one another, or purchase the stock (including copper plates and moulds) of failing firms. Potteries with their own engravers would also supplement their designs with bought-in or exchanged

*Colour Plate 3*

XXXI

XXXII

XXXIII

XXXIV

XXXV

XXXVI

Cock

XXXVII

XL

XXXIX

XLI

XLII

*Colour Plate 4*

15

copper plates. This explains the deteriorating definition of some (overworked) moulds and transfers towards the end of the 19th century, and it is also the reason why one can rarely attribute a piece to any factory on the sole basis of a border mould or transfer print.

Once produced, it is likely that children's wares were sold by the same methods as other inexpensive ceramics. Few would have made the grade into china shops or retailers' showrooms; instead they would have been carried in the panniers of pack-horses and donkeys and sold by itinerant salesmen from door-to-door, in local markets and fairs, and in public houses.

The figure of the pot-seller on a Swansea plate (618) represents another type of salesman who, too poor to own a horse or donkey, carried his pots in a large wicker basket on his own back. Such 'poor crate-men' were familiar figures in the 18th century and were still to be seen hawking their wares in Mayhew's London.

Categories such as commemoratives and souvenirs were usually sold from stalls or booths in appropriate places, just as they are today. It is thought that Staffordshire theatrical figures were sold outside the London theatres, for example, and there is no reason to doubt that plates and mugs representing attractions like Paul Pry, Jim Crow and negro minstrel groups were sold in the same way. Most of the temperance, Band of Hope and Sunday school subjects were probably given as prizes within particular groups and associations.

## CHILD LABOUR

The employment of children as young as six, seven and eight years old in the potteries has been all too well documented: in looking at this array of wares intended *for* children, we should pause to consider how much of their production was *by* children. I have already mentioned the employment of children in painting, either to add colour to borders or to fill in the transfers, but many were also involved in the actual production of the pottery, with all the risks to their health and development that this entailed.

Philanthropists' campaigns to improve the lot of child workers were slow to take effect in the potteries, and throughout the middle decades of the 19th century children – boys and girls under thirteen – were used ruthlessly as cheap labour. Their jobs included lighting fires first thing in the morning, wedging clay (to bash out the air bubbles), mould-running (carrying moulds both empty and filled between the craftsmen's benches and the 'stoves' or heated rooms where they were dried), jigger-turning (working the plate-making machines), and assisting the dippers, printers and potters. They were paid between 3s. 6d. and 6s. for a six-day week, working for at least nine hours a day and sometimes as many as sixteen.

## SOURCES

Few of the engravers working for the ceramic industry produced their own designs for transfer prints. Their habit was to copy from books, periodicals and popular prints with just enough variation from the original to escape accusations of infringing copyright. Copyright laws had existed since Hogarth's day, but they did little to deter most of the engravers who either added or subtracted details of a design to evade them, or else treated them with brazen disregard. In any case, children's china was probably of too humble a nature to warrant litigation, and much is likely to have been as anonymous and untraceable then as now: perhaps this was another reason why so few pieces are marked.

In the early decades of the 19th century children's book and picture sheet illustrations, in the form of copper-plate engravings, wood-blocks or, more rarely, lithographs, were the most usual source of ideas for the ceramic decorators. Picture sheets, printed on one side of the paper with six or more pictures with accompanying verses or short texts could be folded and cut to make a small picture book, pasted on wood and cut to make a jigsaw puzzle (or, in appropriate cases, figures and scenes for toy theatres), or cut out for scrap books and other decoration. They were sold plain sometimes to be coloured at home or, more expensively, hand coloured.

The publications of John Harris and William Darton (and many others, but these two dominated children's book publishing at the time) aimed their attractive volumes and sheets at the affluent and respectable middle classes, and their subjects were echoed time and time again on plates and mugs. The different 'My' series are notable examples (see Family Life).

Most of the early source illustrations in books or on picture sheets are by unknown artists. It was not until the 1860s that illustrators' names were generally acknowledged by publishers, and even then patchily; many anonymous sources have been found right up to the end of the 19th century. Engravers' names are even more sparse. This is not often the case with prints, rather then book illustrations, where artist, engraver and publisher may be acknowledged.

The overwhelming impression of the subject matter throughout the century is one of moral and educational fervour. In spite of encouragingly frequent lapses into humour, mischief or pure ornament, the majority of mugs and plates convey a message of approval for worthy behaviour, warnings against evil-doing and calls to Christian duty. In some, especially among the educational themes, propaganda and humour are cunningly combined.

The predominantly improving and didactic themes of the early 19th century sources are given a self-consciously sentimental flavour during the 1830s and 1840s with such subjects as *Now I'm Grandmother* and others in the Frolics of Youth series. By this time decorative prints as well as book illustrations were much favoured as source material for children's pottery.

The impetus given to toy-book production by developments in colour printing around mid-century seems to have impinged surprisingly little on the producers of children's ceramics. Instead they turned with enthusiasm to the wood-engraved illustrations in young people's periodicals, especially evangelical publications like *The Children's Friend* published by Partridge (whose editor, the Rev. Carus Wilson, happened to be vicar of Tunstall in the Potteries), *The Child's Companion* (Religious Tract Society) and *The Little Gleaner* (Houlston). *Peter Parley's Annual*, founded by the American Samuel Griswold Goodrich and published on both sides of the Atlantic from the 1840s to the 1860s was instructive rather than sermonising, and was an occasional source of ceramic illustration.

Among the transfers inspired by popular prints one might have expected to recognise sources in the colour prints of Baxter, le Blond or Kronheim: not a single example has been discovered. Another surprise has been the rarity of sources among contemporary oil paintings. Only one Landseer has been traced where I hoped for at least a handful, while Morland, Wilkie, Mulready, Frith,

Webster, Birket Foster and their ilk have not been found at all. In January 1890 the *Pottery Trade Gazette* recorded that Sir John Millais was often employed by leading firms to make designs for decorating china, but I have found no evidence on children's wares of the work of Britain's most popular painter.

A great surprise has been the choice of children's stories and verses. The poems of Isaac Watts and Ann Taylor abound, but nursery rhymes, which seem the most obviously suitable of all subjects, are rare: *Old Mother Hubbard, Hey Diddle Diddle, The House that Jack Built* and the *Story of Cock Robin* are the only ones represented in the collection, and not spectacularly at that.

Children's stories are distinctly sparse too. Tales like *Jack the Giant Killer, Puss in Boots, Dick Whittington, Gulliver's Travels* and the fairy stories of Grimm and Andersen which recur often in illustrated children's books of the period, are totally absent. *Cinderella* does not appear until the 1890s. Instead the field is strewn with *Robinson Crusoe, Paul and Virginia* and *Uncle Tom's Cabin*, besides a handful of scenes apparently from 19th century children's stories which have sunk into oblivion. Shakespeare is not to be seen, and Dickens in only one instance; Bunyan is distinctly rare.

The representation of stories from the Bible is just as uneven. The story of Joseph occurs frequently, and there are scenes from the Life of Christ; one rather gory rendering of David holding the bloody head of Goliath, a view of Elijah being fed by the ravens, an endearing Daniel bearding the lion in his den and illustrations of miscellaneous parables. Subjects one most expected, like Adam and Eve in the Garden of Eden, animals processing into Noah's Ark, or Moses in the bullrushes, do not appear at all.

One cannot help suspecting that the relatively large quantities of survivals among temperance, Band of Hope, Robinson Crusoe, Paul and Virginia, and the legions of other 'goody-goody' plates may be because they were simply less popular with children, and therefore less used and broken, than rhymes and nursery stories that were fun rather than moralistic. Who could possibly resist the comic *Dame Trot and her Cat* for example? We have found only one plate from a series that must have been a winner in its time.

XLIII

XLIV

XLV

XLVI

XLVII

XLVIII

XLIX

L

LI

*Colour Plate 5*

LII

LIII

LIV

LV

LVI

LVII

LVIII

LIX

LX

*Colour Plate 6*

# Chapter 1 GIFTS FOR GOOD CHILDREN

**1\*** Straight edge and flat border with painted garland in Pratt colours, and a sepia-printed vignette, carefully painted in Pratt colours, of two boys playing with hoops: 'A PRESENT FOR JOSEPH'. • Mark: a gouged semicircle; no footrim • 6¼ ins. diam.
Dixon Austin, Garrison Pottery, Sunderland, circa 1820–1826.

**2\*** Shape as 1 with painted garland border in Pratt colours and a black-printed vignette of a man driving a donkey: 'A PRESENT FOR CHRISTOPHER'. • Mark: DIXON AUSTIN & Co impressed, and a gouged semicircle; no footrim • 5½ ins. diam.
Dixon Austin.

**3** As 1 with a black print, carefully painted, of two foxes: 'A PRESENT FOR JAMES'. • No mark; no footrim • 6¼ ins. diam.
Dixon Austin.

**4\*** Straight edge and moulded vine garland border painted yellow, orange and green, with a blue print of two boys with hoops: 'A TRIFLE FOR SAMUEL'. • Mark: POUNTNEY & ALLIES in a semicircle above a cross, impressed • 6¼ ins. diam.
Pountney & Allies, Bristol Pottery, Temple Backs, Bristol, circa 1816–1835.

**5\*** Straight edge with crisply moulded dog, fox and monkey border painted in iron red, pale green, pink and dark brown, with a dark brown-printed vignette (painted) inscribed 'A Present for a Friend.' • No mark; double footrim • 7½ ins. diam.
Probably a Tyneside or Wearside pottery; examples with this border, marked Fell, have been found.

**6\*** As 3 with a black-printed vignette of a kilted man with a girl and a dog in a landscape: 'A PRESENT for JANE'. • Mark: DIXON, AUSTIN & Co impressed; no footrim • 6½ ins. diam.

**7** Straight edge painted blue with flat border printed with a chinoiserie pattern in sepia, and a sepia vignette of two girls with a doll in a garden: 'A PRESENT FOR A GOOD GIRL'. • Mark: an impressed asterisk • 6½ ins. diam.
Probably Cambrian Pottery, Swansea, circa 1820.

**8** Straight edge and flat border painted with iron red tulips and tendrils, purple berries and light green leaves with a black print (painted) of a boy with a dog: 'FOR MY DEAR BOY.' • No mark • 5½ ins. diam.
A similar print appears on a 5 ins. plate with an unpainted moulded border of animals and motifs as 5.

**9** Straight edge painted in sepia and plain border, and a blue print, painted in Pratt colours, of birds among reeds: 'A BROTHER'S PRESENT'. • No mark; no footrim • 6¼ ins. diam.
*Private Collection.*

Printed and painted plate. • No mark • 5⅜ ins. diam.
*Private Collection.*

**10*** Rococo edge and moulded border of florets and leaves in sections, painted red, blue, yellow and green, with a sepia-printed vignette inscribed 'A Present for my Dear Child'. • Mark: a vestigial crown, impressed; double footrim • 5¾ ins. diam.

**11** Straight edge with moulded garland border of leaves and florets, painted without regard for the moulding, in iron red, yellow and pale green, and a black print (painted) of children on a seesaw: 'EIN GESCHENCH FUR MEINEN LIEBEN JUNGEN' (a present for my dear child). • Mark: L impressed • 5¾ ins. diam.

**12** Blue wavy grooved edge with flat border and a sepia print of two children flanking the inscription, 'For attention to Learning.' • No mark • 5 ins. diam.

**13** Straight edge painted sepia and flat border, with a sepia print of a boy with a hoop and two children on a seesaw flanking the inscription: 'From an Affectionate Father'. • No mark • 6¼ ins. diam.

The same boy with hoop and children on seesaw print appears in reverse and in blue on a mug in the Willett Collection, Brighton Museum, with the inscription 'A Mark of Respect.'

**14** Wavy edge and moulded border of round-petalled blobbed daisies, painted with bronze and pink lustre lines, and the inscription, 'John Wise Linton Moncrieff Williamson Born at Annan Jany 23d 1854'. • Mark: SEWELL indistinctly impressed • 7¾ ins. diam.

St. Anthony's Pottery, Newcastle-upon-Tyne, 1804–circa 1828.

**15*** Rococo edge with continuous daisy garland border painted iron red, pale green, yellow and blue and a sepia print (painted) of a basket of flowers: 'A Present for a Good Girl.' • Mark: a gouged semi-circle • 7¼ ins. diam.

See 883 and 885 for companion plates to this.

**16** Octagonal, with straight edges painted blue and a wide border of lambrequins, fleurs de lys, rope and other patterns on a lattice background, with a black print of a cat catching rats: 'A PRESENT FOR A GOOD GIRL'. • Mark: LONDON in a semicircle above an anchor, impressed • 6½ ins. diam.

This mark could denote the Middlesbrough Pottery Co., Yorkshire, 1834–1852, or a Tyneside pottery such as Fell of Newcastle, 1817–1890, or Carr of North Shields 1844–circa 1900. Two other firms used a similar LONDON and anchor mark: Isaac & Thomas Bell, Albion Pottery, Newcastle 1860–1863 and Malkin, Walker & Hulse, British Anchor Pottery, Longton, 1858–1864, but this plate is evidently of an earlier period.

**17*** Straight edge with black-printed border and two pink lustre lines, and a black print (slightly painted) of a child in a feathered hat with a model ship and a dog, inscribed in iron red, 'Emma Arle Mowbray.' • No mark; no footrim • 6 ins. diam.

The combination of pink lustre in the decoration and the name Mowbray, a local one, points to a Sunderland origin for this plate.

**18** As 16 with a black print of a boy with a rabbit: 'A PRESENT FOR A GOOD BOY'. • Mark: LONDON in a semicircle above an anchor, impressed • 6½ ins. diam.
(see note for 16)

10

11

12

13

14

15

16

17

18

**19\*** Cylindrical, with loop handle and leaf terminals, black line to rim and an iron red print of two children playing with a doll and a tea-set: 'The good Childs reward'. • No mark • 2¼ ins. ht.; 2½ ins. diam.

**20** Cylindrical, with round-rimmed base and plain loop handle with an iron red print of cherubs with a garlanded woman. 'For my dear Girl'. • No mark • 2¼ ins. ht.; 2⅛ ins. diam.

**21\*** Canary yellow cylindrical, with pointed ear-shaped handle, silver lustre lines and a black print of a boy reading in a landscape: 'A Present for my dear Boy/YOUTH'. • No mark • 2¼ ins. ht.; 2½ ins. diam.

**22** Canary yellow cylindrical with round-rimmed base, loop handle with leaf terminals and an iron red-printed inscription within a (cropped) decorative cartouche: 'Be a good child/Love and fear God/Mind your book/Love your fchool'. • No mark • 2⅛ ins. ht.; 2¼ ins. diam.

**23\*** As 22 with a sepia print of two birds in a tree, and the inscription 'For a good girl'. • No mark • 2¼ ins. ht.; 2 ins. diam.

**24\*** Cylindrical, with loop handle and leaf terminals, pink lustre lines and a sepia-printed farmyard scene: 'FOR MY DEAR GIRL'. • No mark • 2½ ins. ht.; 2⅜ ins. diam.

**25** Cylindrical with reeded loop handle, pink lustre lines and a sepia print (painted) of a woman seated in a flowery bower with a child: 'FOR MY DEAR GIRL.' • No mark • 2¾ ins. ht.; 2½ ins. diam.

**26** Cylindrical with plain loop handle, copper lustre rim and a black print of a seated woman holding a doll out to a child: 'THE GOOD CHILDS REWARD'. • No mark • 2⅜ ins. ht.; 2½ ins. diam.
This print is from an illustration for *My Mother* by Ann Taylor, a picture sheet/booklet issued by William Darton junior, 1815. (See 65).

**27\*** Cylindrical with plain loop handle, black line to rim and a black print (painted) of three boys playing soldiers, or Fugleman, a game of the Follow-my-Leader type: 'A PRESENT TO WILLIAM'. • No mark • 2⅝ ins. ht.; 2½ ins. diam.
This print is from the title-page of *The Knife-Grinder's Budget*, a chapbook printed for T. and J. Allman, London 1829.

**28** Cylindrical with plain loop handle, black line to rim, and a black print of acrobats and jugglers: 'A PRESENT FOR MY DEAR GIRL'. • No mark • 2¾ ins. ht.; 2⅝ ins. diam.

**29** Shaped base and loop handle with leaf terminals and a blue-printed landscape with a reserved tablet inscribed 'Present for being good in Church.' • No mark • 2¾ ins. ht.; 2¾ ins. diam.

**30\*** Cylindrical with reeded loop handle and leaf terminals, pink lustre lines and an iron red-printed landscape with a reserved tablet in-

scribed 'Present for Knitting well.' • No mark • 2½ ins. ht.; 2½ ins. diam.
A companion mug is recorded with the inscription 'Present for Sewing well.'

**31** Cylindrical with plain loop handle and sepia-printed pattern round the rim and the rectangular inscription: 'While you your/Childish games attend/Remember well/Your latter end'. • No mark • 2⅝ ins. ht.; 2⅜ ins. diam.

**32** Cylindrical with loop handle and leaf terminals, orange and brown horizontal bands and a sepia-printed inscription: 'For a Kifs, take this.' • No mark • 2⅝ ins. ht.; 2½ ins. diam.

**33** Cylindrical with loop handle and leaf terminals, iron red rim and a sepia-printed (and painted) decorative inscription: 'INNOCENT PLAY/Abroad in the meadows, to see the young lambs/Run sporting about by the side of their dams./With fleeces so clean and so white;/Or a nest of young doves in a large open cage,/When they play all in love, without anger and rage,/How much we may learn from the sight.' • No mark • 2½ ins. ht.; 2½ ins. diam.

**34** Cylindrical with plain loop handle, pink lustre lines and a sepia-printed tablet with the inscription, 'BE WILLING TO DO WELL WITHOUT PRAISE'. • No mark • 2¼ ins. ht.; 2¼ ins. diam.

**35** Cylindrical with reeded loop handle, blue lines to rim and base and a sepia-printed decorative tablet with the inscription, 'I bought this/Pretty little toy/A present for/My darling boy'. • No mark • 2⅜ ins. ht.; 2½ ins. diam.

**36** Cylindrical with reeded loop handle and leaf terminals, pink lustre rim and handle decoration, and a sepia-printed (and painted) flowery surround to the inscription, 'Let others worship glittring dust/And boast of earthly toys/Christ is my Rock my Hope my Trust/And Spring of all my Joys'. • No mark • 2½ ins. ht.; 2½ ins. diam.

The good Childs reward

For my dear Girl

A Present for my dear Boy

YOUTH

Be a good child
Love and fear God
Mind your book
Love your school

FOR A GOOD GIRL

19    20    21    22    23

FOR MY DEAR GIRL

FOR MY DEAR GIRL

THE GOOD CHILDS REWARD

A PRESENT TO WILLIAM

A PRESENT FOR MY DEAR Girl

24    25    26    27    28

Present
for being good
in Church.

Present
for Knitting
well.

While you your
Childish games attend
Remember well
Your latter end

For a Kiss, take this

29    30    31    32

BE WILLING
TO DO WELL
WITHOUT PRAISE

I bought this
Pretty little toy
A present for
My darling boy

others worship glittring
And boast of earthly toys
hrist is my Rock my Hope
And Spring of all my Joys

33    34    35    36

**37** Slight rococo edge with moulded border of flower sprigs painted pale green, red, blue and yellow, with a sepia-printed decorative inscription, 'HENRY.' • No mark; double footrim • 4¾ ins. diam.

**38** Rococo edge and moulded border of flowers and fruits in sections, painted blue, red and dark green, with a black-printed decorative cartouche with the name 'ANN'. • Mark: ROGERS impressed; double footrim • 5¼ ins. diam.
John Rogers, Dale Hall, Longport, circa 1814–1836. Plates like this may be found in larger sizes.

**39** Nearly straight edge with slightly moulded border of leaves in arcades, and a black-printed vignette of a dog and the name 'MARY'. • Mark: an impressed asterisk/cross; triple footrim • 4 ins. diam.

**39a** Octagonal with rope-twist edge, and blobbed daisy border painted red, blue and green, and a black print of a girl and boy, under a vine trellis flanking the name 'John.' • Mark: impressed 8/33; footrim • 6¾ ins. diam.
Compare with the mug 46.

**40** Parian moulded mug with everted rim, loop handle, beaded borders and applied trophies of toys, with a central cherub's head: 'A GOOD CHILD'S MUG'. • No mark • 2⅝ ins. ht.; 2⅞ ins. diam.

**41** Round-rimmed base and loop handle with leaf terminals, and 'William' in an iron red reserve. • No mark • 3 ins. ht.; 2⅞ ins. diam.

**42** Shaped base and plain loop handle with blue sponged lattice pattern containing red and green flower-heads. • No mark • 2¾ ins. ht.; 2¾ ins. diam.

**43** Drab-ware, concave sided with shaped base, beaded rim and reeded loop handle with leaf terminals. Two identical moulded cream-coloured medallions, one on each side, show a child with a cat. • No mark • 3 ins. ht.; 3¼ ins. diam.

**44** Cylindrical, with shaped base, loop handle with leaf terminals, and a sepia-printed decorative surround to 'GEORGE'. • No mark • 2¾ ins. ht.; 2¾ ins. diam.
Possibly Scott, Southwick Pottery, Sunderland, circa 1800–1897.

**45** Cylindrical with plain loop handle and a sepia-printed decorative inscription 'A PRESENT FOR ELIZABETH'. • No mark • 2½ ins. ht.; 2⅜ ins. diam.

**46\*** Round-rimmed base, plain loop handle and black lines to base, inside rim and handle, with a red print of a girl and boy under a vine flanking the inscription 'Anne.' • No mark • 2⅜ ins. ht.; 2¼ ins. diam.
For a similar print see 39a.

**47** Round-rimmed base with loop handle and leaf terminals, and a sepia-printed cartouche with the inscription 'SAMUEL'. • No mark • 2⅜ ins. ht.; 2¼ ins. diam.

**48** Shaped base with reeded loop handle and leaf terminals, pink lustre lines and borders and a black-printed decorative inscription 'ALICE'. • No mark • 3 ins. ht.; 3 ins. diam.
Possibly Scott, Sunderland.

37

38

39

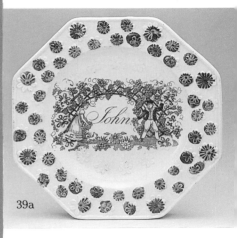
39a

40

41

42

43

44

45

46

47

48

**49** Concave sided with shaped base and reeded loop handle with leaf terminals, moulded lines of beading and moulded motifs on the body, painted dark green, red, pale blue and pink, and the inscription 'ELIZABETH ASH'. • No mark • 3½ ins. ht.; 3¾ ins. diam.

**50** Shaped base with plain loop handle, moulded motifs around the top border and black prints of flower sprays. • Mark: COPELAND & GARRETT LATE SPODE printed in a circle • 3¾ ins. ht.; 2⅞ ins. diam.

**51** Round-rimmed base with reeded lines above, a flat-topped ear-shaped handle and blue lines to inner rim, base and handle. The same sepia print (painted), of two ladies in a landscape, appears on both sides in blue reserves, with the name 'Rebecca' between. • No mark • 3½ ins. ht.; 3¼ ins. diam.

**52** Porcelain, with shaped base, spurred loop handle and gold lines to base, top rim and handle, and 'Ellen' in gold. • Mark: GRAINGER & Co Manufacturers WORCESTER and 24 Princess Street MANCHESTER • 2⅝ ins. ht.; 2⅝ ins. diam.

**53** Porcelain, with shaped base, rounded top rim and jagged loop handle with gold lines to rim and base and decorating the handle, with the inscription in gold: 'A Present for a Good Boy.' • No mark • 3⅛ ins. ht.; 3 ins. diam.

**54\*** Porcelain, cylindrical, with spurred loop handle decorated with gilding, and gilded lines to rim and base, and the gilded inscription 'GAM Apl 9, 1823' beneath a beehive and between two flower sprays, all finely enamelled. • No mark • 3¼ ins. ht.; 3 ins. diam.
Possibly Coalport.

**55** Porcelain with shaped base and spurred handle decorated with gilding, and gilded lines to base and rim, and the gilt-decorated inscription 'Ann Noble'. • No mark • 2¾ ins. ht.; 3 ins. diam.

**56** Shaped base and loop handle with leaf terminals and green prints, on one side, swans on a lake in front of a castle, on the other, a boy with his dog, and in the middle the inscription within a scrolled cartouche: 'A PRESENT FOR A GOOD BOY'. • No mark • 2¾ ins. ht.; 2⅝ ins. diam.
Mugs like this and 58 may be found with grey-blue prints.

**57** Slightly concave with round-rimmed base, plain loop handle, black lines to rim, base and handle, and black prints of 'PRINCESS', a child on a pony attended by a lady on one side, and a pair of Chinese acrobats on the other, with a decorated inscription, 'JAMES' in the middle. • No mark • 3 ins. ht.; 3¼ ins. diam.

**58** As 56 with green prints of a child and a bird cage on one side, three boys looking at a bird's nest of young on the other, and the scroll-decorated inscription 'A PRESENT FOR A GOOD BOY' in the middle. • No mark • 2¾ ins. ht.; 2¾ ins. diam.

**56** Opposite side.

**57** Opposite side.

**58** Opposite side.

# Chapter 2 FAMILY LIFE

**59** Straight edge with moulded garland border of florets and leaves, with a print of a mother with a little boy. • No mark • 7½ ins. diam.
*Private Collection.*

**60\*** Edge and border as 59 above, painted in light green, blue, yellow and brown, with an iron red print of a mother and child in the style of Adam Buck. • No mark; double footrim • 6½ ins. diam.

**61** Erratic edge with moulded border of sprigs and a sepia print of a family outside a house: 'HAPPY FAMILY". • No mark • 4¾ ins. diam.
A larger plate with the same border as this (painted in green, red and blue) has a green print of a weeping mother and a comforting child beside another, perhaps dying, in bed.

**62** Rococo edge with continuous garland border, painted light green, dark red and light blue, with a blue print of a mother on an ottoman, hugging a child. • No mark; double footrim • 6¼ ins. diam.

**63\*** Straight edge with dog, fox and monkey border, painted brown, iron red, yellow, green and blue, with a red print

(painted) of a mother with a child on a toy horse. • Mark: X painted; double footrim • 4¾ ins. diam.

**64\*** Straight edge with moulded garland border of leaves, and a print of a woman nursing a baby beside a table and a curtained bed: 'And can I ever cease to be Affectionate and kind to thee/Who wast so very kind to me?/My Mother'. • Mark: 2 impressed • 5¾ ins. diam.
The print is from an illustration to *My Mother* by Ann Taylor, a picture sheet published by William Darton junior, 1815.
*Private Collection.*

**65** Straight edge with moulded garland and spotted floret border and a print of a mother and child with a doll: 'Who drest my doll in clothes so gay/And taught me pretty how to play and minded all I had to say/MY MOTHER'. • No mark • 5½ ins. diam.
This is another illustration from *My Mother* by Ann Taylor (see 26 and note to 64).
*Private Collection.*

**66** Lobe edge with moulded border of florets in segments, painted with green lines and yellow spots, and a brown print of a mother nursing a baby: 'When pain and sickness made me cry/Who gaz'd

upon my heavy eye/And wept for fear that I should die? My Mother'. • No mark • 6½ ins. diam.
The verse is from *My Mother* (see note to 64) and the print seems to be derived from the picture sheet illustration, with the image in reverse.
*Private Collection.*
These prints from *My Mother* also appear on lobe-edged plates with florets and stars in compartments and on bat-printed tea wares (Willett Collection, Brighton).

**67** Straight edge with plain border painted with red lines and manganese print of a father and child: 'MY FATHER/Who took me in the fields to walk,/And listened to my infant talk,/Making me chains of thistle's stalk./MY FATHER.' • Mark: FERRYBRIDGE • 6½ ins. diam.
Ferrybridge Pottery, Yorkshire, 1792 onwards; this mark, with the reversed D was used in 1804.
This print has also been found on a plate with a garland and spotted floret border as 65.
The verse and illustration come from a jigsaw puzzle/picture sheet by Mary Belson (Elliott) published by William Darton junior, 1812.
A mug in the Willett Collection bears another print from *My Father*.
*Private Collection.*

59

60

HAPPY FAMILY

61

62

63

4

65

66

67

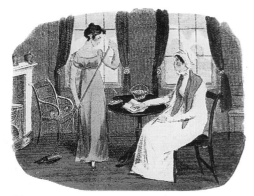

**68** Straight edge and plain concave border painted with red lines, and a red print of a woman sitting at a table talking to a girl with a broom: 'MY DAUGHTER./As Years advance who'll with me bear./The trouble of domestic care./And all my Joy and sorrow share./MY DAUGHTER.' • No mark; double footrim • 5¾ ins. diam.
The same print occurs on a plate with a gadrooned edge and plain border. The illustration is from *My Daughter* by Richard Gregory, published by William Darton, 1812.

**69\*** Indented edge and moulded border of crowns, fleurs de lys, bows and flower

sprays painted in Pratt colours, and a blue print of a mother and child: 'Pleas'd with her Doll as Child could be/Who did with sweet alacrity/Put doll to Bed and work with me/My Daughter'. • Mark: C impressed • 6¼ ins. diam.
The illustration is from *My Daughter* by Richard Gregory (see note to 68).
*Private Collection.*

**70\*** Erratic edge with border of florets and leaves in compartments, painted dark green and mauve, with a green print of an elderly mother and her daughter: 'When Age my Faculties suspend./Who will her kind Afsistance lend/And prove a never failing Friend. MY DAUGHTER'. • No mark; double footrim • 5½ ins. diam.
Probably Goodwins & Harris, Lane End, circa 1831–1838.
Another version of this print is to be found on an octagonal plate with pink lustred daisy border (as 81), with the inscription: 'Who'll treat me with Maternal Care/Who'll lead me to the House of Prayer/And seat me with attention there/My Daughter'.
The illustration and both verses are from *My Daughter* by Richard Gregory (see note to 68).
A set of four garland-bordered plates in the Willett Collection, Brighton, are each decorated with a print from *My Daughter, My Son, My Grandmother* (see page 37) *My Grandfather* (see page 39). They are marked A. STEVENSON WARRANTED STAFFORDSHIRE in a circle around an impressed crown (for Andrew Stevenson, Cobridge circa 1816–1830).

**71** Rococo edge with indistinctly moulded rose, tulip and aster border, and a black print (painted) of a mother and child: 'When first alone I dar'd to go/With out stretch'd arms & tottring toe/What did my trembling courage show/MY CHILDHOOD'. • No mark; double footrim • 6¼ ins. diam.
The verse and illustration come from *My Childhood* a jigsaw puzzle/picture sheet by William Upton (Willian Darton junior, 1812).

**72\*** Straight edge with well moulded garland border of large blooms painted in Pratt colours, and a black print similar to 71. • No mark • 7¾ ins. diam.
(see note to 71).

**73** Gadrooned edge and plain border painted with two black lines, and a black print of children playing with a hoop, a kite and a ball: 'When first the ball or hoop or kite/With speechless rapture pleas'd my sight/What was it kindled such delight/MY CHILDHOOD'. • No mark • 5¾ ins. diam.
The verse and illustration are from *My Childhood* (see note to 71).

**74** Straight edge with well moulded fruiting vine border and a blue print of a boy leading a girl on a horse: 'Who taught his Sisters first to ride/Who did the Little Pony

68

69

70

71

72

73

74

75

76

guide/And with them every Gift divide./MY SON.' • No mark • 6 ins. diam.

From *My Son* by Richard Gregory, published by William Darton junior, 1812. The poem was also included in *Grateful Tributes; or, Recollections of infancy* by Mary Belson (Elliott), (William Darton & Son, circa 1830–1836).

**75** Octagonal with rope-twist edge painted green, and moulded border of line-petalled blobbed daisies. The sepia print of a boy and a girl (slightly painted) is entitled 'THE COUSINS'. • No mark • 6 ins. diam.

**76** Wavy edge with moulded border of blobbed daisies and a red print of 'THE COUSINS' as 75. • No mark; double footrim • 6 ins. diam.

**77\*** Straight edge with moulded garland border of large and small flowers with a blue print of a girl with a child on a rocking horse: 'Who saw me mount the Rocking Horse/And then stood by to check its course,/Lest her dear boy should get a tofs?/MY SISTER.' • Mark: a round-limbed swastika, impressed • 5¼ ins. diam.

This verse and print is from *My Sister* by Mary Belson (Elliott), a picture sheet published by William Darton junior, London 1812.

*Private Collection.*

**78\*** Indented edge and moulded border of crowns, fleurs de lys and flower sprays, painted in Pratt colours, with a blue print illustrating 'MY SISTER' as preceding print. • No mark • 6½ ins. diam.

**79\*** Straight edge with moulded border of rose, shamrock, harp, thistle and flower sprigs, crudely painted in iron red, green and yellow, with a black print of a child on a ladder, with a distressed girl holding it: 'When up the Ladder I would go/How wrong it was I now well know/Who cried but held it fast below MY SISTER'. • No mark; double footrim • 4½ ins. diam.

Larger versions of this plate may be found, some with unpainted borders and painted prints; the same print occurs on octagonal plates with dimpled daisy borders.

The verse and the print are from *My Sister* by Mary Belson see note to 77 above.

Once too I threw my top too far,
It touch'd thy cheek, and left a scar?
Who tried to hide it from Mamma,

**80** Straight edge with moulded anthemion border and blue line to edge, and a blue print of a girl with a little boy in a garden: 'Who was it when we both were young/First prais'd me with her artless tongue/And on my neck delighted hung/MY SISTER'. • No mark; no footrim • 6¼ ins. diam.

**81** Octagonal with rope-twist edge and dimpled daisy border, pink lustred, and a blue print illustrating 'MY SISTER' as 80. • No mark; double footrim • 5¼ ins. diam.

**82** Octagonal with herringbone edge and moulded border of large and small florets, clumsily painted red and blue, with a central black print illustrating 'MY SISTER' as 80 and 81. • No mark; double footrim • 6½ ins. diam.

**83** Rococo edge with indistinctly moulded border of roses, tulips and asters, splodged in red, green, yellow and blue, and a sepia print of a girl with a little boy: 'For it was ever our delight/To love each other day and night/Nor would I do a thing to spite/MY SISTER'. • Mark: X impressed; double footrim • 6¼ ins. diam.

The same plate may be found with an unpainted border and a painted print, sometimes marked with an asterisk impressed; the print also occurs on an unmarked octagonal plate with gadrooned edge and a border of line-petalled daisies.

**84\*** Finely potted with straight edge and continuous vine border. The black transfer is a version of 'MY SISTER' as 83. • No mark; no footrim • 6¼ ins. diam.

**85** Rococo edge with indistinctly moulded rose, tulip and aster border with a yellow line to the edge, and a sepia print (painted) of two children with a dog: 'MY SISTER'. • No mark; double footrim • 6 ins. diam.

**86** Rococo edge with indistinctly moulded border of roses, tulips and asters and a black (painted) print of an old lady comforting a child, a dog lying dead nearby: 'Who took me ... out to ride/ Because I griev'd when Puggy died/And bought me sugar plums beside/MY GRANDMOTHER'. • No mark; double footrim • 6¼ ins. diam.
Illustration from *My Grandmother* by William Upton, a picture sheet used for a jigsaw puzzle, published by William Darton junior, London 1813.

**87\*** Finely potted straight-edged plate with moulded border of continuous leaves and acorns, and a blue print of an old lady giving a doll to a little girl: 'THE PRESENTS/Who came to see me far and near./With cakes and Toys, throughout the year./And call'd me her sweet little dear?/ MY GRANDMOTHER.' • No mark • 5½ ins. diam.
Possibly Brameld, circa 1820.
The same print occurs on a plate with a rose garland border as 95 and on one with a finely moulded garland border of small

flowers and leaves, with the (black) print painted in Pratt colours.
The illustration is from *My Grandmother* by William Upton (see note to 86). Another print in this series, on a plate with a moulded border of florets and leaves in sections, shows an old lady with a child in a landscape: 'Who gave to me a pretty Doll,/A Babyhouse and Cage for Poll,/And let me on her Bosom loll?/MY GRANDMOTHER'.

**88** Octagonal with rope-twist edge and border of florets and stars, the florets painted in pink lustre, and a sepia print of 'The Cottagers'. • Mark: DAVENPORT impressed around an anchor, and DAVENPORT printed in sepia. • 6¾ ins. diam.
Other plates in this series illustrate 'PLAYING AT MARBLES' and 'HUNT THE SLIPPER'.
*Private Collection.*
Another plate may be mentioned here, although it is not illustrated: it has a rococo edge and blobbed daisy border and a blue print of a lady on an ottoman, holding a baby: 'GRANDMAMMA'S TALES./ Hush a bye baby, my baby of bliss/Sleep little pretty one sleep while I kiss./Papa in the orchard with Rosa is gone,/And I pretty baby, I still will sing on.' The same print occurs, without the inscription, on a indistinctly moulded daisy-bordered plate of 5¼ ins.

**89\*** Straight edge with moulded border of shamrocks and flower sprays painted green, red and yellow, with sepia print

(painted) of two children playing with a kitten beneath the decorated inscription: 'Who would his fav'rite kitten bring/And tie a paper to a string/Making her run in a merry ring/My Brother'. The picture is entitled 'Poor Kittens Mistake'. • No mark • 7½ ins. diam.
The illustration is from *My Brother* by Mary Belson (Elliott) a picture sheet published by William Darton junior, London, 1812. *Private Collection.*

**90** Straight edge with painted border of green and brown acorns and a sepia print (painted) of a boy on all fours pulling a child in a miniature Lincolnshire wagon: 'What pleasure filled my little heart,/When seated in my wooden cart,/To see thee act the horses part./My Brother'. • No mark • 4½ ins. diam.
This is a reversed version of an illustration to *My Brother* by Mary Belson (see note to 89).
*Private Collection.*

**91\*** Octagonal with rope-twist edge and blobbed daisy border painted iron red and yellow, with blue centres, and a sepia print (slightly painted) of My Brother as 90 preceding, but printed the same way as the book illustration upon which is it based. • Mark: C impressed • 6¼ ins. diam.
The same print has been noted on a plate with a moulded garland border of large blooms painted in Pratt colours as 72.

**92** Rococo edge with moulded border of pendant rose florets and thistles, with one green and three brown painted stripes, and

86

87

88

89

90

91

92

93

94

a green print within a brown painted circle of a girl with a little boy in skirts: 'MY BROTHER'. • No mark • 6 ins. diam.

**93** Octagonal with rope-twist edge and moulded border of line-petalled daisies, with yellow line to edge and a sepia print (painted) of 'MY BROTHER' similar to 92. • No mark • 6 ins. diam.

The same print (and palette) is to be found on erratic-edged plates with continuous garland borders.

**94** Finely potted, wavy-edged plate with moulded border of three rows of blobbed, round-petalled daisies and a black print of 'MY BROTHER', similar to 92 and 93. • No mark; double footrim • 4¾ ins. diam.

Larger versions of this plate are to be found.

**95\*** Straight edge with moulded border of continuous rose garland painted in pink, yellow and green, and a blue print, slightly painted, of an old man with a child, sailing a toy boat in a tub of water outside a cottage: 'THE BOAT./Who made for me a little Boat,/And did my joy-struck eye denote./To see it on the water float?/MY GRANDFATHER.' • No mark • 5½ ins. diam.

Possibly Brameld.

The same print was used in blue on a vine-leaf bordered plate. The print is taken from *My Grandfather*, an illustrated poem by William Upton probably published as a picture sheet by William Darton junior, 1812–1815.

**96\*** Finely potted hexagonal with moulded border of swags of flowers alternating with pendant fuchsias. The blue print shows a boy receiving a watch from an old man, a dog in attendance: 'THE NEW WATCH./Who when I could both read and spell/And in my writing got on well,/Bought me a watch, the time to tell?/MY GRANDFATHER'. • No mark • 5 ins. diam.

A version of this print occurs on octagonal plates with dimpled daisy borders. Illustration from *The Grandfather* by William Upton (see note to 95).

**97\*** Straight edge with moulded border of rose florets, thistle and shamrock, with alternating flower sprigs, painted green, red and yellow, and a black print of an old man giving a present to a child on leading strings held by a woman: 'Who when a Babe in leading strings/Would haste to me on pleasure's wings/And brought me many pretty things/My Grandfather'. • No mark; double footrim • 5 ins. diam.

Illustration from *The Grandfather* by William Upton (see note to 95).

**98.** Rococo edge with continuous moulded garland border painted with a green line, and an iron red print illustrating 'The Boat' – another version of the print in 95. • No mark; double footrim • 5¼ ins. diam.

Illustration from *The Grandfather* by William Upton (see note to 95).

**99\*** Scallop edge with moulded border of segments containing florets painted dark green and red, and a green print of an old man watching a child on a hobby horse outside a cottage: 'Who when he saw me sad or cross/Would spin the top, or trapball toss,/and let me make his cane my horse/MY GRANDFATHER.' • No mark • 6½ ins. diam.

The same print, entitled 'THE COCKHORSE', has been noted on a plate with a garland and spotted floret border in Pratt colours, and on an octagonal plate with an arcaded lambrequin border. The same print was used, in green, on a plate with a border of florets and leaves in compartments, with the verse: 'Who when the Yard-Dog at me flew/Declar'd he'd thrash him black and blue/And with the Horsewhip beat him too? MY GRANDFATHER'.

The illustration is from *My Grandfather* by William Upton (see note to 95).

**100\*** Wavy edge with moulded border of flower sprays and eagles in sections, painted blue, green and red, and a red print

of two children with an old traveller: 'THE OLD GRANDFATHER.' • No mark • 4½ ins. diam.
Probably Cambrian Pottery, at Swansea 1824–1831.

**101** Plate with erratic edge and indistinctly moulded border of roses, tulips and asters, painted with a red line, and a sepia print (slightly painted) of a girl standing by the sea: 'Who said Sophia had teeth of ivory/In which her lovers took delight/MY GRANDFATHER'. • No mark • 5 ins. diam.
The same rather indistinct print occurs on plates with borders of blobbed daisies.

**102** Octagonal with rope-twist edge and indistinctly moulded border of dimpled daisies, painted with a red line. The black, slightly painted, print illustrates *My Grandfather* as 99. • No mark • 4¾ ins. diam.
Illustration from *The Grandfather* by William Upton (see note to 95).

**103** Wavy edge with blobbed daisy border and a black print of a girl with a cat in a garden: 'Who tould [sic] you of All things deAth/Should NeVeR be FoRgot/MY GRANDFATHER'. • No mark • 6 ins. diam.

**104** Straight edge with moulded border of roses, thistles and shamrock in a continuous garland, and a black print of a family round a table: 'The sire turns o'er with patriarchal grace/The big ha bible ance his father' pride.' • No mark • 5½ ins. diam.
The text is from *The Cotter's Saturday Night* by Robert Burns.

**105** Edge and border as 104 with orange lustre, and a sepia print of a family at a table: 'But now the supper crowns their simple board/The halesome parrich chief of Scotias food.' • No mark • 5¾ ins. diam.
Text from *The Cotter's Saturday Night* by Robert Burns.

**106** As 104 with a black print of two men drinking at a table, watched by a woman: 'And here's a hand my trusty friend And gies a hand O thine/And wee'll tak aright guid willie waught For Auld lang syne.' • No mark • 5½ ins. diam.
This plate is also to be found with a green print.
Text from *Auld Lang Syne* by Robert Burns.

**107** As 106 with an orange lustre border. • No mark • 6¾ ins. diam.

**108** Wavy edge with moulded border of three rows of blobbed round-petalled daisies and a black print of a man dandling a child, watched by a woman: 'The lisping infant prattling on his knee,/Does a his weary kiaugh and care beguile.' • No mark • 6½ ins. diam.
This print is found on plates with borders as 104 etc, sometimes in green and sometimes with orange lustre borders.
The text is from *The Cotter's Saturday Night* by Robert Burns.

**109** Edge and border as 104 with orange lustre, and a green print of a highlander being welcomed into a cottage interior: 'Wr kindly welcome Jenny brings him ben/A strappin youth he taks the mother's eye'. • No mark • 6¾ ins. diam.
The same print is found on smaller plates, without lustred borders.

**110** Wavy edge with moulded border of three rows of blobbed daisies and a sepia print of a woman supervising a little girl holding a baby in a kitchen. • No mark • 6½ ins. diam.

**111** Slight rococo edge and moulded border of rose sprays painted green, red and blue, with a black line to the rim and a black print of a family by a cottage fireside, signed T. Robson. • Mark: MIDDLESBRO' POTTERY in a semicircle around an anchor, impressed. • 5¾ ins. diam.
Middlesborough Pottery, Yorkshire, 1834–1852.

Larger versions of this plate are to be found.
Thomas Robson was a Sunderland engraver who worked for a number of potteries in the North East. The first recorded piece by him was for Phillips & Co., Garrison Pottery, Sunderland, 1813–1819, and he continued to provide engravings for this firm after it became Dixon Phillips & Co. (circa 1840–1865). He seems to have made a number of engravings for the Middlesborough Pottery during the 1830s and 40s. He also produced topographical prints of the North East, and maps, and he was the author of a finely engraved book, *The British Herald*, published in Sunderland in 1850. He died circa 1869.

**112** Slightly wavy edge and moulded border of blobbed round-petalled daisies, with a black print of a family at a hearthside. • No mark; double footrim • 5¼ ins. diam.

**113*** Cylindrical with loop handle and leaf terminals, and blue-printed patterns inside the rim and on the handle. The blue print shows a little girl at her mother's knees, outside a cottage: 'At my desire who'd leave off play/To my advice attention pay/And learn to read and learn to pray/MY DAUGHTER'. • No mark • 2⅜ ins. ht.; 2½ ins. diam.

The illustration is from *My Daughter* by Richard Gregory, a picture sheet published by William Darton, London, 1812 (see also page 33).

**114*** Cylindrical with loop handle and leaf terminals, and a copper lustre band round the rim. The black and painted print of a mother and child in a garden is entitled 'A MOTHERS LOVE'. • No mark • 2½ ins. ht.; 2⅜ ins. diam.

**115** As 114 with an illustration of 'THE FATHERS RETURN'. • No mark • 2½ ins. ht.; 2¼ ins. diam.

**116** As 113 with a blue print of a little boy receiving a watch from an old man: 'Who when I could both read and spell/And in my writing got on well/Bought me a watch the time to tell/MY GRANDFATHER'. • No mark • 2⅜ ins. ht.; 2½ ins. diam.
The illustration is from *My Grandfather* by William Upton, a picture sheet probably published by William Darton junior, 1812–1815 (cf. 96).

**117** Loop handle with shaped base and a black print of a mother breast-feeding a baby with an older child at her feet and a woman standing by with refreshment. • No mark • 2¾ ins. ht.; 2⅝ ins. diam.

**118** Round moulded base and loop handle and a print of a family going to church: 'SUNDAY MORNING'. • No mark • 2½ ins. ht.; 2⅜ ins. diam.

**119*** As 118 with a black print (painted) of a family in a cottage interior greeting father coming home from work with a scythe over his shoulder: 'SATURDAY NIGHT'. • No mark • 2½ ins. ht.; 2½ ins. diam.

**120*** Copper lustre with shaped base and spurred loop handle, with reserves on a yellow ground containing sepia-printed (and painted) scenes after Adam Buck – a mother holding out cherries to a child on one side, and a mother with a child (? eating cherries) on the other. • No mark • 2⅝ ins. ht.; 2⅝ ins. diam.

Printed and painted plate with moulded border. • No mark • 7½ ins. diam. *Private Collection.*

113

114

115

116

117

118

119

120

**121** Straight edge with swagged garland and medallion border and a black print (slightly painted) of four children within a flower-decorated circle: 'INFANCY'. • No mark • 6 ins. diam.

**122** As 121 with a print of three young people: 'YOUTH'. • No mark • 6 ins. diam.

**123** Rococo edge with moulded border of birds and lambrequins, and a print of a mother and father and two children: 'MANHOOD'. • No mark • 6½ ins. diam.

**124** Edge and border as 123 with a print of an old man: 'OLD AGE'. • No mark • 6½ ins. diam.
These prints form a set, and all may be found with either of the two borders illustrated.

**125\*** Straight edge with moulded border of flower heads and leaves alternating with pairs of cornucopias, painted light green, iron red, purple and yellow. The black print, painted in the same colours, shows a baby in a cradle rocked by an old man, two children and a man: 'Infancy, Youth, Manhood, and Old Age.' • Mark: X painted • 6¼ ins. diam.
A version of this print was used by Baker, Bevans & Irwin, Glamorgan Pottery, Swansea, 1813–1838.

*The New Book.*

A NEAT little book, full of pictures, was bought
For a good little girl that was glad to be taught.
She read all the tales, and then said to her mother,
I 'll lend this new book to my dear little brother.

He shall look at the pictures, and find O and I,
I 'm sure he won't tear it, he 's such a good boy.
Oh no ! brother Henry knows better indeed ;
Although he 's too young, yet, to spell or to read.

From 'THE COWSLIP; OR MORE CAUTIONARY STORIES IN VERSE', a childrens book first published in 1811.

121

122

123

124

125

45

# Chapter 3 EARLY DAYS

The title of a large series of plates, clearly produced by a number of different factories, has given us a name for a whole category of images in which children are simply behaving as children – not with their families, nor with toys, or at any particular sport or occupation, but at games of make-believe, mischief or sheer boisterousness.

**126** Erratic edge and moulded border of flower sprigs alternating with vertical curlicues, crudely painted in light green, red and pale blue. The black print (also painted) shows a boy rejoicing to be let out of school: 'OUR EARLY DAYS/A HALF HOLIDAY'. • No mark • 6½ ins. diam.
This print, and 'Anxious Moments' (see 131) appear on jugs from Moore's Wear Pottery and Scott's, Southwick.

**127\*** Rococo edge with border of moulded motifs painted light green, red and yellow, with a sepia print of 'A HALF HOLIDAY' as 126 in reverse. • Mark: a floret, printed in brown • 5¼ ins. diam.
The same plate has been found with a red print and a blue-printed triangular mark.

**128** Straight edge with moulded border of two rows of blobbed round-petalled daisies, spotted in red and green, with a green print of 'A HALF HOLIDAY' as 127. • Mark: indecipherable blob, impressed • 6½ ins. diam.

**129** Rococo edge with border of moulded flower sprigs and motifs, painted pink, yellow, pale blue and pale green, with a sepia print of a boy crossing a churchyard: 'OUR EARLY DAYS/RATHER ALARMED'. • Mark: a floret, printed in green • 7 ins. diam.

**130** Rococo edge with moulded border of roses, tulips and asters and a black print of 'RATHER ALARMED' as 129. • No mark • 7¼ ins. diam.
Possibly Scott, Southwick Pottery, Sunderland.

**131** Straight edge and flat border with two pink lustre lines to border and a black print of a boy apparently catching birds: 'No 4 OUR EARLY DAYS/ANXIOUS MOMENTS'. • No mark; double footrim • 7 ins. diam.
A version of this print occurs on a plate with the same edge and border as 130.

**132** As 127 with an unpainted border and a brown print of a boy attending to bellows in front of the fire: 'OUR EARLY DAYS/THE EXPERIMENTAL PHILOSOPHER'. • No mark • 5¼ ins. diam.

**133** Slightly erratic-edged toy plate with an all-over green print of a boy with his slate at the school door: 'OUR EARLY DAYS/TOO LATE FOR SCHOOL'. • No mark; double footrim • 4 ins. diam.

126

127

128

29

130

131

132

133

47

**134** Wavy edge with a moulded border of three rows of blobbed daisies and a blue/grey print of a little girl lifting her skirts to show a man's boots: 'FROLIC'S [sic] OF YOUTH/DON'T I LOOK LIKE PAPA'. • Mark: NORTH SHORE POTTERY in semicircle around initials GFS & CO, impressed • 6½ ins. diam.
George Smith, North Shore Pottery, Stockton-on-Tees, Durham, circa 1855–60.

**135** Rococo edge with a moulded lattice and cartouche border and a black print of a little girl with spectacles and a walking stick: 'OUR EARLY DAYS/NOW I'M GRANDMOTHER'. • No mark • 8 ins. diam.
Probably Ainsworth, Stockton Pottery, Stockton-on-Tees, Durham, 1865–1901.

**136** Straight edge with moulded border of two rows of blobbed round-petalled daisies, spotted red and blue. The green print shows a girl with a skipping rope, playing with a dog: 'OUR EARLY DAYS/THE ROMP'. • Mark: indecipherable blob, impressed • 6½ ins. diam.

**137** Rococo edge with moulded border of roses, tulips and asters, painted light green, red, purple and blue. The sepia print shows a little girl dressing up her dog in a bonnet: 'OUR EARLY DAYS/THE PET'. • No mark • 7 ins. diam.

**138*** Rococo edge with border of moulded motifs painted light green, pale blue and yellow, and a red print of a child in a large chair, wearing specs, smoking a long clay pipe and reading a newspaper: 'OUR EARLY DAYS/NOW I'M GRANDFATHER'. • Mark: a triangular motif, printed in blue. • 5¼ ins. diam.
The same print was used on daisy-bordered plates, as 136.
The source for this illustration is a print, first issued as an aquatint circa 1828–30 and subsequently published in lithographed form as *Our Early Days No1*, by W. Clerk, 202 High Holborn, circa 1840.

**139** Rococo edge with red line to rim and moulded border of tendrilled flower sprigs. The black print is a version of 'THE ROMP' as 136. • No mark • 7¼ ins. diam.
The same print occurs on a wavy-edged daisy-bordered plate.

**140** Octagonal with moulded border of primrose florets, spotted in pale blue, red and light green, with a black print (slightly painted) of a girl with a book in her hand teaching her dolls on a table: 'OUR EARLY DAYS/KEEPING SCHOOL.' • No mark • 7¼ ins. diam.
This is a reversed version of a print used on daisy-bordered plates marked for the Middlesborough Pottery Co.; on one with the impressed mark LONDON surrounding an anchor (possibly Middlesborough, see note to 16), and on a plate with painted sprigs on an unmoulded border.

**141** Rococo edge with moulded border of roses, tulips and asters with a green print of a child sitting in a large armchair, knitting and wearing specs: 'FROLIC'S [sic] OF YOUTH/NOW I'M GRANDMOTHER'. • No mark • 6 ins. diam.

Possibly Scott, Southwick Pottery, Sunderland.
The same print was used, in sepia, on an alphabet bordered plate with a reeded and feathered edge; in black on a vitruvian scroll and alphabet bordered plate, and in green on a straight-edged plate with rose, tulip and aster border marked DAVENPORT.
The source of this image is a decorative print of circa 1840, companion to *Now I'm Grandfather* (see note to 138).

**142** Straight edge with commemorative moulded border: 'ALBERT EDWARD PRINCE OF WALES BORN Nov 9 1841' and a black print of 'THE ROMP' similar to 136. • No mark • 6½ ins. diam.
Possibly Swillington Bridge, Yorkshire, 1791–circa 1845.

134

135

136

137

138

139

140

141

142

**143\*** Octagonal with deep moulded border of patterns, painted with two green lines. The sepia print (painted) shows a mother and large dog watching a child in a draped interior: 'THE FIRST STEP'. • Mark: Diamond registration mark for Bailey & Ball, Longton, March 1847, printed • 8 ins. diam.
Bailey & Ball, Longton, circa 1843–1850.
This plate is to be found with different coloured lines to the border and in smaller sizes.
The image is taken from an unidentified hand-coloured print, probably cut from a picture sheet of circa 1830, also entitled *The First Step*, that appeared in a 19th century scrap book.

*The First Step*

**144** Rococo edge with moulded border of roses, tulips and asters, painted red, dark green and blue, with a black print of a child playing with a doll: 'THE LITTLE NURSE'. • No mark; triple footrim • 5¼ ins. diam.

**145\*** As 143 with blue lines to the border and a sepia print (painted) of a child watering flowers in a garden: 'THE YOUNG FLORIST'. • Mark: as 143 • 7¾ ins. diam.

**146** Rococo edge with well moulded border of roses, tulips and asters, and a sepia print of a boy cutting into 'A PIGEON PIE'. • Mark: a crown with POTTERY impressed; triple footrim • 6½ ins. diam. Attributed to Swillington Bridge Pottery, Yorkshire. 1791–circa 1895.

**147** Indistinctly moulded version of the border in 146, painted in dark green, blue, pink and yellow, with a sepia print of a boy eating plum pudding: 'CHRISTMAS DAY'. • No mark • 7¼ ins. diam.

**148\*** Straight edge with vitruvian scroll and alphabet border, painted with red lines, with a black print as 147. • Mark: T&B GODWIN NEW WHARF impressed • 6 ins. diam.
Thomas & Benjamin Godwin, New Wharf and New Basin Potteries, Burslem, 1809–34.

**149** Edge and border as 148 with a sepia print of two children under an umbrella. • Mark: EDGE MALKIN & CO impressed • 7¼ in diam.
Edge Malkin & Co, Newport and Middleport Potteries, Burslem, Staffordshire, 1871–1903.

U begins Urn, that at tea-
time Jane brings,
When we all love to hear how it
hisses and sings.

The print source is *The Mother's Pictorial Alphabet*, illustrated by Henry Anelay and engraved by Ames Johnston, published by S. W. Partridge, London, 1862 (Dover Reprint, introduced by Peter Stockham, 1974): 'U begins Urn, that at tea-time Jane brings,/When we all love to hear how it hisses and sings./Also Umbrella, that kept us so dry/When the heavy rain poured from the black angry sky.'

**150** Wavy edge with moulded border of three rows of blobbed daisies and a black print of children and a dog looking at a newspaper: 'CHILD LIFE'. • Mark: LONDON in a semicircle, above an anchor, impressed. • 6 ins. diam.
This could be one of five potteries which used similar marks (see note for 16).

**151** Wavy-edged plate with border of three rows of blobbed daisies and an inner band of vertical sprigs, and a black print of children making a snowman: 'THE MAN OF SNOW'. • No mark • 7¼ ins.
The print is based on the frontispiece (and an illustration later in the book) of *Nursery Carols*, by The Rev John S. B. Mansell, with illustrations by Ludwig Richter and Oscar Pletsch, published by Bell & Daldy, London, 1873. The influence of German artists on children's book illustration was strong at this time: here it has percolated to ceramic decoration.

143

144

145

146

147

148

149

150

151

**152*** Octagonal with rope-twist edge and border of florets and stars, clumsily painted in red, green, pale blue and yellow. The sepia print shows three children admiring a caricature of a man standing outside the window: 'FROLIC'S OF YOUTH/THE YOUNG ARTIST'. • Marks: DAVENPORT in a semicircle above an anchor, surmounted by 12 and with 5 and 2 either side of the anchor, impressed, and DAVENPORT printed in sepia. • 6 ins. diam.
Davenport, Longport, Staffordshire, 1852. The same plate has been found with a green print.

**153** Rococo edge with continuous garland border painted with a green line, and a sepia print of a boy pulling children in a basket: 'THE NEW OMNIBUS'. • No mark; double footrim • 4½ ins. diam.
A version of this print has been found in black on a straight-edged plate with a moulded border of primrose florets.

**154** Octagonal with pink lustred rope-twist edge and moulded border with dimpled daisies and stars, and a black print of a girl running off with a boy's hat in a garden: 'Quarrelsome Children'. • No mark • 6¼ ins. diam.

The illustration is from *The Cowslip*, 'or, More Cautionary Stories', in verse by the author of that much-admired little work entitled *The Daisy*. The author was Elizabeth Turner and *The Cowslip* was first published in 1811.

**155*** Rococo edge with moulded border of fruit and flowers in compartments, painted light green, red and blue. The green print shows two boys playing soldiers and tilting at a pile of pots: 'FROLIC'S OF YOUTH/THE DOWNFALL OF CHINA'. • Mark: WEDGWOOD & CO impressed • 6¾ ins. diam.

Wedgwood & Co., Unicorn and Pinnox Works, Tunstall, Staffordshire, circa 1860. This print occurs on a marked Davenport plate of the same type as 152. The subject refers to the Opium Wars of 1839–1842 in which the Chinese were defeated and, among other things, ceded Hong Kong to the British (cf the lithograph by Thomas Fairland on the same subject).

**156** Slightly erratic edge with indistinctly moulded border of flower sprigs alternating with pendant thistles, crudely painted in light green, red and blue. The green print shows four boys in harness, driven by another: 'THIS BOY, I THINK, LOOKS VERY GRAND,/DRIVING OUT HIS FOUR-IN-HAND.' • Mark: YMP impressed • 7½ ins. diam.
Ynysmedw Pottery, near Swansea, Wales, circa 1850–70.

**157*** Rococo edge with flowers and leaves in compartments, painted dark green and red, and a red print of children pinching chestnuts from a brazier while the woman vendor sleeps: 'THE TEMPTING MOMENT.' • No mark • 6¾ ins. diam.

**158** Straight edge with moulded border of lobes and florets and a black print of children: 'DOES IT RAIN'. • Mark: LONDON impressed around an anchor, in a fan shape • 6½ ins. diam.
Possibly Middlesborough Pottery, Malkin Walker & Hulse, Longton, Isaac & Thomas Bell, Albion Pottery, Newcastle, Carr & Sons, North Shields, or Fell & Co, Newcastle (see note to 16).
*Private Collection.*

**159** Grooved and feathered edge and moulded border of vertical sprigs. The black print (painted) shows four boys playing at jousting: 'THUMP AWAY JACK – TAKE CARE OF HIS HEAD –/TIS ALL IN GOOD FUN. NOW HIT HIM HARD, NED.' • Mark: four squares, impressed • 8¼ ins. diam.

**160** Straight-edged plate with a moulded border of formalised fruiting vine and a sepia print of two children beside a boat, pulling in a fishing net containing a mermaid. • No mark • 6¾ ins. diam.

152

153

154

155

156

157

58

159

160

**161** Straight edge with unmoulded border and toothed pattern printed in red round the rim. The central black print shows a boy taking a girl and her doll for a ride in a boat. • No mark • 5 ins. diam.

**162** As 161 with larger-scale pattern round the rim and a sepia print of two boys fishing. • No mark • 5 ins. diam.

**163** As 162 with a sepia print of a boy in military dress stepping out with a girl. • No mark • 5 ins. diam.
Others in this series include two boys dressed as Turks, with a bugle and bayonet, two boys in a boat, and a boy and girl with a balloon (as 165 below).

**164** Straight edge with a moulded border of continuous shamrock and a red print of a boy mending a fishing net. • No mark • 6 ins. diam.

**165** Straight edge with moulded border of flattened blobbed daisies and a black print of a girl and boy in military dess holding a balloon. • No mark • 6½ ins. diam.

**166** Straight edge with a moulded border of roses, thistles and shamrock in a continuous garland and a green print of a girl holding a gate. • No mark • 5¾ ins. diam.

**167** Edge and border as 164 with a red print of a woman in a conservatory with a child with a hoop. • No mark • 6 ins. diam.
Others in this series include a kilted boy sitting down with his dog and crook, a girl holding a baby and reading a book, and a child with a dog carrying a basket of provisions.

**168** Straight edge with vitruvian scroll and alphabet border, with black line to edge, and a sepia print of three little girls: 'THE GRACES'. • No mark; double footrim • 6¼ ins. diam.
Probably Godwin, Burslem.
This print is to be found on similar plates, some smaller, with red lines in the border and red transfers, marked T & B GODWIN NEW WHARF.
The three sister goddesses, Aglaia, Thalia and Euphrosyne of Greek mythology, the embodiment and bestowers of beauty and charm, were portrayed by Botticelli, Raphael, Rubens and Canova, among others; the subject is here given a children's interpretation by a Victorian popular artist whose identity we have yet to discover.

**169** Rococo edge with moulded animal border and green line to edge. The green print shows two children in a landscape, with another in the background: 'CHARLES & HARRY: "Ellen, I cannot lend you this,"/I heard young Harry say, "The ball is mine –/I tell you Miss. With it you shall not play."' • No mark • 5 ins. diam.
*Private Collection.*

**170** Straight edge with vitruvian scroll and alphabet border. The black (painted) print, enclosed within a red painted circle, shows a boy in a large top hat with a little girl and a dog: 'PLAYING AT LOVERS'. • No mark • 7¼ ins. diam.

**171** Wavy edge with moulded border of three rows of blobbed daisies and a red print (slightly painted in yellow) of children 'PLAYING AT "MORNING CALLS"/ IN THE OLD BARONIAL HALLS.' • No mark • 6½ ins. diam.
This print was also used in blue on a straight-edged daisy-bordered plate.

**172** Straight edge with moulded border of two rows of blobbed daisies, and green line to edge. The green print (painted) shows children floating walnut-shell boats in a tub of water: 'SHIP-BUILDING'. • No mark • 7¼ ins. diam.
The same plate is to be found in smaller sizes, with black prints, and with red lines to the edge; the same print (in sepia) occurs on a vitruvian scroll and alphabet bordered plate.
This print appeared in *Warne's Holiday Album* – 'A Book of Easy Reading for Children by Aunt Friendly', circa 1860, as an illustration to a story entitled The

Walnut-shell Fleet. It was used again in the *Alphabet of Fruits*, one of 'Aunt Louisa's London Toy Books', published by Frederick Warne & Co., Kronheim & Co., 1875: 'W for the WALNUTS at Christmas we eat,/And make of the shells such a capital fleet.'
For other prints from the same source see 518, 609 and 611.

**173** Straight edge with indistinctly moulded vitruvian scroll and alphabet border (as 170), with a black print of a weeping girl holding a doll, a town cryer in the distance: 'LOST'. • No mark • 6¼ ins. diam.
This print was also used on larger plates in the same series as 170.
It appeared as an illustration to the story of 'Little Margaret' in *The Sunday Scholar's Companion*, August 1873. This magazine, published by the Church of England Sunday School Institute, Fleet Street, London, included natural history, poems, songs (with music), pictures and, of course, improving stories.

**174** Wavy edge with moulded border of flower sprays and garlands, painted in light green, yellow and red, with a sepia print of a boy and girl and a dog playing soldiers: 'JUVENILE COMPANIONS'. • No mark; triple footrim • 7¾ ins. diam.
A similar print was used on a vitruvian scroll and alphabet bordered plate, probably by Thomas Godwin of Burslem, with

the subtitle 'THE YOUNG SERGEANT'; another version was used on an alphabet bordered plate by Elsmore and Forster, Tunstall, 1853–71.

**175** Straight edge with arcaded border of florets and leaves, painted with two red lines. The sepia print shows a child in a kilt with a toy sword. • No mark • 6½ ins. diam.

**176** Wavy edge with border of radiating lines and a polychrome print (partly painted) of a boy playing soldiers in a landscape. • Marks: W S & Co's QUEEN'S WARE STOCKTON impressed, and No 101 PASTIMES W S & Co printed in green in a decorative cartouche. • 6½ ins. diam.
William Smith & Co., Stafford Pottery, Stockton-on-Tees, circa 1825–1855.
This is an early and successful example of colour-printing on a plate; for more from the same factory, see page 69.

**177** Rococo edge with continuous garland border and green line to edge, with a sepia print of a boy playing with a model cannon: 'LILLIPUTIAN ARTILLERY'. • Mark: an asterisk, impressed; double footrim • 4½ ins. diam.
This illustration appeared as the tail-piece to the section on 'Artificial Fireworks' in *The Boy's Own Book* (1829).

**178** Straight edge with swagged garland and medallion border with a black line to the edge, and a black print (painted) of two children chasing butterflies: 'JUVENILE COMPANIONS/NOW THEN I SHALL CATCH IT'. • No mark • 5 ins. diam.
This print also appears on alphabet bordered plates.

PLAYING AT LOVERS

PLAYING AT MORNING CALLS
IN THE OLD BARONIAL HALL

SHIP-BUILDING

171

172

LOST!

JUVENILE COMPANIONS

173

174

175

LILLIPUTIAN ARTILLERY

JUVENILE COMPANIONS
NOW THEN I SHALL CATCH IT

176

177

178

**179** Shaped base and plain loop handle with a black print of 'THE GARDENER' on one side and 'MY PRETTY BABE' on the other, see 199. • No mark • 2½ ins. ht.; 2½ ins. diam.
The 'voided' effect of this print, in which the figures appear white with touched-in details against the solid printed background is unusual on children's wares, and is parallelled in the penwork of the time. In this, scenes were painted with a similar voiding technique on the surfaces of boxes and small furniture.

**180** Cylindrical with plain loop handle, black line to the rim and a black print of a girl 'DANCING FOR APPLE PYE'. • No mark • 2⅝ ins. ht.; 2⅝ ins. diam.

**181** Canary yellow cylinder with plain loop handle, silver lustre rim and handle, and an iron red print of cavorting cherubs, one with a bearded mask: 'THE FRIGHT'. • No mark • 2¼ ins. ht.; 2¼ ins. diam.

**182** Shaped base and loop handle with leaf terminals, and a manganese print of a lady with a parasol talking to three children, also with a parasol. • No mark • 2¾ ins. ht.; 2½ ins. diam.

**183** Slightly tapered, with plain loop handle and a sepia print (painted) of children dressed up in 18th century costume: 'NEW YEAR'S GIFT', • No mark • 3 ins. ht.; 2½ ins. diam.

**184** Cylindrical with plain loop ..andle and a black print of a boy and a girl dressed up in 18th century costume posting letters into trees: 'LETTER'. • No mark • 2⅜ ins. ht.; 2⅜ ins. diam.

**185** Cylindrical with ring handle and 'voided' black print covered all over in orange lustre. The print shows children 'DANCING'. • No mark • 2⅝ ins. ht.; 2½ ins. diam.

**186** Round-rimmed base with ring handle and a black print of four children at a meal. • No mark • 2¾ ins. ht.; 3 ins. diam.

179               180               181               182

183               184               185               186

**187** Cylindrical with loop handle and leaf terminals, and a green print of children playing shops. • No mark • 2½ ins. ht.; 2⅜ ins. diam.

**188** As 187 with a red print of two children sitting in a wheelbarrow. • No mark • 2½ ins. ht.; 2⅜ ins. diam.

**189** As 187 etc with a green print of children at a washtub. • No mark • 2⅜ ins. ht.; 2½ ins. diam.

**190** As 187 etc with a sepia print of children reading to their dog and dolls. • No mark • 2½ ins. ht.; 2⅝ ins. diam.

**191** As 187 etc with a green print of children playing houses under an umbrella. • No mark • 2½ ins. ht.; 2⅝ ins. diam.

**192** Shaped base and reeded loop handle with leaf terminals, and a black print of a child in a frilly crinoline behind a chair

watching a chimney sweep emerge from the fireplace. On the opposite side of the mug is the inscription in a scrolling cartouche: 'He that refuseth instruction despiseth his own soul.' • No mark • 3½ ins. ht.; 3½ ins. diam.
This image appears on an undated and unattributed decorative print of the mid-19th century.

**193** Cylindrical with plain loop handle and a red print of 'WILLIAM & HIS STORY BOOK'. • No mark • 3¼ ins. ht.; 2⅞ ins. diam.

**194** As 193 with a green print of a little boy with a parasol tugging at a little girl's dress. • No mark • 2¾ ins. ht.; 2¾ ins. diam.

**195** Round-rimmed base and moulded line below rim, flat-topped ear-shaped handle, brown line decoration and a pale blue border round the top. The sepia prints show a child on a rocking horse with a girl watching on one side, and a boy and a girl playing with a kitten on the other. • No mark • 3⅛ ins. ht.; 3⅜ ins. diam.
This print is from *My Sister* by Mary Belson (see 77).

**196** The opposite side of 195.
This print is from *My Brother* by Mary Belson (see 89).

**197** Shaped base and loop handle with leaf terminals and a sepia print (painted) of children 'PLAYING WITH A MOUSE'. • No mark • 2⅝ ins. ht.; 2¾ ins. diam.

**198** Shaped base and loop handle, and a green print of a child with a broken pitcher being comforted by another. • No mark • 2¾ ins. ht.; 3 ins. diam.
*The Broken Pitcher* was the title of a Victorian popular song for children.
See note for 521.

**199** The opposite side of 179.

187 188 189 190 191

192 193 194 195

196 197 198 199

# Chapter 4 GAMES AND PASTIMES

The images on children's wares give an indication of the most popular outdoor games they played. Hoops, kites and whipping tops seem to be in the lead, with hobby horses, battledore and shuttlecock, and stilts following close behind. Other games illustrated, such as hustlecap or la grace, have disappeared altogether. Hunting, shooting and fishing subjects must have had an obvious relevance in a period when these activities were a normal part of everyday country life, but what of tiger and elephant hunting? These scenes are in the well-established tradition of illustrations of Indian scenery and sporting life, and provide strong evidence of the continuing reality – even for children – of British India: there must have been few middle- and upper-class families at this period without relatives among the British Raj.

**200** Straight edge painted red, with moulded border of rose sprays alternating with rococo curlicues, and a sepia print of boys flying kites. • No mark; double footrim • 7½ ins. diam.

**201** Straight edge and indistinctly moulded daisy border with a manganese print of boys bowling hoops with a man watching. • No mark • 6 ins. diam.
The same print is recorded on a mug. This print was illustrated in *The Book of Sports* by William Martin (new edition, revised and with additions, Darton & Clark, circa 1840).

**202** Vitruvian scroll and alphabet border with a sepia print (painted) of boys with a kite. • Mark: EDGE MALKIN & CO impressed • 7¼ ins. diam.
Edge Malkin & Co., Newport and Middleport Potteries, Burslem, 1871–1903.

The print comes from an illustration by Henry Anelay in *The Mother's Picture Alphabet* (S. W. Partridge, London, 1862; Dover Reprint, 1974): 'K begins Kite that we saw in the sky:/It vanished almost, it was soaring so high.'

**203** Wavy edge with border of blobbed daisies and an inner band of sprigs, and a black print of two boys with hoops. • Mark: . . E & Co; triple footrim • 6¾ ins. diam.
Probably Moore & Co., Wear Pottery, Southwick, Sunderland, 1803–1874.

**204** Wavy edge and border of three graduated rows of pointed-petalled blobbed daisies, with a black print of a boy with a hoop shaking apples off a tree. • Mark: 48 impressed; double footrim • 8 ins. diam.
The mark is likely to indicate the date, 1848.

**205** Straight edge with blue plant motif around the border and a black print of children playing in a garden, one with a hoop: 'THE LITTLE PLAYFELLOWS.' • Mark: Bristol KX (or XX) impressed, and 8/87 above. • 6½ ins. diam.
Pountney & Co., Bristol Victoria Pottery, Temple Backs, Bristol.
The border of this plate probably provides an example of Pountney's special glaze effects and the numbers in the mark denote its date: August 1887.

**206\*** Straight edge with shamrock leaf and floret border and a blue print of a boy with a hoop and a girl with a doll: 'Why should I love my sport so well/So constant at my play:/And lose the thoughts of heav'n and hell/And then forget to pray?' • No mark • 4¾ ins. diam.
*Private Collection.*

**207** Straight edge with blobbed daisy border and a sepia print of a boy with a bubble pipe. • Mark: BTP Co impressed • 5 ins. diam.
Bovey Tracey Pottery Company, Devon, 1842–1894.

**208** As 207 with a sepia print of a boy bowling a hoop. • Mark: BTP Co impressed • 5 ins. diam.
Bovey Tracey Pottery.

**209** Wavy edge and blobbed daisy border with a sepia (painted) print of a child riding a hobby horse. • No mark • 4¾ ins. diam.
Another plate in this series shows a girl sketching.

MINOR SPORTS.    21

SPORTS OF AGILITY AND SPEED.

MANY of the previous sports with balls and tops, are in part games of agility and speed, and so also are several of those which will be found among the Miscellaneous Minor Sports; but the following pastimes are exclusively games either of speed or agility, for which no implements are necessary.

LEAP-FROG.

This is a most excellent pastime. It should be played in a spacious place, out of doors if possible, and the more there are engaged in it, provided they be of the same height and agility, the better is the sport. We will suppose a dozen at play:—Let eleven of them stand in a row, about six yards apart, with all their faces in one direction, arms folded, or their hands resting on their thighs, their elbows in, and their heads bent forward, so that the chin of each rests on his breast, the right foot advanced, the back a little bent, the shoulders rounded, and the body firm. The last begins the sport by taking a short run, placing his hands on the shoulders of the nearest player, and leaping with his assistance (of course, springing with his feet at the same time) over his head, as represented in the cut. Having cleared the first, he goes on to the second, third, fourth, &c. in succession, and as speedily as possible. When he has gone over the last, he goes to the proper distance, and places himself in position for all the players to leap over him in their turn. The first over whom he passed, follows him over the second, third, fourth, &c.; and when he has gone over, the one who begun the game places himself in like manner for the others to jump over him. The third follows the second, and so on until the parties are tired.

**210** Rococo edge and continuous daisy garland border painted red, pale green and blue, with a green print of boys playing leapfrog. • No mark; double footrim • 7 ins. diam.
This was an illustration in *The Boy's Own Book* – 'A complete Encyclopaedia of All the Diversions . . . of Boyhood and Youth' (Vizetelly, Branston & Co., London, 4th edition, 1829). Under the heading 'Minor Sports – Sports of Agility and Speed' leapfrog was rated 'a most excellent pastime'. The print was used again in *Mother Goose's Melodies* (Munroe and Francis, 1833) to illustrate 'Boys and girls come out to play'.

**211** Indented edge and moulded border of feathered curlicues enclosing rose and pansy sprays, with black lines, and a black print of three boys playing: 'In mirth and play no harm you'll know: When duty's task is done/PLAYING AT HUSTLE CAP.' • No mark; triple footrim • 5¼ ins. diam.
The same print appears on a rococo-edged plate with a rose, tulip and aster border. Hustle cap was a game like pitch and toss, in which halfpence were placed in a cap and thrown up.

**212** Erratic rococo edge with moulded flower sprig border painted maroon, pale blue and pale green, and a green print of boys playing a game with a ball on a string, perhaps cup and ball or bilboquet. • No mark • 7 ins. diam.

**213*** Edge and border as 210 with a sepia print of boys walking across the fens on stilts. • No mark; double footrim • 4½ ins. diam.
This illustration, entitled 'Walking on Stilts' appeared in *The Boy's Own Book* (Vizetelly, Branston & Co., London, 4th edition, 1829).

74          GYMNASTICS.

boy is, the longer it is necessary to have his stilts. By means of these odd additions to the natural leg, the feet are kept out of the water, which lies deep during winter on the sands, and from the heated sand during the summer; in addition to which, the sphere of vision or so perfect a flat is materially increased by the elevation, and the shepherd can see his sheep much further on stilts than he could from the ground. Stilts are easily constructed: two poles are procured, and at some distance from their ends, a loop of leather or rope is securely fastened; in these the feet are placed, the poles are kept in a proper position by the hands, and put forward by the action of the legs. A superior mode of making stilts is by substituting a piece of wood, flat on the upper surface, for the leather loop; the foot rests on and is fastened by a strap to it; a piece of leather or rope is also nailed to the stilt, and passed round the leg just below the knee: stilts made in this manner do not reach to the hands, but are managed entirely by the feet and legs. In many parts of England, boys and youth frequently amuse themselves by

Walking on Stilts.

**214*** Octagonal with straight edges and moulded border of rose, thistle and shamrock sprays, painted iron red, pale green

and yellow, alternating with tendrilled sprigs, and a black print of a boy playing with a whipping top. • No mark • 5¼ ins. diam.
This print has also been found on a straight-edged plate with plain border and black lines, marked with an impressed cross and POUNTNEY & ALLIES (Bristol, 1816–1835).

**215** Slightly rococo edge and sectioned border painted with two black lines, and a black print of a boy and a girl sailing model ships. • No mark • 5 ins. diam.

**216** Rococo edge and moulded daisy garland border, with a black print of three boys playing ninepins: 'CHILDREN'S PLAY/NINEPINS'. • No mark; double footrim • 4¾ ins. diam.

**217** Rococo edge with animal border and a sepia print of 'THE YOUNG SAILORS'. • No mark • 6¾ ins. diam.
*Private Collection.*

**218** Toy plate with straight edge and plain border with a manganese print of boys playing ball. • No mark • 4 ins. diam.
The same print, in blue, appears on a 7¼ ins. plate with indented edge and border of rococo curlicues and rose sprays painted red, green and yellow.

**219** Nearly straight edge with blobbed daisy border and green print of a boy outside a cottage playing with a 'WHIPPING TOP.' • No mark • 5½ ins. diam.

**220** Straight edge with moulded border of ferns and vertical sprigs, and a blue print of people near a river with sailing dinghies. • No mark • 5¾ ins. diam.
Possibly Ynysmedw Pottery, near Swansea, circa 1850–1870.

210

211

212

214

215

216

218

7

219

220

65

**221*** Straight edge and border of swagged garlands and posies, painted iron red, yellow, green and purple without regard for the moulding, and a blue print of children playing 'THE SHUTTLE COCK'. • Mark: painted l • 5½ ins. diam.

**222*** Rococo edge with bead moulding and garland border painted iron red, pale green, pink and yellow, and a sepia print (painted) of a man and two women playing blind man's buff. • Mark: painted 5; double footrim • 5 ins. diam.
This print was used, in black, on a gadrooned edge plate, by the Cambrian Pottery, Swansea, 1831–1850.

**223*** Rococo edge and moulded border of roses, tulips and asters, painted red, green and blue, and a black print of children playing with a swing: 'CHILDREN'S PLAY/A SEE SAW'. • Mark: l impressed: triple footrim • 5½ ins. diam.
A version of this print, with the same curious title, occurs in blue on a straight-edged plate with moulded leaf border.

**224** Indented edge with moulded border of rococo curlicues alternating with rose sprays painted red, green and yellow, and a blue print (clumsily painted) of children on a seesaw within a decorative surround. • No mark • 6½ ins. diam.

**225** Edge and border as 224 with brown line, and a sepia print of children playing with a swing. • No mark; double footrim • 8½ ins. diam.

**226** Twelve-sided plate with moulded floret border painted yellow, iron red, pale green, and purple, with a sepia print (painted) of two boys on 'THE SEESAW'. • No mark; double footrim • 6½ ins. diam.

**227*** Rococo edge and continuous daisy garland border painted maroon, pale green and blue, with a black print of a girl on a rocking horse and a boy with a whip looking on, in a landscape. • No mark; double footrim • 4½ ins. diam.

**228** Toy plate with slightly erratic edge and plain border, and a black print of a girl playing shuttlecock. • No mark • 3¾ ins. diam.

**229** As 228 with a black print of children playing boats at the seaside. • No mark • 3¾ ins. diam.

**230** Straight edge with moulded border of roses, thistles and shamrock, and a manganese print of a boy on a swing. • No mark • 4¾ ins. diam.

JEUX D'ENFANS.

Colin maillard.

Les quilles.

La balançoire.

La chasse au papillon.

A page from *Alphabet des Images* (Arnauld de Vresse, Paris, circa 1850).

221

222

223

4

225

226

227

228

229

230

**231** Rococo edge and border of roses and buds, painted red, green and blue, with a black print of 'CHILDREN'S PLAY/THE ROPE'. • No mark; triple footrim • 6¼ ins. diam.

**232** Octagonal with pink lustred edge and moulded border of roses, thistle and shamrock sprays alternating with tendrils, and a black print of a girl skipping. • No mark • 5¼ ins. diam.

**233*** Straight edge and moulded garland border painted iron red, pale green, pink and yellow, with a black print of three girls skipping: 'FEMALE SCHOOLFELLOWS./ See those skippers in a row.' • No mark • 6½ ins. diam.
Possibly James & Ralph Clews, Cobridge, 1818–1834.
A companion plate has a print of two boys playing marbles and two, with hoops, watching: 'DIFFERENT SPORTS/What only two at marbles play'.

**234** Wavy edge and border of round-petalled blobbed daisies, with a colour print of a boy reading in a landscape with cottages in the background, sometimes known as *The Village Poet*. • Marks: W. S. & Co's WEDGEWOOD impressed, and No 100 PASTIMES W. S. & Co printed. • 8 ins. diam.
William Smith & Co., Stafford Pottery, Stockton-on-Tees, Yorkshire, circa 1825–1855.
This plate and others marked WEDG-WOOD or WEDGEWOOD date from before 1848 when a court action by Wedgwood resulted in an injunction preventing William Smith from using the most prestigious name in pottery on any of his wares. Smith's subsequent use of the name Queens Ware must have been almost as annoying for Wedgwood.

**235*** As 234 with a colour print of a girl skipping. • Marks: As 234 • 8 ins. diam.
William Smith, Stockton.
The same colour print also occurs on wavy edged plates with radiating lines in the borders, also by William Smith of Stockton (see 176).

**236** As 235 with a colour print of a girl with a portfolio in a landscape with ruins in the background, sometimes known as *The Lady Artist*. • Marks: as 235 • 8 ins. diam.
Other examples in this series include a colour print of a girl feeding poultry (see 397) and one of a boy taking a picnic in a landscape with a windmill in the background and a whipping top in the foreground. The latter is marked as 234 but with 'No 101 Pastimes' (see below, courtesy of Peter Stockham).

**237** Rococo edge and border of roses, tulips and asters painted red, green, yellow and purple, with a manganese print of people in exotic costume playing chess in a landscape. • No mark • 7½ ins. diam.
Possibly John Carr, Low Lights Pottery, North Shields, Northumberland, circa 1845–1900.

**238*** Rococo edge with continuous daisy garland border, painted pale green, red and pale blue, with a blue print of boys swinging round a pole. • No mark; double footrim • 7 ins. diam.

**239** Slightly erratic edge with border of flowers and leaves printed in sepia and painted red, blue and pale green, and a sepia print (painted) of a girl sketching under a tree. • Mark: WOODLAND within a cartouche, and J. M. & Co beneath • 6½ ins. diam.
Possibly Joseph Mayer & Co., Burslem, circa 1841.

**240\*** Twelve-sided with iron red edge and moulded floret border, painted iron red, yellow, pink and pale green, with a black print (painted) of a woman with a decanter and glass: 'PLEASURE'. • Mark: M painted; double footrim • 6½ ins. diam.
The source for this image is an early 19th century decorative print by A. Courcell.

**241** Octagonal with herringbone edge and floret border painted in pink, blue and yellow, and a black print (painted) of two women in a landscape, one playing a guitar and the other holding some music. • No mark; double footrim • 6¾ ins. diam.

**242\*** As 240 with a print of a man playing a violin. • No mark; double footrim • 6½ ins. diam.

**243** Straight edge with printed alphabet border and a red print of children playing banjos. • Mark: a printed retailer's mark – H. C. Edmiston • 6¼ ins. diam.

**244** Slight rococo edge and tendrilled flower sprig border, and a sepia print (slightly painted) of a 'Tudorbethan' man playing his lute to a girl in a landscape. • No mark • 7½ ins. diam.
This print has been noted on a mug attributed to Dawson, Sunderland.

**245** Straight edge with moulded border of florets painted red, dark blue and yellow, and a sepia print of a girl dancing, within a decorative border. • Mark: DAWSON impressed; no footrim • 6¾ ins. diam.
John Dawson & Co., South Hylton & Ford Potteries, Sunderland, circa 1799–1864 (this mark pre-1848).

**246\*** Vitruvian scroll and alphabet border, with a black print (painted) of a little girl standing at a piano: 'THE PRETTY CHILD ON TIPTOE STANDS,/TO REACH THE PIANO WITH HER HANDS.' • Mark: ELSMORE & FOSTER • 7 ins. diam.
Elsmore & Foster (or Forster), Clayhills Pottery, Tunstall, 1853–1871.

**247** Straight edge with red painted line and radiating moulded lines to the border, and a green print of two children dancing. • Mark: FELL & Co above an anchor • 6¼ ins. diam.
Thomas Fell, St. Peter's Pottery, Newcastle-upon-Tyne, 1817–1890 (this mark post-1830).

**248** Vitruvian scroll and alphabet border with a black print (painted) within a red circle, of 'HIGHLAND DANCE'. • No mark • 7¼ ins. diam.
This is a companion plate to 170.

240

241

242

243

244

245

246

247

248

**249** Straight edge and rose, honeysuckle and swagged garland border, painted iron red, green and turquoise, with a black print (painted) of a female archer with a shepherd and sheep. • No mark • 7 ins. diam.
Probably Baker, Bevans & Irwin, Glamorgan Pottery, Swansea, 1813–1838.

**250\*** Octagonal with beaded edge painted yellow, and sepia-printed border of chinoiserie patterns, medallions, curlicues and leaves, painted in Pratt colours. The central roundel, also printed in sepia, shows two lady archers and a man. • Mark: a diamond impressed • 6½ ins. diam.
Ferrybridge Pottery, Yorkshire, 1792 onwards.
The print comes from an illustration in *The Sporting Magazine*, Volume 3, 1794.

**251** Straight edge with moulded border of two rows of blobbed daisies and a sepia print (slightly painted) of two archers in an exotic landscape. • No mark • 5¾ ins. diam.

**252** Straight edge and moulded border of roses, thistles and shamrock, with a green print of a boy tying on ice skates on a frozen river. • No mark • 6½ ins. diam.

**253\*** Rococo edge with moulded border of fruit and flowers in sections, painted iron red, green, yellow, purple and pink, with a sepia print (painted) of a man fishing in a landscape with a large house in the background. • No mark • 7¼ ins. diam.

**254** Straight edge with crisply moulded border of flower sprays alternating with scalloped panels painted with black lines, and a black print of a man drying his fishing net on a rustic bridge, with a cottage and a turret in the background. • Marks: BAKER BEVANS & IRWIN impressed, and Opaque China B B & I within a cartouche, printed. • 6 ins. diam.
Baker, Bevans & Irwin, Swansea.

**255** Reeded and feathered edge with vertical sprig border and a sepia print of boys playing 'FOOT-BALL'. • No mark • 6½ ins. diam.
This print was used by J & G Meakin, Hanley, 1851 onwards.

**256** Octagonal with straight edges painted red and a moulded garland and medallion border, with a sepia (painted) scene of 'CRICKET'. • No mark • 8 ins. diam.

**257** Indistinctly moulded alphabet border with a sepia print (painted) of a rugby scene. • No mark • 5¾ ins. diam.
Probably Allerton, Longton, 1859–1942.
A version of this print, with more figures in the background, has been found on a straight-edged plate with a fern and vertical sprig border.

249  250  251

252  253  254

255  256  257

**258** Cylindrical with plain loop handle and green prints illustrating 'THE GAME AT MARBLES' on one side, and 'CHERRIES RIPE' (see 594) on the other. • No mark • 2⅞ ins. ht.; 3 ins. diam.

**259** Round-rimmed base with plain loop handle and black prints of 'JUVENILE GAMBLERS' on one side, and 'MY PRETTY BIRD' (see 847) on the other. • No mark • 2⅝ ins. ht.; 2½ ins. diam.

**260** Cylindrical with loop handle and leaf terminals, and a green print of four boys 'PLAYING AT MARBLES'. • No mark • 2½ ins. ht.; 2½ ins. diam.

**261** As 258 with green prints of 'THE TOP SPINNER' on one side and 'THANK YOU MADAM' (see 591) on the other. • No mark • 3 ins. ht.; 3 ins. diam.

**262** Shaped base and loop handle with leaf terminals, and a black print of a boy bowling a hoop on one side and three children in a garden on the other: 'A PRESENT FOR A GOOD BOY'. • No mark • 2⅝ ins. ht.; 2⅝ ins. diam.
The print of the hoop-bowling boy also appears in sepia on a plain cylindrical mug 'FOR A GOOD BOY' (277), and on a plate (208).

**263** Tapered with shaped base and plain loop handle, pink lustre lines and a black print of children looking at 'The Burning Glass.' • No mark • 2½ ins. ht.; 2¼ ins. diam.

**264** Shaped base with plain loop handle and a black print of a boy with a hoop and a man talking to him, his hand on the boy's shoulder. • No mark • 2¾ ins. ht.; 2¾ ins. diam.

**265\*** Cylindrical with plain loop handle and a sepia print (painted) of three boys playing with 'THE PEG TOPS'. • No mark • 2⅝ ins. ht.; 2⅝ ins. diam.

**266** Shaped base and loop handle with leaf terminals, red lines to rim and handle, and a red print of boys playing boisterously in a landscape, with 'J K L' above and 'FOR MY NEPHEW' below. • No mark • 2¾ ins. ht.; 2¾ ins. diam.

**267** Tapered, with round-rimmed and reeded base, and pointed ear-shaped handle, with a black print of boys playing 'BLIND MAN'S BUFF'. • No mark • 2½ ins. ht.; 2½ ins. diam.

**268** Round-rimmed base with plain loop handle and a red print of boys sitting on a bench playing cards. • No mark • 2¾ ins. ht.; 2¾ ins. diam.

**269** Shaped base with plain loop handle and black prints, of a scene outside a tavern with skittles on one side, and a cottage interior with a harbour view on the other. • No mark • 2⅝ ins. ht.; 2¾ ins. diam.
The source for these prints are illustrations of the Franklin maxims 'Dost thou love life, then do not, squander time' ... and

'Employ time well if thou meanest to gain leisure' ... on a picture sheet by Robert Dighton, published by Bowles & Carver, London 1795 (see 1080).

**270** Shaped base and plain loop handle with a black print (painted) of children on a seesaw 'INNOCENT SPORT'. • No mark • 2 ins. ht.; 2¼ ins. diam.

**271** Cylindrical with plain loop handle and a black print of children on a seesaw with a dog watching. • No mark • 2¾ ins. ht.; 2¾ ins. diam.

**272** Cylindrical with loop handle and leaf terminals and a black print of two boys on a see-saw: 'GOOD EXERCISE'. • No mark • 2¾ ins. ht.; 2¾ ins. diam.

**273** Apricot-coloured, cylindrical, with plain loop handle and black prints of a girl on a swing on one side and a bird on a mistletoe sprig on the other. • Mark: SWING, printed on a garter enclosing C. P. Co Ltd. • 3¼ ins. ht.; 2⅞ ins. diam. Campbellfield Pottery Co. Ltd., Springburn, Glasgow, Scotland, 1850–1905; this mark post-1884.

258

259

260

261

262

263

264

265

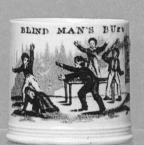

266

267

268

269

270

271

272

273

**274** Cylindrical with flat-topped ear-shaped handle and red-printed borders and prints, of football on one side and cricket on the other. • Mark: F & R printed on a garter enclosing SPORTS • 3¼ ins. ht.; 3⅜ ins. diam.
Ford & Riley, Newcastle Street, Burslem, 1882–1893.

**275** Cylindrical with plain loop handle and a green print of a girl on one side and a boy on the other, painting flowers in a pot in the middle, the pot inscribed: 'COME SISTER SUE/AND WE'LL CHANGE THE HUE/OF THE FLOWER IN THAT BLUE POT./I'M SURE WE SHALL FIND/THAT MOTHER WON'T MIND/SO WE MAY AS WELL DO IT AS NOT'. • No mark • 3 ins. ht.; 3 ins. diam.

**276** Shaped base with plain loop handle, sepia-printed borders and two (printed and painted) cricketing scenes. • No mark • 3¼ ins. ht.; 3¼ ins. diam.

**277** Cylindrical with plain loop handle and green prints of a boy and a girl playing shuttlecock: 'KEEP IT UP', on one side and a boy bowling a hoop: 'FOR A GOOD BOY' (see 262) on the other. • No mark • 3 ins. ht.; 3 ins. diam.

**278** Cylindrical with plain loop handle and a sepia print of a boy on a penny farthing or ordinary, followed by a boy on a bicycle with two horizontally placed wheels and a perch for the rider between. • No mark • 2¾ ins. ht.; 2¾ ins. diam.

**279** Round-rimmed base with plain loop handle and a black print of boys playing a ball game with a small flat bat, possibly a form of rounders. • No mark • 2⅞ ins. ht.; 3 ins. diam.

**279a** Shaped base with plain loop handle and a sepia print, with painted details, of girls playing tennis. • No mark • 2¾ ins. ht.; 2½ ins. diam.
*Private Collection.*

**274** The opposite side.

**276** The opposite side.

274

275

276

277

278

279

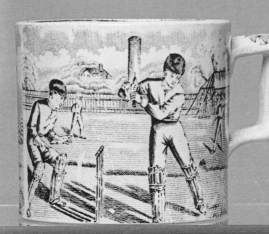

9a

274

276

**280** Straight edge with arcaded border of florets and leaves, painted with red lines, and a sepia print of 'FOX HUNTING'. • No mark • 6½ ins. diam.

**281** As 280 with a green print of 'WILD BOAR HUNTING'. • No mark • 6½ ins. diam.

**282** As 280 etc with a sepia print of 'WILD GOOSE SHOOTING'. • No mark • 6½ ins. diam.

**283** Straight edge with green line and moulded border of rococo curlicues alternating with rose sprays, and a green print of a fox-hunting scene. • No mark • 7½ ins. diam.
Versions of this print were used by J. & G. Meakin of Hanley and by Evans & Glasson, Swansea; it is also to be found, in brown, on unmarked plates with the same border as 283 but with a slightly indented edge.

**284** Straight edge with indistinctly moulded vitruvian scroll and alphabet border, with a sepia print of a man shooting birds, with dogs watching. • No mark • 7¾ ins. diam.
Probably Charles Allerton, Park Works, Longton, 1859–1942.

**285** Straight edge painted green, and moulded border of blobbed round-petalled daisies in three graduated rows, with a blue print of 'SPORTSMAN'. • Mark: H impressed • 7½ ins. diam.
Possibly Bovey Tracey Pottery, Devon, 1842–1894.
This print may be found on smaller plates, sometimes in green; some are marked BTP & Co.

**286** Straight edge and moulded border of scallops and florets, with a black print of 'THE HUNTSMAN'. • Mark: a castle over an anchor • 6¾ ins. diam.

W. H. and J. H. Ainsworth, Stockton Pottery, Stockton-on-Tees, 1865–1901.
A companion plate, also marked, illustrates 'THE WILD HORSE'.

**287** Octagonal, with rope-twist edge painted red, and moulded border of large and small florets, with a black (painted) print of a man with a gun and a spaniel retrieving a bird. • No mark • 5½ ins. diam.

**288** Shapely rococo edge with moulded border of painted posies and unpainted baskets of flowers, and a blue print of 'DOG FOX and GAME'. • No mark; double footrim • 6½ ins. diam.
This print comes from an illustration on a sheet of four hand-coloured 'Copper Plate Pictures for Children' published by Darton, 1825.

280

281

282

283

284

285

286

287

288

**289** Indented edge painted brown, with moulded border of rose sprays and rococo curlicues and a sepia print of wild horse hunting. • No mark • 7½ ins. diam.

**290** Erratic edge and border of tendrilled flower sprigs, with a sepia print (painted) as 289, with the title, 'WILD HORSE HUNT'. • No mark • 8¼ ins. diam.

**291** Wavy edge and three-row blobbed daisy border with an inner row of sprigs, and a black-printed scene of 'Hawking'. • Mark: MOORE & Co impressed • 7½ ins. diam.
(Samuel) Moore & Co., Wear Pottery, Southwick, Sunderland, 1803–1874.

**292** Straight edge painted pink with a plain border and a manganese print of a tiger-hunting scene. • No mark • 6¼ ins.
The same print, in sepia, is to be found on straight-edged plates with rose spray and rococo curlicue borders.

**293** Nearly straight edge with a rose spray and rococo curlicue border and a blue-printed scene of a 'TIGER HUNT'. • No mark • 4¾ ins. diam.

**294** Edge and border as 290 with a sepia print of another view of a 'TIGER HUNT'. • No mark • 6½ ins. diam.
Others in this series were Buffalo Hunt and Stag Hunt; the prints were used by several different factories but the engravings probably came from a common source. The Shelton engraver Elisha Pepper is known to have supplied four hunting scenes in this series to the Dutch factory of Petrus Regout (see note to 496).

Illustration from an early 19th century scrapbook, see colour plate CLXIV.

89

290

291

292

293

294

## PUZZLES

**295** Vitruvian scroll and alphabet border with a black print of silhouette figures: '6. WHAT FRUIT DOES OUR SKETCH REPRESENT?' • No factory mark, but the answer to the riddle: '6. A PEAR: (PAIR)'. • 6 ins. diam.
This and the two following plates are part of a series produced by an unidentified Staffordshire pottery. Six different riddle illustrations are recorded.

**296** As 295 with the riddle: '2. WHY IS THIS GEOMETRICAL FISHING?' Answer on underside: '2. BECAUSE IT IS A TRIANGLE'. • 6 ins. diam.

**297** As 295 etc with the riddle: '1. WHY IS THIS POOR LITTLE RABBIT SO TERRIBLY FRIGHTENED?'. Answer on underside: '1. BECAUSE HE IS NOT GAME'. • 6 ins. diam.

**298** Rococo edge painted pale green and continuous daisy garland border, with a sepia print (painted) of three girls holding up banners: 'CHARADES/My first is on the Reindeer's head/My second is a measure,/My total is a favourite dance/That's always seen with pleasure./HORNPIPE.' • No mark; double footrim • 4½ ins. diam.
This illustration appeared in *The Girl's Book of Diversions* by Miss Leslie (Thomas Tegg, 1835) and later in *The Girl's Own Book* by Mrs Child (18th edition, William Tegg, 1858).
The word charade is used here in its original sense, meaning 'a riddle in which a word is enigmatically described or

represented in action' [*Oxford Dictionary of English Etymology*].

**299** Slight rococo edge and dark blue acorn and oakleaf printed border and circular design of cavorting cherubs: 'FIND SEVEN CHILDREN'. • No mark • 7¼ ins. diam.
This is based on a reversed version of an undated lithograph entitled *Seven Boys, An Allegory of the Pleiades, or Seven Stars*, from a painting by Francis Floris, published as Royal Album No 12 by Alfred Carlile, London. (See illustration on opposite page).

**300** As 298 but with an unpainted border, and a black print of two girls playing a game with sticks and rings: 'RIDDLE/I ever live man's unrelenting foe/Mighty in mischief though I'm small in size/And he at last that seeks to lay me low/My food and habitation both supplies/. . .' [WORM]. • No mark; double footrim • 4½ ins. diam.
This illustration shows two girls playing the game La Grace, and it is taken from *The Girl's Book of Diversions* (see 298): 'The Graces. This is played with two small hoops and four sticks. Each player takes a pair of sticks and a hoop, and stands opposite to her adversary. The sticks are held one in each hand so as to cross; the hoop is hung on their points, and then tossed over to the other player, who must endeavour to catch it on the points of *her* sticks, having first tossed her own hoop towards her opponent. The hoops are thus alternatively thrown backwards and forwards, and received on the points of the

sticks which are always held across each other . . . This game affords very good and healthful exercise, and, when well played, is extremely graceful. It is, however, too difficult for small children, unless they be uncommonly alert.' Another writer described 'La Grace' as 'a new game, common in Germany, but introduced into this country from France. It derives its name from the graceful attitudes which it occasions. . . In America is it called The Graces or The Flying Circle.' [*The Girl's Own Book* by Mrs Child (Tegg, 4th ed. 1832)].
Another illustration of 'LA GRACE' appears on a straight-edged plate with blobbed daisy border.

**301** Rococo edge with moulded border of roses, tulips and asters, painted red, green and blue, with a green print of children sitting outside: 'CHARADES/My first is productive of light/My second to wood has affiance/My whole is high polished and bright/And my first on its aid has reliance/CANDLE-STICK'. • No mark • 6 ins. diam.
This is an illustration from *The Girl's Book of Diversions* (see 298).

**302** Slightly rococo edge and plain border with a red print of children playing blind man's buff: 'RIDDLE/I'm in every one's way yet no one I stop/My four horns each day/Horizontally play/And my head is nail'd on at the top/A TURNSTILE'. • Mark: (?) W W impressed • 5 ins. diam.
Possibly Wilkinson & Wardle, Denaby Pottery, nr Mexborough, Yorkshire, 1864–1866.
Some of these and similar riddles have been found on alphabet bordered plates.

295

6. WHAT FRUIT DOES OUR SKETCH
REPRESENT?

296

2. WHY IS THIS GEOMETRICAL FISHING?

297

WHY IS THIS POOR LITTLE RABBIT SO TERRIBLY FRIGHTENED?

298

CHARADES
My first is on the Antiquary's head
My second is a measure

My total is a favourite dance

299

FIND SEVEN CHILDREN

300

RIDDLE

301

CHARADES
My first is productive of light,
My second to wood has affinite

302

RIDDLE

# Chapter 5 CHILDREN'S STORIES AND NURSERY RHYMES

JOHN GILPIN

**303** Vitruvian scroll and alphabet border, with black line, and a black print (slightly painted) of 'JOHN GILPIN'S ARIVAL [sic] AT WARE'. • No mark; double footrim • 6¼ ins. diam.
Probably Godwin, Burslem.
This and the following John Gilpin prints are from George Cruikshank's illustrations to *The Diverting History of John Gilpin* (Charles Tilt, 1828).
The popular humorous ballad by William Cowper (1731–1800) about the wedding anniversary adventures of a London draper 'of credit and renown' was based on an anecdote about a Mr. Beyer, a real-life linen draper of Paternoster Row, who was caricatured in a succession of illustrations during the 19th century.

**304** Straight edge painted black, with garland and medallion border, and a sepia print (slightly painted) of 'JOHN GILPIN PURSUED AS A HIGHWAYMAN'. • No mark • 5¾ ins. diam.

**305** As 303 with a black print (slightly painted) of 'JOHN GILPIN GOING PAST EDMONTON'. • No mark; double footrim • 6¼ ins. diam.
Probably Godwin, Burslem.

**306** Nearly straight edge with border of flower sprays alternating with vertical curlicues, painted blue, pale green and red, with a green print of 'OLD MOTHER HUBBARD/She went to the Hosier's to buy him neat hose;/And when she came back he was drest in his clothes.' • No mark • 6¼ ins. diam.
The print is based on an illustration in *The Comic Adventures of Old Mother Hubbard and her Dog* (John Harris, 1819).
*Old Mother Hubbard*, possibly by Sarah Catherine Martin (1768–1826) is one of the few nursery rhymes attributed to a named author; it is also one of the few that recurs on children's wares with regularity. First published in 1805 (by John Harris), its instant popularity ensured a succession of editions and variants.

**307** Heavily potted alphabet border, with a manganese print illustrating the 'DIVERTING HISTORY OF JOHN GILPIN/FROM AND RETURN HOME.' • No mark • 7¼ ins. diam.
The same series of prints can be found on garland and medallion bordered plates of 8¼ ins. size, and on plates with rose, thistle and shamrock borders lustred in orange: on one of these, the illustration of John Gilpin pursued as a highwayman is mis-titled 'FROM AND RETURN HOME'.

**308** Nearly straight edge with moulded border of three graduated rows of blobbed daisies, and a black print of 'OLD MOTHER HUBBARD/See the Dame's Dog is dead and lost all his powers:/As he lies on a Bier the Dame strews it with Flowers'. • No mark • 6 ins. diam.
The same print is to be found on a plate with a border as 306.
It also comes from John Harris's 1819 edition of *Old Mother Hubbard*.

303

304

305

306

307        308

309        310        311

**309** Straight edge with beaded rim and continuous vine border, with a sepia print of Dame Trot with Spot the dog and her cat: 'Another time the Dame came in/When Spot demurely sat/Half lather'd to the ears and eyes/Half shaven by the Cat'. • Mark: a crown with CLEWS WARRANTED STAFFORDSHIRE impressed. • 5½ ins. diam. James and Ralph Clews, Cobridge, 1818–1834. The print is from an illustration in *The Comic Adventures of Old Dame Trot and Her Cat* (John Harris, London, 1820 and subsequently).
*Private Collection.*

**310** Straight edge with moulded border of alternate arabic and roman numerals, with a red print illustrating 'THE HOUSE THAT JACK BUILT/This is the man all tatter'd and torn/that kissed the maiden all forlorn.' • No mark • 5½ ins. diam.

**311** Rococo edge painted green, and continuous daisy garland border, with a sepia print illustrating 'Hey diddle diddle. The Cat and the Fiddle./The Cow jump'd over the moon./The little Dog laugh'd. To see such fine sport./And the Dish ran away with the Spoon.' • No mark; double footrim • 5¼ ins. diam.

**312** Straight edge and blobbed daisy border, with a blue print of 'THE FOX AND THE STORK'. • No mark • 6½ ins. diam. This print and the following are based on illustrations in Croxall's edition of *Aesop's Fables*, 1818.

**313** Straight edge with black-printed alphabet border and a black print of 'AESOP'S FABLES/THE SHEPHERD'S BOY'. • Mark: T & B GODWIN NEW WHARF; double footrim • 5¼ ins diam. Thomas & Benjamin Godwin, New Wharf, Burslem, circa 1809–1834. An inscribed label on the underside of the plate reads: 'in 1830 given to me by Mary Lee My Grandmother'.

**314** Wavy edge and blobbed daisy border with a green print illustrating 'THE HORSE AND THE STAG'. • No mark • 6¾ ins. diam. The print is based on an illustration in Croxall's edition of *Aesop's Fables* (1818).

**315** Nearly straight edge painted with a blue line, and plain border painted with red and black semicircles, and a black print of 'PILGRIM'S PROGRESS/THE WICKET GATE'. • No mark • 7½ ins. diam. The print is from an illustration in *The Picture Scrap Book or Happy Hours at Home* (Religious Tract Society, circa 1860).

**316** Octagonal with pink lustred rope-twist edge and moulded border of large and small florets, and a black print (painted) illustrating 'LARK AND YOUNG ONES'. • No mark • 7 ins. diam. The print is after Thomas Bewick's engraving for The Lark and Her Young Ones in his book of *Fables*, 1818.

**317** Straight edge and plain border painted with two blue lines, and a black print of 'CHRISTIAN AND HOPEFUL CROSSING THE RIVER TO MOUNT SION/PILGRIM'S PROGRESS.' • No mark • 6½ ins. diam.

**318** Erratic edge with moulded border of florets and dots in lines and semicircles painted red and pale green, and a sepia print of a lion attacking a turbanned man: 'ARABIAN NIGHTS'. • No mark • 6¾ ins. diam. This is almost certainly an illustration to the 'History of Prince Amgiad and of Prince Assad' in the *Arabian Nights*, in which Amgiad with his scimitar (not shown in this picture) rescues the Emir Giondar from the clutches of a lion.

**319** Straight edge and sepia-printed alphabet border, and sepia print (painted) to illustrate 'CRUSOE RESCUES FRIDAY'. • Mark: Rd No 69963 B. P. Co TUNSTALL ENGLAND, printed • 8¼ ins. diam. Brownhills Pottery, Tunstall, 1872–1896; this design was registered in 1887.

**320** As 319 with a sepia print (slightly painted) of Robinson Crusoe making a basket: 'CRUSOE AT WORK'. • Mark: Rd No 69963 B. P. Co. • 7¼ ins. diam. Brownhills Pottery, Tunstall, 1872–1896.

312    THE FOX AND THE STORK

313    ABCDEFGHIJKLMNOPQRSTUVWXYZ   ÆSOP'S FABLES   THE SHEPHERD'S BOY

314    THE HORSE AND THE STAG

315    PILGRIM'S PROGRESS   THE WICKET GATE

316    LARK AND YOUNG ONES

317    CHRISTIAN AND HOPEFUL CROSSING THE RIVER TO MOUNT SION   PILGRIM'S PROGRESS

318    ARABIAN NIGHTS

319    ABCDEFGHIJKLMNOPQRSTUVWXYZ   CRUSOE RESCUES FRIDAY

320    ABCDEFGHIJKLMNOPQRSTUVWXYZ   CRUSOE AT WORK

## ROBINSON CRUSOE

Daniel Defoe's novel, written in 1719, was based on the adventures of a Scottish sailor, Alexander Selkirk, who joined Dampier's expedition to the South Seas in 1703 and who, after a quarrel with his captain, lived on the island of Juan Fernandez for 52 months before being picked up. *The Life and Adventures of Robinson Crusoe* was one of the first, and one of the most enduring, adventure stories.

**321** Octagonal with wavy edge and wide border of moulded patterns, with two red painted lines. The black print shows Robinson Crusoe on the raft. • No mark • 6 ins. diam.
This plate design was registered by Bailey & Ball, Longton, in 1847; although unmarked, we can assume that plates of this shape illustrated here were made by them.

All the prints can be found on large and small sized plates, and with different coloured lines in the borders; the prints may be black or sepia, and are almost always painted.
The prints on all the plates except 329 and possibly 335 are based on J. J. Grandville's illustrations for *Robinson Crusoe*, first published in French in 1840 and in English (by George Routledge) in 1853. These were highly regarded by other artists of the time, including Charles Altamont Doyle (1832–1893) whose fine watercolour copies of 24 of them, bound in an album, were sold at Christie's in 1991.

**322** As 321 with a sepia print of Robinson Crusoe on the raft. • Mark: a green blob • 7¾ ins. diam.

**323** As 321 etc with a black print (painted) shows Robinson Crusoe at a table. • No mark • 6 ins. diam.

**324** Straight edge painted red and indistinctly moulded border of flower sprays, with a manganese print (painted) of Robinson Crusoe reckoning time. • No mark • 7 ins. diam.

**325** As 321 etc with a sepia print of Robinson Crusoe digging. • Mark: a blue arrowhead • 6 ins. diam.

**326** As 321 etc with a black print of Robinson Crusoe followed by the kid. • Mark: a blue painted X • 7¾ ins. diam.

I could never see a bird near the place as long as my scare-crows hung there.

**327** As 321 etc with a sepia print of Robinson Crusoe watching his first crop. • Mark: diamond registration mark for Bailey & Ball, April 1847. • 8 ins. diam.

**328** As 321 etc with a black print of Robinson Crusoe carrying corn. • Mark: a yellow V • 6 ins. diam.

**329** Rococo edge with moulded border of roses, tulips and asters painted red, green and blue, with a black print within a circle of Robinson Crusoe with his dog. • No mark; triple footrim • 7½ ins. diam.

I thrust her off with the oar I had into the channel.

321     322     323

324     325     326

327     328     329

**330** Rococo edge and indistinctly moulded border of roses, tulips and asters, with a black print of 'ROBINSON CRUSOE REPAIRING HIS WARDROBE'. • No mark; triple footrim • 5¼ ins. diam.
Illustration from Grandville's *Robinson Crusoe* (see 321).
Another version of this print has been found on an indistinctly moulded vitruvian scroll and alphabet bordered plate.

**331** As 321 etc with a black print of Robinson Crusoe in his boat. • No mark • 6½ ins. diam.

**332** As 321 with a sepia print of Robinson Crusoe startled by his parrot. • No mark • 7¾ ins. diam.

**333** Vitruvian scroll and alphabet border with blue line, and a sepia print of 'ROBINSON CRUSOE & FAMILY DINING'. • No mark • 7 ins. diam.

**334** As 321 etc with a black print of 'ROBINSON CRUSOE AND FAMILY AT DINNER.' • Mark: three green blobs • 7½ ins. diam.

**335** Vitruvian scroll and alphabet border with a black print of 'ROBINSON CRUSOE./At dinner with his little fami[ly]'. • No mark • 6¼ ins. diam.
This may have been inspired by Grandville's illustration, but the engraver has departed some way from the image, if not the idea, apart from reversing it.

**336** Nearly straight edge with indistinctly moulded border of two rows of blobbed daisies and a sepia print (painted) of 'ROBINSON CRUSOE AND HIS MAN FRIDAY'. • No mark • 6¼ ins. diam.

**337** As 321 with a sepia print of 'ROBINSON CRUSOE MILKING.' • No mark • 7¾ ins. diam.

**338** Nearly straight edge with blobbed daisy border and a black print of Robinson Crusoe rescuing a Christian man from the cannibals. • No mark • 6 ins. diam.

330

331

332

333

334

335

336

337

338

LXI     LXII     LXIII     LXIV

LXV     LXVI     LXVII     LXVIII

LXIX     LXX     LXXI     LXXII

LXXIII                 LXXIV                 LXXV

LXXVI                 LXXVII                LXXVIII

LXXIX                 LXXX                 LXXXI

*Colour Plate 8*

LXXXII      LXXXIII      LXXXIV

LXXXV      LXXXVI      LXXXVII

LXXXVIII      LXXXIX      XC

*Colour Plate 9*

XCI

XCII

XCIII

XCIV

XCV

XCVI

XCVII

XCVIII

XCIX

C

CI

*Colour Plate 10*

CII

CIII
CHRISTMAS DAY

CIV
THE SENTINEL

CV
CAT AND KITTENS

CVI

CVII
THE LITTLE JOCKEY

CVIII
Who saw me mount the Rocking Horse
And then stood by, to check its course,
Lest her dear boy should get a tofs?
My Sister.

CIX
My Sister

CX
Pleas'd with her Doll, as Child could be,
Who did with sweet alacrity,
Put Doll to Bed, and work with me!
My Daughter

*Colour Plate 11*

CXI

CXII

CXIII

CXIV

CXV

CXVI

CXVII

CXVIII

CXIX

*Colour Plate 12*

CXX

CXXI
THE ALDERMANS HOBBY

CXXII
THE SUMMER STYLE

CXXIII
THE LADYS ACCELERATOR
WONDERS WILL NEVER CEASE

CXXIV
THE REAL DANDY HOBBY

CXXV
A VISIT TO CARLTON HOUSE

CXXVI
QUEEN ADELAIDE

CXXVII
CAROLINE REGINA

CXXVIII

*Colour Plate 13*

CXXIX          CXXX          CXXXI

CXXXII          CXXXIII          CXXXIV

CXXXV          CXXXVI          CXXXVII

*Colour Plate 14*

CXXXVIII          CXXXIX          CXL

CXLI          CXLII          CXLIII

CXLIV          CXLV          CXLVI

*Colour Plate 15*

CXLVII CXLVIII CXLIX

CL CLI CLII

CLIII CLIV CLV

*Colour Plate 16*

CLVI

CLVII

CLVIII

CLIX

CLX

CLXI

CLXII

CLXIII

CLXIV

*Colour Plate 17*

CLXV      CLXVI      CLXXVIa

CLXVII      CLXVIII      CLXIX

CLXX      CLXXI      CLXXII

*Colour Plate 18*

## UNCLE TOM'S CABIN

The American Harriet Beecher Stowe's anti-slavery novel was first published in serial form in the *National Era* in 1851–52, and in book form in 1852, with illustrations by George Cruikshank. It became the best selling novel of the 19th century. An ardent temperance as well as anti-slavery campaigner, Harriet Beecher Stowe and her husband visited England in 1853, 1856 and 1859, expressly to encourage support for the prohibition movement which had taken root in England following the introduction of the prohibitionist 'Maine Law' in that state of America in 1851.

**339** Slightly rococo edge with moulded border of three rows of blobbed daisies and a blue print illustrating 'UNCLE TOM'S CABIN./HALEYs BARGAIN FOR ELIZAs CHILD.' • Mark: a circle divided into three sections, impressed • 7 ins. diam.

This print is from one of George Cruikshank's illustrations for *Uncle Tom's Cabin* (Cassell, 1852). All the others on this page, except 342 and 345 are from the same source.

**340** Wavy edge and blobbed daisy border, with a sepia print (painted) of 'UNCLE TOM'S CABIN./PRAYER MEETING IN UNCLE TOM'S CABIN.' • No mark • 6½ ins. diam.
This plate is also found in a larger size.

**341** As 339 with a green print of 'UNCLE TOM'S CABIN/THE DEATH OF UNCLE TOM.' • No mark • 7 ins. diam.
This plate is also to be found in a smaller size.

**342** Straight edge with plain border painted with red lines, and a manganese print illustrating 'UNCLE TOM'S CABIN;/THERE IS ANOTHER PROPRIETOR OF SOULS'. • No mark • 6½ ins. diam.
This print also appears on a plate with the same border and impressed mark as 345, and on a 'vitruvian scroll and alphabet bordered plate (unmarked). Another vitruvian scroll and alphabet bordered plate has the *Uncle Tom's Cabin* print, 'Lizzy's Bridge'.

**343** As 340 with sepia print (painted) of 'UNCLE TOM'S CABIN./EMMELINE ABOUT BEING SOLD.' • No mark • 7¾ ins. diam.

**344** Erratic edge lustred pink and continuous daisy garland border painted red, green, blue and yellow, with a sepia print of 'UNCLE TOM'S CABIN/EVA DRESSING TOM'. • No mark; double footrim • 6¼ ins. diam.

A version of this print appears in black on an erratic-edged plate with an unmoulded border painted with black lines; this is a companion plate to an illustration of the 'DEATH OF UNCLE TOM' – a different one from 341.

**345** Rococo edge and moulded border of strapwork and cartouches, and a black print of UNCLE TOM'S CABIN;/THE VISION OF UNCLE TOM'. • Mark: a castle and anchor, impressed • 8 ins. diam.
W. H. & J. H. Ainsworth, Stockton Pottery, Stockton-on-Tees, 1865–1901.

**346** Rococo edge and moulded border of birds and pendant lambrequins, spotted in blue, green, pink and brown, with a sepia print (painted) illustrating 'UNCLE TOM'S CABIN/TOM AND EVA/YOUR LITTLE CHILD IS YOUR ONLY TRUE DEMOCRAT'. • No mark • 8¼ ins. diam.

## PAUL AND VIRGINIA

The five *Paul and Virginia* plates on this page represent a large group illustrating the phenomenally successful pastoral romance written by the French natural philosopher and follower of Rousseau, Jacques-Henri Benardin de Saint-Pierre in 1788. It focuses on the lives (and, of course, love affair) of two young people brought up in Mauritius, free from social prejudice, religious superstition and other conventions of European society. The story was as popular in England as on the Continent and was illustrated by several different artists during the 19th century; it was also adapted for theatrical productions.

**347** Wavy edge and blobbed daisy border, with a manganese print of Paul and Virginia: 'Their Youth'. • Mark: W. S. & Co's QUEEN'S WARE STOCKTON impressed, and PAUL and VIRGINIA printed • 6½ ins. diam.

William Smith, Stafford Pottery, Stockton-on-Tees, Yorkshire, circa 1825–1855.

**348** Octagonal with lustred rope-twist edge and moulded border of large and small dimpled florets, and a sepia print (painted) of 'PAUL & VIRGINIA'. • No mark • 6¼ ins. diam.
The source for this print is the frontispiece of St. Pierre's *Paul and Virginia* in the edition illustrated by Corbould and Heath (J. F. Dove, 1828).

**349\*** Edge and border as 347 with a sepia print of 'Virginia attending the Sick Poor.' • Mark: W. S. & Co's QUEEN'S WARE STOCKTON impressed • 7 ins. diam.
Other images in the *Paul and Virginia* series produced, with varying borders, by William Smith of Stockton, include 'Discovered by Fidelio'; 'Virginia comforting Paul'; 'Virginia and her Goats'; 'Virginia at the Fountain'; 'Passage of the Current'; 'The Bird's Nest', and 'The Body of Virginia found in the Sand'.

**350** Wavy edge with moulded wavy lines enclosing a single row of daisies, and a black print of 'The Mar ... [?] Slave and Virginia'. • Mark: indistinct shield, impressed, and a blue-printed squiggle • 6¾ ins. diam.

**351** Straight edge and sepia-printed alphabet surrounding an off-centre illustration of 'NURSERY TALES/CINDERELLA'. • Mark: Rd No 75,500 TUNSTALL ENGLAND B. P. Co., printed • 7¼ ins. diam.
Brownhills Pottery, Tunstall 1872–1896.
This is one of a series that also includes Jack and Jill, Miss Muffet, Whittington and his Cat, Little Red Riding Hood, Old Mother Hubbard and Little Jack Horner. Similar series were devoted to 'Bible Pictures' and 'Wild Animals' (see 721).

**352** Rococo edge with moulded border of baskets of flowers alternating with flower sprays and butterflies in tendrilled cartouches. The sepia print illustrates the 'Death of Paul'. • Mark: an indecipherable

impressed mark, and PAUL and VIRGINIA and 13 printed • 6½ ins. diam.
William Smith, Stafford Pottery, Stockton-on-Tees, Yorkshire, circa 1825–1855.

**353** Straight edge with moulded border of ferns and vertical sprigs, and a sepia print (painted) of two men attacking a wolf. • Mark: Y P impressed • 5¾ ins. diam.
Ynysmedw Pottery, nr Swansea, circa 1850–70.
The inspiration for this print may have come from an illustration to *Little Red Riding Hood* by W. Tomlinson, circa 1880.

**354** Octagonal with rope-twist edge and moulded border of dimpled florets and stars, lustred in two shades of pink, with a red print of 'CHILDREN IN THE WOOD'. • Mark: anchor and DAVENPORT impressed • 6¾ ins. diam.
Davenport, Longport, Staffordshire, circa 1840–50.

**355** Straight edge and plain border painted with two black lines, and a black print illustrating 'COCK ROBIN/Who will dig his grave I said the Owl/With my spade and shovel And I'll dig his grave/This is the Owl so brave That dug Cock Robin's grave.' • Mark: X impressed • 6 ins. diam.

347

348

349

350

351

352

353

354

355

ENIGMAS

The plates on this page represent stories that have so far eluded us. The first four recount the adventures of a schoolboy called George and his birthday cake. It must have been familiar to many Victorian children, but we have been unable to trace the origins, either of its text or its pictures. The three in the bottom row are part of another series whose elusiveness is tantalising.

**356** Wavy edge with three rows of blobbed daisies and a black print of a servant and schoolboys: 'YOUR MAMMA SENDS HER LOVE, AND, SHE BID ME TO [?SAY]/SHE HAS SENT YOU A PRESENT, TO GRACE YOUR BIRTHDAY, AND A CHARMING PLUM CAKE IT IS.' • No mark • 5¼ ins. diam.

**357** As 356 with a black print illustrating 'NOW VEX'D AT HIS FOLLY, AND LOSS OF HIS CAKE/HE RESOLVED ALL HIS OLD FOOLISH TRICKS TO FORSAKE, AND NEVER TO DO SO AGAIN.' • No mark • 5¼ ins. diam.

**358** As 356 etc with a black print illustrating 'GEORGE RAN TO THE SPOT, BUT HIS FATE HAD BEEN SEAL'D/FOR A PLOUGH-BOY, IN PASSING, WHILE GEORGE LEFT THE FIELD, HAD CARRIED IT OF [sic] AS HIS PRIZE.' • No mark • 5¼ ins. diam.

**359** As 356 etc with a black print illustrating 'GEORGE IS GONE OUT TO PLAY, AND I HARDLEY KNOW WHERE/BUT I THINK I CAN SEE HIM YES HEAR I DECLARE MASTER GEORGE AND HIS PLAY MATES ARE COME.' • No mark • 6½ ins. diam.
Another in the series has its black print crudely painted, and shows George in the schoolmaster's study: 'MY BIRTH DAY IS COME I HAVE THEREFORE TO PRAY/THAT YOU WILL PERMIT ME A SHORT TIME TO PLAY IF ITS PROPER TO GRANT MY REQUEST.'

**360** Octagonal with rope-twist edge and blobbed daisy border, and a red print of 'CHARLOTTE & LUCY LOOKING AT THE KITTENS.' • No mark • 5¾ ins. diam.

**361** Rococo edge with moulded border of roses, fuchsia and vertical columnar sprays, and a sepia print illustrating 'OH, HERE IS OLD ROBERT, HE'S COME WITH OUR PONY/TO MEET US HALF WAY: AND HERE, TOO, HIS TONY.' • No mark • 7 ins. diam.
This print is also to be found, in red, on a wavy-edged, daisy-bordered plate.

**362** Rococo edge with flower and curlicue border painted pale green, iron red and blue, and a black print of 'TOM SUCKLED BY THE GOAT.' • No mark • 4½ ins. diam.
*Private Collection.*

**363** As 362 with a black print (very slightly painted) of a peg-legged veteran 'TEACHING NED HIS EXERCISE.' • Mark: a floret, impressed • 4½ ins. diam.

**364** As 362 with a black print (slightly painted) of 'LITTLE HENRY NOTICED BY THE LADY'. • Mark: a floret, impressed • 4½ ins. diam.
Others in this series include 'A SOLDIER VISITING HOME'; 'CURING THE TARTARS HORSE', and 'LITTLE JACK'S MONKEY KILLED'.

356

357

358

360

361

362

363

364

111

**365** Cylindrical with plain loop handle and black prints of the sparrow and his arrow on one side, the dead Cock Robin on the other, and the verse in the middle: 'THE DEATH OF COCK ROBIN/WHO killed Cock Robin?/I, said the Sparrow:/With my bow and arrow/I killed Cock Robin./All the birds of the air/Fell a sighing an sobbing,/When they heard the sad Fate/of poor COCK ROBIN.' • No mark • 3⅛ ins. ht.; 3¾ ins. diam.

**366** As 365 with black prints of the bull on one side, the dove on the other and the verse in the middle: 'THE DEATH OF COCK ROBIN./WHO'll be chief mourner?/I, said the Dove,/For I mourn for my love./I'll be chief mourner./WHO'LL toll the bell?/I, said the Bull/Because I can pull. So Cock Robin, Farewell.' • No mark • 3⅛ ins. ht.; 2¾ ins. diam.

**367** As 365 with sepia prints of the priest marrying the man all tattered and torn on one side, the cock on the other and the verse in the middle: 'THE HISTORY OF THE HOUSE THAT JACK BUILT/This is the Cock that crowed in the morn that waked the Priest all shaven and shorn that married the Man all tattered and torn that kissed the Maiden all forlorn that milked the Cow with the crumpled Horn that tossed the Dog that worried the Cat that killed the Rat that eat the Malt that lay in the House that Jack built'. • No mark • 2¾ ins. ht.; 2⅝ ins. diam.

**368** Shaped base and broken (loop) handle with black prints of the maiden all forlorn on one side, the man all tattered and torn on the other, and the verse in the middle: 'THE HISTORY OF THE HOUSE THAT JACK BUILT/This is the Man all tattered and torn that kissed the Maiden all forlorn' . . . • No mark • 2⅝ ins. ht.; 2⅞ ins. diam.

**369** Shaped base and plain loop handle with red prints (painted) of the dog worrying the cat that killed the rat on one side, the cow with the crumpled horn tossing the dog on the other and the verse

in the middle: 'THE HISTORY OF THE HOUSE THAT JACK BUILT/This is the Cow with the crumpled Horn that tossed the Dog' . . . • No mark • 2½ ins. ht.; 2½ ins. diam.

**370** Shaped base and plain loop handle, with a sepia-printed alphabet flanking a view (painted) of Robinson 'CRUSOE ON THE RAFT'. Mark: Rd. No. 69963 B. P. Co • 2½ ins. ht.; 2⅞ ins. diam. Brownhills Pottery, Tunstall, 1887.

**371** Shaped base and loop handle with leaf terminals, and black-printed patterns inside and outside rim and on handle, and a view of 'ROBINSON CRUSOE AND HIS MAN FRIDAY/Now Friday do exactly as you see me do/Are you ready Friday let fly then'. • Mark: an underglaze blue crescent-shaped blob • 2¾ ins. ht.; 2⅞ ins. diam.

**372** Slightly tapered with plain loop handle and a sepia print of a woman feeding a hen, watched by three gentlemen, with the verse on the opposite side: 'Higglepy, Piggleby, my black hen./She lays eggs for gentlemen:/Sometimes nine, and sometimes ten./Higglepy, Piggleby, my black hen!' • No mark • 3 ins. ht.; 2½ ins. diam.

**365** The opposite side.

**366** The opposite side.

**367** The opposite side.

**368** The opposite side.

**373** Cylindrical with flat-topped ear-shaped handle and blue-printed flower and leaf border inside rim, and views of ROBIN HOOD AND THE BUTCHER' on one side, and 'ROBIN HOOD AND THE SHERIFF' on the other. • No mark • 3¼ ins. ht.; 3¼ ins. diam.

**374** Shaped base and plain loop handle with a green print of 'OLD MOTHER GOOSE WHEN SHE WANTED TO WANDER/WOULD RIDE THROUGH THE

AIR ON A VERY FINE GANDER.' • No mark • 2⅝ ins. ht.; 2¾ ins. diam.

**375** Shaped base and loop handle with leaf terminals, and a black print of four men in the forecourt of an inn. • No mark • 2½ ins. ht.; 2¾ ins. diam.
This is one of the illustrations by Phiz (H. K. Browne) for the first edition of Dickens's *Pickwick Papers* (1837).

**369** The opposite side.

365

366

367

368

369

370

371

372

365

366

367

368

373

374

375

369

# Chapter 6 EDUCATION

**376** Straight edge and moulded border of rose sprays alternating with scrolling frond motifs, painted in Pratt colours, and a black print illustrating 'THE HORN BOOK/ The Infant prattler jumps and skips/(A Mother's kisses on his lips)/And pleased to learn the Horn-book trips/THE SCHOOL-BOY!' • Mark: a crown and WARRANTED impressed • 7½ ins. diam. Probably James & Ralph Clews, Cobridge, 1818–1834.

This and the prints on the next two plates are from *The School-boy* by William Upton (Darton, 1820).

**377** As 376 with the black print 'JUST BREECHED/Just Breeched, and proud to show his cloaths/(His mind sweet budding like the Rose.)/To join his little Play-mates, goes/THE SCHOOL-BOY!' • Mark: a crown and WARRANTED impressed • 7½ ins. diam. Probably Clews. It was customary, until the early 20th century, for small boys to be dressed in frocks over long pantaloons, or in knee-length skirts; at the age of five or six they were 'breeched', that is, given long trousers or breeches to wear. At about the same time their school education began.

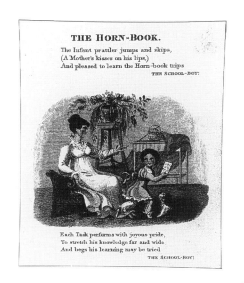

**378** As 376 etc with a black print illustrating 'BREAKING UP./The blithsome Holidays appear,/(The Jubilee days of Childhood's year.)/To welcome Home with blessings dear,/THE SCHOOL-BOY!' • Mark: a crown and WARRANTED impressed • 7½ ins. diam. Probably Clews.

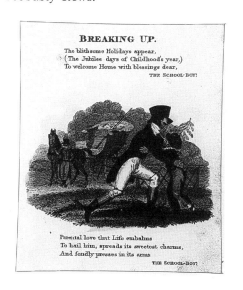

**379** Rococo edge and moulded border of flowers and fruits in compartments, painted dark green, red and yellow, and a sepia print illustrating 'ADVERBS./are words add-ed to Verbs, Participles, and Adjectives/Many adverbs end in *ly*. Ellen works *neatly*, sings *sweetly*, sews *industriously*'. • No mark • 8 ins. diam. This and the following five prints are from *The Paths of Learning Strewed with Flowers* or *English Grammar Illustrated* (John Harris, 1820).

**380** As 379 with a sepia print illustrating 'ADJECTIVE./Means the *quality* of a thing/ A *Good* Girl, relieving a *poor lame* Man, *good* is the quality of the Girl, *lame* and *poor* of the Man.' • Mark: an anchor impressed • 8 ins. diam.

**381\*** As 379 with a black print illustrating 'VERB./To Walk, To ride, To laugh, To cry/A Verb means the act of doing anything. Charles rides well, the Horse gallops: the words *ride* and *gallop* are Verbs'. • No mark • 8 ins. diam.

**382** As 379 with a black print illustrating 'NOUN/The name of any *thing, person,* or *Place*/Nouns mean *things*: whatever we can touch or see, as *Gentleman, Dog, Flower, Field, Kate* or *Ann*'. • No mark • 8 ins. diam.

**383** As 379 with a sepia print illustrating 'ARTICLES./*a, an, the/an apple.*/The Article *a* becomes *an* before a Vowel, and is called an indefinite article because it means any thing; as *a Cow, an Apple.*' • No mark • 8 ins. diam.

**384\*** As 379 with a black print illustrating 'MARKS and STOPS./A comma is marked thus , a Semicolon, thus ; a Colon, thus : a Period, or full stop thus . a Note of interrogation, thus ? a note of Admiration, thus !' • No mark • 8 ins. diam.

**376**

THE HORN-BOOK.

The infant prattlers jump and skip,
A Mother's kisses on the lip,
And pleased to learn the horn-book try.
THE SCHOOL BOY.

**377**

JUST BREECHED

Just Breeched, and proud to show his clothes,
His mind never looking like the Rose,
To join his little Play-mates, dance.
THE SCHOOL BOY.

**378**

BREAKING UP

The Welcome Holidays appear,
(The Jubilee days of Childhood's year,)
To welcome Home with Merriment dear,
THE SCHOOL BOY.

**379**

ADVERBS,
are words added to Verbs, Participles,
and Adjectives

Many adverbs end in ly. Ellen works
neatly, sings sweetly, sews industriously.

**380**

ADJECTIVE.
Means the quality of a thing

Affection, relieving a poor lame Man good is
the quality of the Girl lame and poor of the Man.

**381**

VERB.

To walk        To laugh.
To ride        To cry.

A Verb means the art of doing anything Charles
rides well, the Horse gallops, the words, ride,
and gallop are Verbs

**382**

NOUN,
The name of any thing person or Place

Nouns mean things, whatever we can touch or
see as Gentleman Dog Flower Field Kirk, &c Ann

**383**

ARTICLES
a    an    the
an    apple

The Article a becomes an before a Vowel and
is called an indefinite article because it
means any things as a Cow, an Apple

**384**

MARKS and STOPS,
A comma is marked thus , a Semicolon thus ;

a Colon, thus :    a Period or full stop thus .    a Note of
Interrogation, thus ?    a note of Admiration thus !

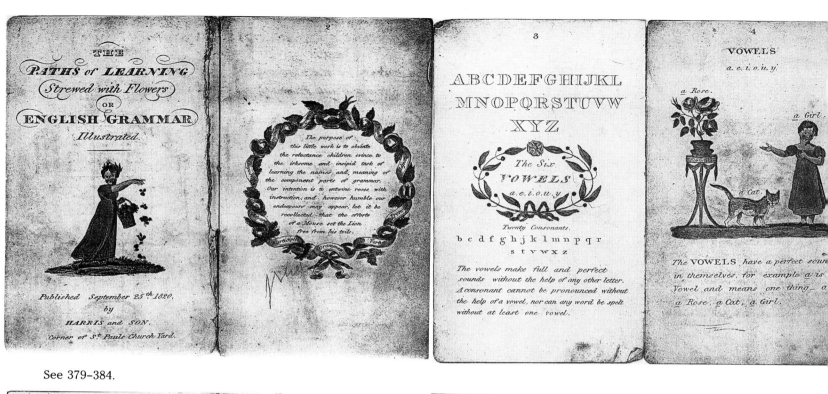

**THE PATHS of LEARNING Strewed with Flowers OR ENGLISH GRAMMAR Illustrated.**

Published September 25th 1820,
by
HARRIS and SON,
Corner of St Pauls Church Yard.

The purpose of this little work is to obviate the reluctance children evince to the irksome and insipid task of learning the names and meaning of the component parts of grammar. Our intention is to entwine roses with instruction, and however humble our endeavours may appear, let it be recollected that the efforts of a Mouse set the Lion free from his toils.

**ABCDEFGHIJKL MNOPQRSTUVW XYZ**

The Six VOWELS a. e. i. o. u. y.

Twenty Consonants.

b c d f g h j k l m n p q r s t v w x z

The vowels make full and perfect sounds without the help of any other letter. A consonant cannot be pronounced without the help of a vowel, nor can any word be spelt without at least one vowel.

**VOWELS** a. e. i. o. u. y.

a Rose. a Girl. a Cat.

The VOWELS have a perfect sound in themselves, for example a is a Vowel and means one thing — a a Rose, a Cat, a Girl.

See 379–384.

**ADJECTIVES**
have three degrees of comparison

Short 1. Shorter 2. Shortest 3.

MARY is short. — Positive degree. 1.
JAMES is shorter. Comparative degree. 2.
FRANK is shortest. — Superlative degree. 3.

**PRONOUN**
I. thou. he. she. my. thy. it.

PRONOUN is a word used instead of a noun, to avoid the too frequent repetition of the same word, as Jane has a Garden and she waters it. — she and it are Pronouns, for Jane and Garden.

**VERB**
to ride, to walk, to laugh, to cry.

A VERB, means the act of doing any thing, Charles rides well, the Horse gallops; the words ride and gallop are Verbs.

**PARTICIPLES**
are derived from Verbs.

Past marched. Present marching.

There are two participles. — 1st the past, ending in ed as marched, armed. 2ly the present, ending in ing — as walking. — holding.

116

## 5

### ARTICLES

*a    an    the.*

*an Apple*

*a Cow*

The ARTICLE *a* becomes *an* before a Vowel, and it is called an indefinite article, because it means any thing, as *a* Cow, *an* Apple.

## 6

### ARTICLE

*the.*

THE is called a definite Article because it means some particular thing, as I caught a Pigeon, but not *the* Pigeon with strings round its neck.

## 7

### NOUN

*is the name of any thing, person or place.*

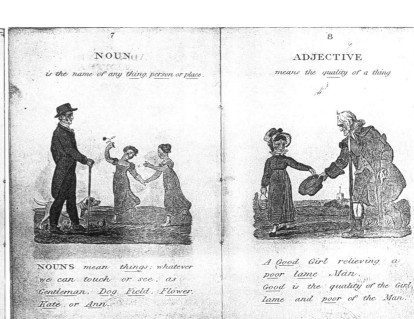

NOUNS mean things; whatever we can touch or see, as Gentleman, Dog, Field, Flower, Kate, or Ann.

## 8

### ADJECTIVE

*means the quality of a thing*

A *Good* Girl relieving a poor *lame* Man.
*Good* is the quality of the Girl *lame* and *poor* of the Man.

## 13

### ADVERBS

*words add-ed to Verbs, Participles and Adjectives.*

Many adverbs end in *ly.* Ellen works *neatly,* sings *sweetly,* sews *industriously.*

## 14

### PREPOSITION

*at    to    from    of    for    by*

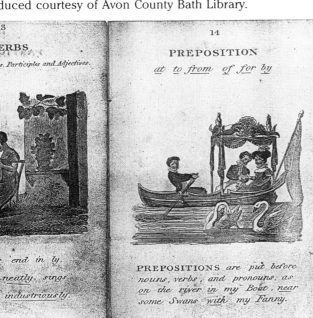

PREPOSITIONS are put before nouns, verbs, and pronouns, as *on* the river *in* my Boat, *near* some Swans *with* my Fanny.

## 15

### CONJUNCTION

*and, but, if, yet,*

CONJUNCTIONS are words that join sentences and words together, you *and* I rode together *but* we did not reach London, *yet* we saw it. — *and, but, yet,* are all conjunctions

## 16

### INTERJECTIONS

*oh! alas! O! la! fie! hush! behold!*

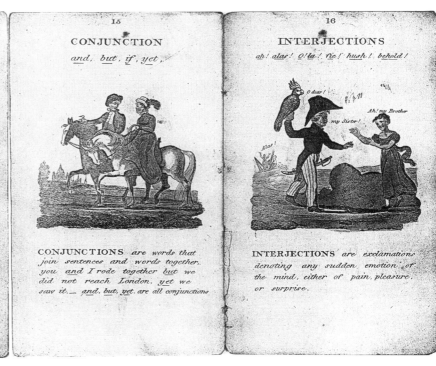

INTERJECTIONS are exclamations denoting any sudden emotion of the mind, either of pain, pleasure, or surprise.

**385** Straight edge with rose, thistle and shamrock border lustred in orange, with a black print showing 'A LECTURE ON ARITHMETIC'. • No mark • 5¾ ins. diam. This and the prints on the following five plates are part of the same humorous series illustrating mathematical concepts.

**386** Wavy edge and three-row blobbed daisy border with a black print showing 'DIVISION'. • Mark: an asterisk impressed; double footrim • 6¾ ins. diam.

**387** As 385 with a black print illustrating 'SUBSTRACTION'. • No mark • 5½ ins. diam.

**388** Rococo edge and indistinctly moulded rose, tulip and aster border, with a sepia print of a parson with tithe pigs, illustrating 'DECIMALS'. • No mark • 6½ ins. diam.

**389** As 388 with a sepia print illustrating 'VULGER FRACTIONS'. • No mark • 6½ ins. diam.

**390** As 388 etc with a sepia print illustrating 'ADDITION'. • No mark • 6½ ins. diam.

**391** Erratic edge and indistinctly moulded border of tendrilled flower sprays, and a green print of a boy reading a book. • No mark • 4½ ins. diam.

The print also appears on small alphabet bordered plates.

This is a reversed version of an illustration in *The Mother's Picture Alphabet* with illustrations by Henry Anelay (Partridge, 1862): 'B begins Bible, the book we so prize;/That teaches us all to be holy and wise.' A similar image later appeared in the evangelistic magazine, *The Little Gleaner*, January 1872 (Houlston, London).

**392** Erratic edge and moulded border of florets and leaves in compartments, painted iron red, pink lustre, pale green and yellow, with a sepia print of three cherubs looking at a globe, in the manner of Cipriani. • No mark • 4½ ins. diam.
This may have been a 'stock block' used also for the decoration of a map or atlas.

**393** Straight edge with single-row blobbed daisy border and a sepia print of the 'SCHOOL BOY.' • Mark: JOHN THOMSON GRANITE impressed round an anchor • 4¼ ins diam.

John Thomson, Annfield Pottery, Glasgow, 1816–1896.

**394** As 391 with a green print of a mother reading to two children. • No mark • 4½ ins. diam.
This is a version of the title page illustration by Henry Anelay in *The Mother's Picture Alphabet* (Partridge, 1862).

386

387

389

390

391

392

393

394

EDUCATION

The following four plates, and 400, give a light-hearted emphasis to the teaching of French. More examples in the same vein are to be found in the Caricature section (page 185).

**395** Vitruvian scroll and alphabet border with a black print (painted) of a flower seller: 'FLEURS – FLOWERS'. • No mark • 6 ins. diam.

**396** Nearly straight edge with moulded border of tendrilled flowers and a sepia print (painted) of children with a cat looking at an alphabet: 'LA LECTURE – READING'. • Mark: a four-petalled floret impressed • 6½ ins. diam.
This print was used by J. F. Wileman, Foley China Works, Fenton, 1869–1892.

**397** Reeded and feathered edge with border of vertical sprigs, and a sepia print (painted) of 'CANDINS – DANDIES'. • Mark: a floret impressed • 6¼ ins. diam.

**398** As 397 with a black print (painted) of 'EMPLOYES – CLERKS'. • Mark: a circle of dashes, impressed • 7¼ ins. diam.
Others in this series illustrate 'LE DOCTEUR – DOCTOR' and 'LES KABYLES – KABYLES' (Berbers).

**399** Straight edged bowl with border of trilobate leaves and a green print of a boy giving a group of children 'THE LESSON'. • No mark • 7 ins. diam.
This is another in the set of bowls illustrating trades (see page 157). The same print has been found on a plate with a border of lines in a zig-zag pattern.

**400** Wavy edge and three-row border of blobbed daisies, with a manganese print of a child on a toy horse: 'LE PETIT ROI SUR SON DADA/THE LITTLE KING ON HIS HOBBY HORSE'. • Mark: LONDON impressed in a fan shape above an anchor • 6¾ ins. diam.
This could be one of five factories, see note for 16.

**401** Straight edge decorated with a black-printed rope, and a black-printed view of the 'INTERIOR OF STRATFORD GRAMMAR SCHOOL.' • No mark; double footrim • 7 ins. diam.

**402** Straight edge and border of ferns and vertical sprigs, and a sepia print (painted) of children playing schools. • No mark • 6¾ ins. diam.

**403** Gadroon edge and alphabet border with a red print of a Dutch boy and girl recoiling from a goose, encircled by the sign language alphabet. • Mark: Rd No 426673 • 7 ins. diam.
Aynsley & Co., Commerce Works, Longton, 1904.
This is an illustration of the sign language (still used today) that has been evolving in Europe since the 16th century. The growth in urban populations resulting from the Industrial Revolution, undoubtedly led to a more powerful lobby for deaf people. This plate (and the mug 417) may have been part of a campaign on behalf of the deaf, or they may have been designed specifically for deaf children.

395

396

397

398

399

400

401

402

403

**404** Lobed edge with florets in reeded segments, painted red and green, with a green print of a boy hurting his fingers in a toothed tool: 'THE SENSES./FEELING.' • No mark • 7 ¼ ins. diam.
This print, and 405, 406 and 409, came from *The Parlour Book or, Conversations on Science and the Arts for the use of schools and families* by William Martin (Darton & Clark, circa 1840).

**405\*** As 404 with the border florets painted yellow and blue, and a red print of children looking through a telescope and a microscope. 'THE SENSES./SEEING.' • No mark • 7¼ ins. diam.

**406\*** As 404 etc with red and green florets, and a green print of a girl at a fortepiano and boys playing the violin and flute: 'THE SENSES./HEARING.' • No mark • 7¼ ins. diam.

**407** Straight edge and moulded border of florets and curlicues on a granular background, with a black print of a girl with a basket of flowers in a garden: 'N stands for Nemophila, Lovely of hue,/Like the sweet

Summer sky in its delicate blue.' • No mark • 6¼ ins. diam.
This and other prints in the series, such as Daisy, Lily and Tulip, are to be found also on alphabet bordered plates. For an illustration of Convolvulus, untitled but from the same source, see 505.
This print is from *The Alphabet of Flowers*, one of 'Routledge's New Series of Shilling Toy Books' with illustrations printed in colour by Leighton Brothers, circa 1868, and was one of the illustrations to The Alphabet of Flowers included in *The Boys' and Girls' Illustrated Gift Book* (Routledge, 1872).

**408** Rococo edge with lattice and scrolled cartouche border, and a sepia print of two boys running from a man behind a fence, with a large 3: 'THE CHILD'S PANORAMA.' • Mark: NORTH SHORE POTTERY in a semicircle above initials (indistinct) • 8 ins. diam.
William Smith junior, North Shore Pottery, Stockton-on-Tees, Yorkshire, circa 1845–1884.

**409** Straight edge painted green with two-row blobbed daisy border and a sepia print of three children smelling flowers: 'THE SENSES./SMELLING.' • Mark: an asterisk impressed • 5½ ins. diam.

This print has also been found, in manganese, on a 5¾ ins. plate with a lobed border as 404 etc.

**410** Straight edge painted blue, with an indistinctly moulded border of ferns and vertical sprigs, and a black print of a 24-hour clock. • Mark: NEW TIME Rd No 22184 B. H. & Co, printed • 5¾ ins. diam.
There were several factories with the initials BH, but the registration number dating this design to 1885 suggests that the plate was made by Buckley Heath, Union Pottery, Burslem, 1885–1890.
Use of the 24-hour clock officially began in 1925, but it had been in use long before this at Greenwich, on the Continent and by the military. Perhaps this plate was part of an early campaign for its more general introduction.

**411** Octagonal with pink lustred rope-twist edge and moulded border of dimpled florets, with a black print (painted) of two cherubs on a clock face with Roman numerals. • No mark • 6¼ ins. diam.

**412\*** Rococo edge with indistinctly moulded border of florets and leaves in compartments, painted green, red and blue, and a manganese print of an 'alphabet tree' encircled by a capital letter alphabet and with the inscription, 'Easy steps to the Tree of learning'. • Mark: GOODWINS & HARRIS impressed • 6¼ ins. diam.
Goodwins & Harris, Crown Works, Lane End, circa 1831–1838.

**404** THE SENSES. / PEEPING.

**405** THE SENSES. / SEEING.

**406** THE SENSES. / HEARING.

**407** N stands for Nemophila, lovely of hue, / Like the sweet Summer sky in its delicate Blue.

**408** THE CHILD'S PANORAMA.

**409** THE SENSES. / SMELLING.

**410**

**411**

**412**

**413** Shaped base and loop handle, with a red print of 'THE SCHOOL IN UPROAR'. • No mark • 2⅝ ins. ht.; 2¾ ins. diam. *Private Collection.*

**414** Cylindrical with loop handle and leaf terminals and black prints (painted) of a pair of boxing negroes on one side (the title is indecipherable), and 'A LECTURE ON ARITHMETIC' on the other (see 385). • No mark • 2⅝ ins. ht.; 2¾ ins. diam. Another image in the series of humorous mathematics, (see page 119).

**415*** Creamware, cylindrical, with loop handle and leaf terminals, pink lustre lines and a sepia print of a girl and a boy 'GOING TO SCHOOL'. • No mark • 2¾ ins. ht.; 2⅝ ins. diam.

**416*** Round-rimmed base with plain loop handle, iron red lines to rim and handle and a blue print (painted and lustred) illustrating 'NOUN', as 382. • No mark • 2½ ins. ht.; 2⅝ ins. diam. An example in the series based on the illustrations to *The Paths of Learning*

*Strewed with Flowers* (John Harris, 1820), see also page 115.

**417** Shaped base with spurred loop handle and black-printed sign language alphabet in squares. • No mark • 2½ ins. ht.; 2⅝ ins. diam. See note to 403.

**418** Shaped base and reeded loop handle with leaf terminals, pink lustre borders and black prints of a floating Noah's ark within a banner title, 'SCRIPTURE HISTORICAL ALPHABET' and a view of Samuel with the priest in the temple: 'S was Samuel, the prophet/and judge by whose hand/Saul was made/King of Israel to rule/o'er the land.' • No mark • 2⅝ ins. ht.; 2⅞ ins. diam.

**419** Shaped base and loop handle with leaf terminals, and black prints: inside the rim, 'A was an ass so stupid & dull. B was a bee with her honey bag full'; the illustration of a cat with a mouse, and a girl with a doll, in a park landscape with a mansion and a battlemented bridge is for 'C was a cat that caught all the mice. D was a doll dressed up very nice'. • No mark • 2¾ ins. ht.; 2¾ ins. diam.

**420** Cylindrical with plain loop handle and a black print (painted) of a boy and a girl dressed as an 18th century shepherd and shepherdess flanking a large H: 'HOULETTE/SHEPHERD'S CROOK'. • No mark • 2⅜ ins. ht.; 2¼ ins. diam.

**421** Round-rimmed base and top edge, and loop handle with leaf terminals, and a black print illustrating 'C was a Cobbler, at work in his Stall' on one side, and 'D was a Dustman who Dust Ho! did call' on the other. • No mark • 3¾ ins. ht.; 3 ins. diam.

**422** Cylindrical with plain loop handle and a green print illustrating 'H FOR HIDE AND SEEK'. • No mark • 3 ins. ht.; 2¾ ins. diam.

**423** As 422 with a green print illustrating 'S FOR SNOWBALLS'. • No mark • 3 ins. ht.; 2¾ ins. diam.

413

**424** Cylindrical with plain loop handle and a grey print of a family of anthropomorphic pigs on one side, and the verse on the other: 'V Stands for the village/Where these piggies dwell./Of the three little piggies/I a tale could tell!'. • No mark • 2⅞ ins. ht.; 2½ ins. diam.

**425** Cylindrical with plain loop handle and a green print of a girl showing her basket of eggs to two children on one side, and the verse on the other: 'E IS AN EGG/IN A BASKET/WITH MORE/WHICH PEGGY/WILL SELL FOR/A SHILLING A SCORE.' • No mark • 3¼ ins. ht.; 3 ins. diam.

414

415

NOUN.
The name of any *thing*, *person*, or *Place*.

...uns mean *things*... whatever we can touch or
...a Gentleman, Dog, Flower, Field, Kate, or Inn.

416

417

418

419

420

421

...RICAL
ALPHABE...    S    S

...ught all the mice. D. was a doll dre...

SHEPHERD'S CROOK

D was a Dustman who Dust Ho! did call    D

422    423    424    425

FOR HIDE AND SEEK

FOR SNOWBALL...

**426** Cylindrical with slightly spurred loop handle and blue prints representing A on one side and B on the other. • No mark • 2¾ ins. ht.; 2¾ ins. diam.

This and the two following illustrations, and 431, 432 and 434, were used in the *Child's Treasury of Knowledge* (Wier & White, Boston, undated, reprinted in *100 Nineteenth Century Rhyming Alphabets in English from the Library of Ruth M. Baldwin* (Southern Illinois University Press, 1972).

**A** stands for Apple, which here you may see.

**427** As 426 with manganese prints representing Q on one side and W on the other. • No mark • 2¾ ins. ht.; 2⅝ ins. diam.

**Q** stands for Quills, from the goose or the swan.

**428** Cylindrical with plain loop handle and green prints representing E on one side and F on the other. • No mark • 2½ ins. ht.; 2½ ins. diam.

**E** is for Elephant, monstrous and high.

**429*** Round-rimmed base and loop handle with leaf terminals and black prints of a tinker on one side and a vintner on the other, with the verse in the middle: 'T was a Tinker;/and mended/a Pot./V was a Vintner;/a very great/Sot.' • No mark • 2¼ ins. ht.; 2⅝ ins. diam.

A companion mug shows 'N was a/ Nobleman, Gallant/Bold./O was an/ Oyster girl, and/a sad Scold.'

**430** Cylindrical with reeded loop handle and leaf terminals, and dark blue prints, on one side 'S STANDS FOR SHEEP WHO OFT SLEEP IN A FOLD' and on the other 'T IS A TIGER SAVAGE AND BOLD'. • No mark • 3 ins. ht.; 2¾ ins. diam.

**431** Cylindrical with flat-topped ear-shaped handle grooved at the sides, and a red print representing L. • No mark • 2¾ ins. ht.; 2¾ ins. diam. (See 426).

**L** is a Ladder, for climbing a wall.

**432** As 431 with a red print representing W. • No mark • 2⅝ ins. ht.; 2⅝ ins. diam.

**W** is a Windmill, that turns with the wind.

**433** Round-rimmed base and loop handle with leaf terminals, and manganese prints representing S on one side and T on the other. • No mark • 3¼ ins. ht.; 3 ins. diam.

**F** begins Fox, and we know he is sly.

**426** The opposite side.

**428** The opposite side.

**434** As 426 with red prints representing T on one side and Z on the other. (See page 131). • No mark • 2¾ ins. ht.; 2¾ ins. diam.

**T** stands for Tiger, striped yellow and black.

**429** The opposite side.

**433** The opposite side.

**435** Cylindrical with plain loop handle and a black print of a lady and gentleman greeting a train marked 'NORTH STAFFORD', illustrating 'Y is YOURSELF, coming home from school,/The lessons all said according to rule.' • No mark • 2¾ ins. ht.; 2⅝ ins. diam.

Is YOURSELF, coming home from the school, When lessons are all said according to rule.

This is an illustration from *Cousin Chatterbox's Railway Alphabet* (Dean, circa 1852, V&A Reprint 1986).
The addition of 'NORTH STAFFORD' to the railway carriage instead of the GW of the original, suggests that a Staffordshire firm made this mug.

**436** Cylindrical with loop handle and leaf terminals, and green prints of a baker with a large pie in a well-appointed kitchen: 'FOUR AND TWENTY BLACKBIRDS BAKED IN A PIE' on one side and 'BAKER' on the other. (See 438).

**430** The opposite side.

426 427 428 429

430 431 432 433

426 428 434 429

433 435 436 430

**437** Cylindrical with loop handle and green prints, F for fiddle on one side, and A for archer on the other. • No mark • 2¾ ins. ht.; 2½ ins. diam.

This and the following 13 prints were all used as illustrations to the alphabet in *Our Darling's First Book* (Blackie, circa 1900), but this is unlikely to have been their first use.

**438** As 437 with red prints, G for goose and B for baker (the same figure as that of 436). • No mark • 2¾ ins. ht.; 2½ ins. diam.

**439** As 437 etc with green prints, H for hen, and C for cow. • No mark • 2¾ ins. ht.; 2½ ins. diam.

**440\*** As 437 etc with blue prints, T for train and O for omnibus. • No mark • 2¾ ins. ht.; 2½ ins. diam.

**441** As 437 etc with red prints, K for kitten and Q for queen. • No mark • 2¾ ins. ht.; 2½ ins. diam.

**442** As 437 etc with blue prints, L for lion and R for rabbit. • No mark • 2¾ ins. ht.; 2½ ins. diam.

**443** As 440 with red prints. • No mark • 2¾ ins. ht.; 2½ ins. diam.

**444** As 437 etc with blue prints, P for punch and U for umbrella. • No mark • 2¾ ins. ht; 2½ ins. diam.

**437** The opposite side.

**438** The opposite side.

**439** The opposite side.

**441** The opposite side.

**442** The opposite side.

**444** The opposite side.

437         438         439         440

441         442         443         444

437         438         439

441         442         444

**445** Shaped base and plain loop handle, with black prints (the same on each side) representing 'C c Cook. Cat. Clock.' • No mark • 2¾ ins. ht.; 2⅞ ins. diam.

**446** As 445 with green prints representing 'H h Horse. House. Hound. Horn.' • No mark • 2½ ins. ht.; 2¾ ins. diam.

**447** As 445 with red prints representing 'M m Mil-ler. Mill. Mouse.' • No mark • 2⅝ ins. ht.; 2¾ ins. diam.

**448** As 445 with red prints representing 'F f Fox. Fan. Fowl. Fence.' • No mark • 2⅝ ins. ht.; 2¾ ins. diam.

**449** Cylindrical, with spurred ear-shaped handle and dark blue prints as 445 etc representing 'Q q The Queen. God bless Her.' • No mark • 2⅞ ins. ht.; 2⅝ ins. diam.

**450** Round-rimmed base with loop handle and leaf terminals, and green prints of a king on one side, a lady on the other, and the inscription within a decorated border in the middle: K WAS A KING/WITH SCEPTRE & CROWN/L WAS A LADY/WHO WORE A NICE GOWN.' • No mark • 3¼ ins. ht.; 3¼ ins. diam.

**434** The opposite side of the mug shown on page 127.

painted red and green with a black print of capital M and MOON. MOUSE. MAN. • No mark • 6¾ ins. diam.
*Private Collection.*

**452** Cylindrical with plain loop handle and a dark blue printed view of 'DUBLIN' surrounded by a decorative alphabet. • No mark • 2⅝ ins. ht.; 2½ ins. diam.

**453** As 452 with a blue print of men on rafts on a lake, with a church in the background. • No mark • 2¾ ins. ht.; 2½ ins. diam.

**454** As 452 with a view of 'COPENHAGEN'. • No mark • 2⅝ ins. ht.; 2½ ins. diam.

**455** As 452 etc with a red-printed decorative alphabet on one side and birds above flowers in the aesthetic style on the other. • No mark • 2¾ ins. ht.; 2⅝ ins. diam.

**456** As 453 with a brown-printed scene of children fishing beside a dinghy, flanked by a decorative alphabet. • No mark • 2½ ins. ht.; 2½ ins. diam.

**457** As 455 with a sepia-printed decorative alphabet and aesthetic birds on willow branches. • 2¾ ins. ht.; 2⅝ ins. diam.

**Z** comes the last, and here it all ends.

**451** Rococo edge with moulded border of florets and leaves in compartments,

**Y** is a Youth, who has many kind friends.

From the *Child's Treasury of Knowledge*. (See note to 426).

445         446         447         448

449         450         434         451

452         453         454

455         456         457

# Chapter 7 MONTHS AND SEASONS

**458** Straight edge with red line and indistinctly moulded border of floral sprays with a manganese print (painted) illustrating 'MARCH'. • No mark • 7 ins. diam.

This and the following four prints are part of a series produced by several different factories, particularly on Tyneside and in Yorkshire potteries such as Kilnhurst, near Swinton.

**459** Straight edge with black line and moulded garland and medallion border, with a black print (slightly painted) depicting 'AUGUST'. • No mark • 6 ins. diam.

This print, and 461 (September), appear on pieces marked for Fell, Newcastle.

**460** Straight edge and moulded alphabet border on a granular background, with a manganese print (painted) illustrating 'APRIL'. • No mark • 7¼ ins.

A version of this print has been found on a straight edged plate with moulded border of ferns and vertical sprigs marked YP (for Ynysmedw Pottery, nr Swansea).

**461** Erratic edge with black line and indistinctly blobbed daisy border, with black (slightly painted) print of 'SEPTEMBER'. • No mark • 6¾ ins. diam.

Prints in this series appear on plates from Ynysmedw Pottery, nr Swansea, circa 1850–1870.

**462** Slightly erratic edge and blobbed daisy border with a sepia print of 'NOVEMBER'. • No mark • 8 ins. diam.

**463** Wavy edge with moulded border of three graduated rows of blobbed daisies and a black print (painted) of 'DECEMBER'. • Mark: P impressed • 6 ins. diam.

Copeland porcelain children's Christmass mugs, printed and painted with festive scenes. The left hand mug: design registered in 1866 • 2⅝ ins. ht.; 3⅛ ins. diam. The right hand mug: 3 ins. ht.; 3 ins. diam.

458

459

460

61

462

463

133

The prints on the plates on this page also represent a series known to have been produced in the Tyneside and Wearside region.

**464** Wavy edge with well-moulded daisy border and a red print of 'APRIL' with a zodiac sign in the background. • Mark: SCOTT impressed • 6½ ins. diam.
Anthony Scott & Co., Southwick Pottery, Sunderland, circa 1838–1897.

**465** Wavy edge with blobbed daisy border and a black print (painted) representing 'JANUARY' with a zodiac sign. • No mark • 7¾ ins. diam.

**466** Wavy edge with blobbed daisy border and inner row of sprigs, with a black print (slightly painted) of 'MARCH' with a sign of the zodiac. • Mark: DIXON & CO impressed • 7 ins. diam.
Dixon & Co., Sunderland or Garrison Pottery, Sunderland, Durham, circa 1807–1865.

**467** As 464 with a red print illustrating 'JULY'. • Mark: SCOTT impressed • 6½ ins. diam.
Anthony Scott, Sunderland.

**468** Straight edge and moulded border of blobbed diamonds in a lattice pattern and a black print representing 'JUNE' with a zodiac sign. • Mark: MONTHS OF THE YEAR and J. & M. P. B. & Co., printed • 6¾ ins. diam.
J. & M. P. Bell & Co., Glasgow Pottery, Dobbies Loan, Glasgow, circa 1850–1870. Another 'June' plate is marked FELL & Co.

**469** As 464 with a red print depicting 'AUGUST'. • Mark: SCOTT impressed • 6½ ins. diam.
The same plate has been found with an impressed asterisk mark.

**470** Straight edge with moulded border of two rows of blobbed daisies and a black print depicting September (without title) with zodiac sign. • Mark: ALBION POTTERY impressed in a circle, enclosing G&A • 5¾ ins. diam.
Probably Galloway & Atkinson, Albion Pottery, Newcastle-upon-Tyne, circa 1865–1872.
A version of this print, entitled 'SEPTEMBER' has been found on a plate with a reeded and feathered edge and border of vertical sprigs, and on a bowl from Scott's Southwick Pottery, Sunderland.

**471** As 465 with a black print (painted) of 'MAY'. • No mark • 5¾ ins. diam.

**472** Straight edge with moulded border of roses, thistles and shamrock, with a red print of 'NOVEMBER'. • No mark • 5¾ ins. diam.

464        465        466

467        468        469

470        471        472

**473** Indented edge with moulded border of rococo curlicues and flower sprays, and a sepia print of children sliding on the ice under a bridge: 'FEBRUARY./SUMMERS SUN IS WARM AND BRIGHT/WINTERS SNOW IS COLD AND WHITE/AUTUMN BRINGS US SHEAVES OF GRAIN/SPRING WILL SCATTER FLOWERS AGAIN/ PLEASANT CHANGES GOD ARRANGES ALL THROUGHOUT THE YEAR.' • No mark • 6¾ ins. diam.

The print is from an illustration to a poem by Jane Euphemia Browne (Aunt Effie) that appeared in *The Picture Scrap Book or Happy Hours at Home* (Religious Tract Society, circa 1860) and later in *The Child's Companion and Juvenile Instructor* for December 1872 (Religious Tract Society).
Other prints in this series have been found on plates with indistinctly moulded alphabet borders; all have the same verse.

**474** Rococo edge and moulded border of roses, tulips and asters, and a green print of a man and a boy with firewood: 'THE SEASONS/FEBRUARY/Now vapours gross obscure the air Or by the northern blast congeald/The trees their hoary honours bear Or sheets of snow blanch o'er the field.' • No mark; double footrim • 6 ins. diam.

**475** Straight edge with red line, and moulded border of ferns and vertical sprigs, with a black print of 'THE SEASONS/MAY/Cheered by the balmy breath of may The featherd [sic] choirs fill every grove/The trees are deckd with blossoms gay The herds in verdant pastures rove.' • Mark: B. W & Co printed in a cartouche • 6¾ ins. diam.
Bates Walker & Co., Dale Hall Works, Burslem, 1875–1878, or Buckley Wood & Co., High Street Pottery, Burslem 1875–1885.
A plate in the same series, illustrating 'JULY' with two children and a dog, has the verse: 'Now growing in full summers heat The sun pours down his genial rays/Yet ripning [sic] crops the trav'ller greet And cooling fruit his thirst allays.'

**476** Straight edge with arcaded border of florets and leaves painted with red lines, and a green print of 'SPRING'. • No mark • 5¾ ins. diam.

**477** As 476 with a sepia print of 'SUMMER'. • No mark • 5¾ ins. diam.

**478** As 476 etc with a manganese print of 'AUTUMN'. • No mark • 5¾ ins. diam.

**479** As 476 etc with a sepia print of 'WINTER'. • No mark • 5¾ ins. diam.
Plates in this series are to be found with different coloured prints.

**480** Cylindrical with round-rimmed base, plain loop handle and a black print (painted) illustrating 'AUTUMN' on one side and 'WINTER' on the other. • No mark • 2½ ins. ht.; 2½ ins. diam.

**481** Cylindrical with round-rimmed base and top edge rim, reeded loop handle, pink lustre decoration and a black print of 'AUTUMN' similar to 478. • No mark • 2¾ ins. ht.; 3 ins. diam.
Probably Sunderland or Tyneside; Maling of Newcastle is known to have used this print.

**482** Cylindrical with straight-topped ear-shaped handle reeded at the sides, with a green print illustrating 'MARCH', a variation of the print on 466. • No mark • 2½ ins. ht.; 2½ ins. diam.

**483** Shaped base and plain loop handle with green-printed harvesting scenes on each side and an inscription in the middle: 'THE SEASONS/*AUGUST*/The bending ears their load sustain/Their cluster'd stores of golden grain.' • No mark • 2½ ins. ht.; 2½ ins. diam.

**483** Opposite side.

**480** Opposite side.

473     474     475

6     477     478     479

480     481     482     483

# Chapter 8 COUNTRY LIFE

## COUNTRY BUILDINGS

**484\*** Straight edge and moulded dog, fox and monkey border painted iron red, purple, green and yellow, with a black print (painted) of a cottage in a landscape. • No mark • 6¾ ins. diam.
Probably Baker, Bevans & Irwin, Glamorgan Pottery, Swansea, 1813–1838.

**485** Lobed edge with moulded bird and butterfly border painted iron red, blue, green and yellow, with a black print of a cottage in a landscape. • Mark: five painted dots; double footrim • 6¼ ins. diam.

**486** Slight rococo edge with moulded border of flower sprays and vertical sprigs painted iron red, purple, green, turquoise and yellow, with a black print (painted) of a house in a landscape. • Mark: a painted squiggle; double footrim • 7¼ ins. diam.

**487\*** Rococo edge with rose, tulip and aster border garishly painted in iron red, dark green, blue and yellow, with a pink lustre painted house in a landscape. • Mark: a circle of dots • 6¼ ins. diam.
Possibly Patterson & Co., Sheriff Hill Pottery, Newcastle-upon-Tyne, 1830–1904.

**488** Indistinctly moulded alphabet border with a pink lustre line, and a painted lustre house among trees. • No mark • 7½ ins. diam.
A lustre cottage and trees in the same style have been noted on a wavy-edged octagonal plate of the Bailey & Ball type.

**489** Rococo edge with moulded border of pendant rose, thistle and shamrock painted iron red, pale green, blue and yellow, with a pink lustre painted house among trees. • Mark: asterisk impressed; double footrim • 7 ins. diam.
A plate in a smaller size with the same border has a pair of lustre cottages, and trees in the same style as this.

**490** Rococo edge and indistinctly moulded rose, tulip and aster border, lustred in pink, with a pink lustred house among green painted trees. • Mark: a circle of dots • 6¼ ins. diam.
Possibly Patterson, Newcastle.

**491** Edge and border as 486 with a blue print of a cottage among trees. • Mark: three painted dashes; double footrim • 5½ ins. diam.

**492\*** Straight edge and moulded garland border of leaves and small florets, lustred in pink, with a pink lustre-painted church. • Mark: 1 impressed • 5½ ins. diam.

GILES's FARM.

A hand-coloured print from an early 19th century scrapbook.

484

485

486

487

488

489

490

491

492

## COUNTRY PEOPLE

**493** Octagonal with rope-twist edge and dimpled floret border, with a black print of a fortune-teller in a landscape. • No mark; double footrim • 6¾ ins. diam.

**494** Twelve-sided, with moulded floret border painted iron red, yellow, pink and pale green, with a black print (painted) of a woman with a basket of fruit and leaves on her head, with a child in a landscape. • No mark; double footrim • 7¼ ins. diam.

**495** Octagonal with rope-twist edge painted red, and blobbed floret border, with a green print (painted) of a woodland scene. • No mark • 7¼ ins. diam.

**496** Slightly wavy edge with three-row border of separated daisies and a manganese print of figures in national costume in a central European landscape, one of them reading a newspaper. • Mark: PR with X above and 5 below, impressed; THE NEWS and PR printed • 8 ins. diam. Petrus Regout, Maastricht, Holland, 1836–1870.
This is part of a series by an anglophile Dutch potter that also included a scene of figures in a landscape with an exotic castle, called FAMILIAR SWAN. Regout's determination to compete with the English in the production of transfer-printed wares not only led him to employ English craftsmen in his factory, but also to purchase engraved copper plates from firms in the Potteries. However, this does not appear to be an English design.

**497** Rococo edge and moulded border of flowers and fruits in compartments, painted in iron red, yellow, purple, green and turquoise, with a sepia print (painted) of three men conversing in a landscape. • Mark: a painted arrowhead • 7¼ ins. diam.
The same print occurs on a straight-edged plate with a rose, honeysuckle and swagged garland border (Baker, Bevans & Irwin, Swansea).

**498** Straight edge and black-printed alphabet border, with a black print of figures in a garden. • Mark: 5/86 and 01, impressed • 6½ ins. diam.

**499\*** Straight edge and moulded garland border painted iron red, blue and pale green, with a black print illustrating 'OLD DAVID'S COTTAGE/And proudly glows his aged cheek.' • No mark • 6½ ins. diam.
Possibly James & Ralph Clews, Cobridge, 1818–1834.
See 233 and 537 for companions to this plate.
*Private Collection.*

**500** Straight edge with dog, fox and monkey border painted with blue lines, and a grey print of two boys, one playing a wind instrument. • No mark • 4¾ ins. diam.
*Private Collection.*

**501** Many-sided, with blue edge and plain border, and a sepia print (painted) of a cart-horse drinking in a pond, with a village in the background. • Mark: ZP impressed • 6¼ ins. diam.
This is probably a Wearside factory.

'The Drowsy Messenger.' A lithograph published by W. Spooner, from a mid 19th century scrapbook.

493

494

495

·6

497

498

499  OLD DAVID'S COTTAGE
And proudly fleers his aged cheek.

500

501

No. 311 [267] "I SEE YOU, MY BOY"

**502** Rococo edge painted black with a rose and jasmine border painted green, red and blue, with a black print of a man lying down in a rocky landscape, and children trying to steal his apples, the engraving signed T Robson. • Mark: MIDDLESBRO' POTTERY impressed • 6½ ins. diam.
This is said to be from a drawing by Jesse Austin, used on colour-printed pot lids, entitled 'I see you, my Boy.' [*The Pictorial Pot Lid Book* by Harold George Clarke, Courier Press, 1955]. The same image, on a print by Henry Linton with a different artist's signature, has been found in a 19th century scrapbook. For a note on Thomas Robson, see 111. Another marked Middlesbrough plate in this series has a black print of hop pickers.

**503** Octagonal with blue edge and indistinctly moulded dimpled floret border, and a sepia print (painted) of 'THE FISHERMAN'S CHILDREN.' • No mark • 7¾ ins. diam.
The same print has been found in black on a daisy-bordered bowl with the impressed mark LP, possibly for Livesley Powell, Hanley, 1851–1866.

**504** Slightly wavy edge with three rows of blobbed daisies and a black print of a woman with a mop and bucket and a man at a pump: 'A LESSON FROM THE PUMP'. • Mark: LONDON impressed in a fan shape around an anchor • 6 ins. diam.

This could be from one of five potteries that used a similar mark: see note to 16. The same print has been found in red on a plate with a reeded and feathered edge and a vertical sprig border.

**505** Reeded and feathered edge with vertical sprig border and a black print (painted) of two little girls in a park, one putting flowers in the other's hair. • Mark: an impressed asterisk • 6¼ ins. diam.
The same plate may be found in a larger size.
This print was an illustration for The Alphabet of Flowers included in *The Boys' and Girls' Illustrated Gift Book* (Routledge, 1872): 'C for Convolvulus, children's delight,/Which opens in day-time, and shuts up at night.' (for another print from the same source see 407).

**506** Wavy-edged octagonal with a wide border of patterns and two red lines, and a black print of a man and a woman in romanticised costume outside a cottage: 'COURTSHIP'. • No mark • 7¾ ins. diam. Bailey & Ball, Longton, mid-19th century.

**507** Straight edge and indistinctly moulded border commemorating 'ALBERT EDWARD PRINCE OF WALES BORN Nov 9 1841', with a black print of a man and a woman courting in a landscape. • Mark: a crown and POTTERY impressed • 6½ ins. diam.
Probably Swillington Bridge, Yorkshire, 1791-circa 1845.

**508** Straight edge with toothed rim and moulded dog, goat and butterfly border, painted black, dark green, red and yellow, with a sepia print of a woman and child in a landscape: 'THE MORNING WALK./To meet the smiling morning's eye,/Whence dart soft living beams of light,/The modest snowdrop, golden daffodil./That blows beside the wand'ring rill.' • No mark • 7½ ins. diam.
Another plate in this series illustrates 'THE HAPPY CHILDREN./I thank the goodness & the grace/Which on my birth have smiled./And made me in these Christian days/A happy English child'. This verse comes from *Hymns for Infant Minds* by Jane and Ann Taylor (1812).

**509** Rococo edge and indistinctly moulded border of florets and leaves in compartments, painted dark green and red, with a manganese print of a kilted Scotsman dallying with a girl: 'Come under my Pladie and sit down beside me/Theres room enough in it dear Lafsie for twa'. • Mark: GOODWINS & HARRIS impressed; double footrim • 6¼ ins. diam.
Goodwins & Harris, Crown Works, Lane End, Staffordshire, circa 1831–1838.

**510** Straight edge painted pink, with an indistinctly moulded border of flowers, leaves and tendrils, with a sepia print (painted) of a man and boy on a donkey in a landscape. • No mark • 7½ ins. diam.

502

503

504

505

506

507

508

509

510

**511\*** Octagonal with rope-twist edge painted green and well-moulded dimpled floret border, with a sepia print of a girl, 'THE PRIDE OF THE VILLAGE.' • No mark • 7¾ ins. diam.
The same plate may be found in 5¾ ins. size.

**512\*** Erratic edge with indistinctly moulded border of flower sprays and vertical sprigs, painted in turquoise, yellow, blue and (the sprigs) pink lustre, with a sepia print of a kilted girl with a spinning wheel: 'SCOTLANDS PRIDE'. • No mark; double footrim • 6¾ ins. diam.
The same print has been found in green on an octagonal plate with a sparse daisy border painted in yellow, greens and purple. A companion print shows a bag-piper entitled 'SCOTLAND'S GLORY', on a plate with a rose, thistle and shamrock border.

**513** Octagonal with rope-twist edge painted pale green and a moulded border of line-petalled daisies, with a sepia print (painted) of a seated girl: 'THE PRIDE OF THE VILLAGE'. • No mark • 7 ins. diam.

**514** Straight edge painted blue with grey-hound, goat and butterfly border, and a sepia print (painted) of a girl in a land-scape with a church in the background: 'THE VILLAGE BELLS'. • No mark • 6¼ ins. diam.

**515** Wavy-edged octagonal with wide border of patterns and two red lines, and a black print (painted) of an encampment and a 'GIPSY GIRL'. • Mark: printed diamond registration mark for Bailey & Ball, Longton, 1847 • 7½ ins. diam.

**516** Rococo edge with moulded border of florets and leaves in compartments, painted green, blue and yellow, with a black print of a girl in a landscape. • No mark • 6½ ins. diam.

**517** Edge and border as 513 with a yellow line to the edge and a sepia print of a child

in a garden: 'THE ORPHAN'. • No mark • 5¼ ins. diam.

**518** Vitruvian scroll and alphabet border with red line to edge and a sepia print (painted) of a 'COTTAGE GIRL' • No mark • 7½ ins. diam.
This appeared as an illustration in the *Alphabet of Fruits*, one of Aunt Louisa's London Toy Books (Warne & Kronheim, 1875): 'N is the NECTARINE kind Jenny took/To the sick girl who lived by the side of the brook.' See also 172, 609 and 611.

**519** As 517 with a sepia print (painted) of 'THE WOODMAN'S DAUGHTER'. • No mark • 5¼ ins. diam.

511

512

513

514

515

516

517

518

519

**520** Rococo edge and moulded border of roses, tulips and asters painted red, green and blue, with a black print of a girl with 'THE FLOWER BASKET'. • No mark; triple footrim • 7½ ins. diam.

**521** Nearly staight edge and indistinctly moulded blobbed daisy border, with a black print of two girls commiserating over a 'BROKEN PITCHER'. • No mark • 6 ins. diam.
This predicament must have been quite common in the days when many country folk had to fetch all their water from a common well – a task often given to children. *The Broken Pitcher* was the name of a popular song of the mid-19th century (for another print on the same subject see 198).

**522** Slightly rococo edge with crisply moulded border of flower sprigs, leaves, reeding, arcades and beads, with a green print (crudely painted) of a coy little girl on a style: 'BOOTS.' • Mark: STAFFORD POTTERY SOUTH STOCKTON, impressed • 7 ins. diam.
William Smith (1825–1855), or George Skinner (1855–1870), Stafford Pottery, Stockton-on-Tees.

**523** Rococo edge with moulded border of trendrilled flower sprigs, and a sepia print (painted) of two children in idealised rustic costume in a fanciful landscape. • No mark • 7½ ins. diam.
This plate, and others in the series, such as 525 (with this border) may also be found in 6½ ins. size; they are probably of Tyneside or Wearside origin: this print is to be found on a mug attributed to Dawson, Sunderland. Just to add a little confusion, examples of these prints may also be found on alphabet bordered plates by J. & G. Meakin of Hanley.

**524** Octagonal with herringbone edge and moulded floret border painted with dots and lines in dark green, red and blue, with a black print of 'THE COTTAGE GIRL.' • No mark; double footrim • 6½ ins. diam.

**525** Slightly rococo edge with a moulded border of flower sprigs and vertical fleur de lys motifs, with a sepia print (painted) of a boy making a wreath in a girl's hair, in a flowery bower. • No mark • 7½ ins. diam.

**526** Straight toothed edge with moulded greyhound, goat and butterfly border painted brown and yellow, with a sepia print (slightly painted) of a girl with flowers in a vase. • No mark; double footrim • 5 ins. diam.

**527*** Rococo edge with moulded border of trailing strawberries, leaves and tendrils, painted green, red and black, and a black print of 'THE ORPHAN CHILD'. • No mark • 7½ ins. diam.
Another plate with the same border pattern shows three children fishing: 'THE FIRST NIBBLE'.

**528** Erratic grooved edge painted blue, with a black print of a boy and a girl in a landscape near a cottage. • No mark • 5¼ ins. diam.

SATURDAY NIGHT.
Returning from Market.

'Returning from Market.' A lithograph by C. Ingrey, from a mid 19th century scrapbook.

520

521

522

523

524

525

526

527

528

### BIRDS' NESTING AND BUTTERFLY CATCHING

The birds' nest subjects on this page may well represent contemporary propaganda against the collecting of nests containing young; the more usual habit of collecting eggs, later in the 19th century and well into the 20th, was perhaps a step towards no birds' nest raiding at all. Butterfly catching had not yet fallen into disfavour.

**529** Erratic edge and moulded border of flower sprays and vertical sprigs, painted turquoise, yellow, blue and (the sprigs) pink lustre, with a sepia print of a girl and a boy looking for 'THE LARKS NEST.' • No mark; double footrim • 7 ins. diam.
A similar print may be found in sepia on a plate with a rococo edge and a rose, tulip and aster border, marked with an impressed asterisk.

**530** Reeded and feathered edge with vertical sprig border and a black print of a girl carrying flowers in her apron and a boy

with a bird's nest containing young. • No mark • 7½ ins. diam.
This print was the illustration to a poem by 'R. P. S.' in *The Children's Friend* in April 1869, which included the lines 'Think of His love, and never tear/The nest from bush or spray,/Nor from their downy, mossy bed steal the young brood away./The child who robs the sweet bird's nest,/I fear perhaps in time,/May grow in sinful cruelty,/And do some dreadful crime.'

**531** Rococo edge and indistinctly moulded rose, tulip and aster border, painted red, pale green and yellow, with a black print of two boys with 'THE BIRD TRAP'. • No mark • 7¼ ins. diam.

**532** Nearly straight edge painted brown, with a moulded border of rose sprays and rococo curlicues, and a sepia print of a boy and a girl chasing a butterfly in a garden. • No mark • 7½ ins. diam.
The same print, entitled 'THE BUTTERFLY' has been noted on a straight-edged, plain-bordered toy plate.

**533** Wavy-edged octagonal, with wide border of patterns and two green lines, and a sepia print (painted) of a girl and a boy with 'THE BIRDS NEST'. • Mark: diamond registration mark for Bailey and Ball, Longton, 1847 • 8 ins. diam.

**534** Slightly rococo edge with moulded border of tendrilled flower sprigs, and a sepia print (painted) of a girl and a boy with a butterfly. • No mark • 5¾ ins. diam.

**535\*** Straight edge and moulded garland border of florets and leaves, painted pale green, iron red, blue and brown, with a black print of a boy and a girl with a bird's nest of young. • No mark; no footrim • 4¾ ins. diam.

**536** Octagonal with a brown line to the edge and an indistinctly moulded border of dimpled florets, with another version of the print (painted) of 535, entitled 'THE BIRDS NEST'. • No mark • 4¾ ins. diam.

**537\*** Straight edge and moulded flowery garland border painted iron red, blue and pale green, with a black print of boys with a bird's nest: 'RURAL CHARACTERS/Too plainly now I see thier [sic] sport.' • No mark; double footrim • 5½ ins. diam.
Possibly James & Ralph Clews, Cobridge Works, Cobridge, 1818–1834.
Old David's Cottage (499) is a companion plate to this one.

529

530

531

532

533

534

535

536

537

149

# Chapter 9 OCCUPATIONS AND TRADES

Some of these, like the illustrations of pottery making, are obvious candidates for this section, while others might have found a place, just as happily, in Country Life, Animals, or even Early Days: apologies to those who find our decisions disagreeable.

**538\*** Straight edge, painted blue, with a moulded garland border of oak leaf and rose sprays, and a sepia print of 'THE REAPER/The ruddy Glow and sun-burned Cheek/The harvest Labourer bespeak,/The sweeping sickle clears the Field,/Whose warming Rows resistless yield.' • No mark • 6¼ ins. diam.

This illustration, and all the others on this page except the two large plates in the bottom row, come from *The Progress of a Quartern Loaf* by Mary (Belson) Elliott (William Darton, 1820), illustrated with six scenes and accompanying verses. Of these, only The Miller has so far defied discovery.

**539** Straight edge with moulded an-themion border and a blue print of the 'REAPER' similar to 538. • Mark: Progress of the Loaf, printed on a scroll • 6½ ins. diam.

**540\*** Straight edge with blue line and moulded garland border, and a blue print of 'THE PLOUGHMAN./The Ploughman's labour first prepares/The bosom of the earth for seed:/This done he has no further cares,/Then other labourers succeed.' • Mark: a crown impressed • 6 ins. diam. Possibly James & Ralph Clews, Cobridge, 1818–1834.

**541\*** Octagonal with indistinctly moulded floret border painted with dots and lines in red, green and blue, and a red print of the 'SOWER./With steady hand the Sower throws/That seed on which so much depends./Following the Plough's deep track he goes/And plenty every step attends'. • No mark; double footrim • 6¼ ins. diam.

**542\*** Vitruvian scroll and alphabet border painted with black lines, and a black print of the 'THRASHER./And see another Friend appears./With active flail the corn to thrash./To separate the clustering ears./And clear the Grain from stalk & trash.' • Mark: ? TWIGG impressed within an oval, and Progress of the Loaf printed on a scroll • 7 ins. diam. Possibly J. Twigg & Co., Newhill Pottery, Nr Swinton, Yorkshire, circa 1822–1866.

**543** Edge and border as 541, with a red print of 'THRASHER' similar to 542. • No mark; double footrim • 6½ ins. diam.

**544** Vitruvian scroll and alphabet border with a black line, and a black print of farming figures, animals and trophies and the inscription 'TRUST IN GOD/THE HUSBANDMAN'S DILIGENCE PROVIDES BREAD'. • No mark; triple footrim • 8¼ ins. diam.

**545** Straight edge and moulded border of horses and riders with dogs and foxes painted with black lines, and a manganese print of the 'BAKER', without a verse. • No mark • 4¾ ins. diam.

**546** Rococo edge with moulded flowers and leaves in compartments, painted iron red, pale green, turquoise and yellow, with a sepia print of a horse and farming trophies and the inscriptions 'GOD SPEED THE PLOUGH' and 'THE FARMERS FRIEND'. • Mark: an X painted • 7¼ ins. diam.

538

539

540

541

542

543

544

545

546

**547** Straight edge with moulded border of rose sprays and rococo curlicues, with a green print of a man and a woman looking at workers 'CUTTING THE WHEAT'. • No mark • 7¾ ins. diam.
This print is taken from an illustration in *The Child's Companion*, August 1865 (Religious Tract Society).

**548** Gadroon edge and plain border painted with two black lines, and a black print of a man driving two horses pulling a roller. • Mark: DILLWYN SWANSEA impressed; RURAL SCENES and 6 printed; double footrim • 5 ins. diam.
Dillwyn, Cambrian Pottery, Swansea, circa 1824–1850.
This is part of a series that also included a woman carrying a hay fork; a girl with a rake; waggoners; reapers; gleaners; binders; a shepherd, and sheep-shearers. The same prints may also be found on plates with rose, tulip and aster borders.

**549** As 547 with a green print showing farm workers sowing 'THE SEED IN THE GROUND'. • No mark • 7¾ ins. diam.

**550** Rococo edge with moulded rose-spray border painted red, green and black, with a sepia print of 'THE REAPER.' • Mark: an asterisk, impressed • 7¾ ins. diam.
*Private Collection.*

**551** Straight edge with toothed rim and moulded border commemorating 'ALBERT EDWARD PRINCE OF WALES BORN Nov 9 1841'. The green print shows a woman

sitting on a donkey 'RETURNING FROM MARKET'. • Mark: a crown and POTTERY, impressed • 7½ ins. diam.
Probably Swillington Bridge Pottery, Yorkshire, 1791-circa 1845.
This and the following print are based on a pair of unidentified hand-coloured lithographs, probably cut from a picture sheet, found in a 19th century scrap book. Two mugs with the same prints appear on page 161.

**552** Rococo edge and indistinctly moulded border of roses and leaves, painted dark green and mauve, with a black print of a girl with a donkey 'GOING TO MARKET.' • No mark • 6½ ins. diam.

**553** Gadroon edge and tendrilled alphabet border, with a manganese print of 'Wood Cutters'. • No mark; double footrim • 5¾ ins. diam.

**554** Rococo edge painted turquoise, and continuous daisy garland border, with a sepia print (painted) of 'WOODCUTTER'S' [sic]. • No mark; double footrim • 5¼ ins. diam.

**555** Indented edge and moulded border of flower sprays in feather-edged sections, with a black print of a 'WOODMAN'. • No mark; triple footrim • 6½ ins. diam.

547 CUTTING THE WHEAT

548

549 THE SEED IN THE GROUND

550 THE REAPER.

551 RETURNING FROM MARKET

552 GOING TO MARKET.

553 Wood Cutters

554 WOODCUTTER'S

555 WOODMAN

## THE POTTER'S ART

These illustrations show the stages in ceramic production and the layout of a typical (but so far unidentified) Staffordshire pottery, as well as the employment of children in most departments. All are based on the images on a set of stereo-scopic (photograph cards) of circa 1860, some of which are illustrated by Geoffrey Godden in *Staffordshire Porcelain*.

**559** As 557 with a sepia print of 'THE POTTERS' ART/PLATE MAKING'. • No mark • 7½ ins. diam.
See *Staffordshire Porcelain*, fig. 522.

**560** Straight edge and plain border painted with blue lines, and a black print of 'THE POTTERS' ART/PRINTING'. • No mark • 7¾ ins. diam.
See *Staffordshire Porcelain*, fig. 520.

**561** As 559 with a sepia print (painted) of 'THE POTTERS' ART/PRINTING'. • No mark • 7½ ins. diam.
This is another version of the print of 560 with the image reversed.

*Illustrations of sources courtesy of Geoffrey Godden.*

**556** Straight edge with indistinctly moulded border of tendrilly sprigs and a black print showing 'THE POTTERS' ART/ SLIP MAKING'. • No mark • 7½ ins. diam.

**557** Rococo edge and tendrilly sprig border with a sepia print (painted) of 'THE POTTERS' ART/TURNING'. • No mark • 6½ ins. diam.

**558** As 556 with a black print of 'THE POTTERS' ART/TRANSFERRING'. • No mark • 7½ ins. diam.

**562** As 557 etc with a sepia print (painted) of 'THE POTTERS' ART/CUP MAKING'. • No mark • 6½ ins. diam.
See *Staffordshire Porcelain*, fig. 515.

**563** Slightly wavy edge with a plain border and a green print (painted) of 'THE POTTERS' ART/THROWING'. • No mark; double footrim • 5½ ins. diam.

**564** As 557 with a sepia print (painted) of 'THE POTTERS' ART/PACKING'. • No mark • 6½ ins. diam.

556

557

558

559

560

561

562

563

564

**565** Straight-edged bowl with a moulded border of trilobate leaves and a green print illustrating 'THE LITTLE DOCTOR'. • No mark • 7 ins. diam.
See 399 for another bowl in this set.

**566** As 565 with a black print of 'THE LITTLE BLACKSMITH'. • No mark • 7 ins. diam.

**567** As 565 with a green print of 'THE LITTLE COOPER'. • No mark • 7 ins. diam.

**568** Straight edge with moulded border of swagged garlands, rose and honeysuckle, painted iron red, green, turquoise, purple and yellow, with a sepia print (painted) depicting 'THE WASHERWOMAN'. • Mark: a squiggle and three dots, painted • 7 ins. diam.
Probably Baker, Bevans & Irwin, Glamorgan Pottery, Swansea, 1813–1838.

**569** Wavy edge and moulded border of flowers, leaves and pairs of cornucopias, with a black print (painted) of blacksmiths at work, with beehives in the background: 'FLEIZ BEZAHLT DIE SCHULDEN/ABER FAULHEIT VERMEHRT' (Diligence pays dividends, but idleness causes debt). • No mark; double footrim • 6¼ ins. diam.

**570** Straight edge painted red with indistinctly moulded alphabet border painted red, and a black print (painted) of 'THE VILLAGE BLACKSMITH.' • Mark 73/5 (indistinct – probably the date, May 1873). • 7 ins. diam.
This print has also been found in manganese on an alphabet bordered plate.

**571** Straight edge with border of moulded flower sprays painted in light, bright colours, and a sepia print (painted) of two women 'Washing.' • Mark: a daisy impressed • 7¾ ins. diam.
*Private Collection.*

**572** Toy plate with slightly erratic edge and indistinctly moulded border of ten- drilled sprigs, and a dark green print of a woman wiping a table in a kitchen. • No mark • 4½ ins. diam.
This illustration appears in an advertisement for *Widow Green, and her Three Nieces* by Mrs Ellis – one of Partridge's Shilling Books. The advertisement, which appeared at the back of *Cousin Bessie* by Mrs Balfour (1862) made the recommendation: 'It is an interesting, an excellent little book to place in the hands of young women going to service. . .' The fact that this image was translated onto a child's plate is an interesting indication of the social groups towards which such china wares were being directed by the 1860s.
For others in this set see 391 and 394.

Shilling Books.

With 24 Engravings. Cloth, 1s.

## Widow Green, and her Three Nieces.

BY MRS. ELLIS.

"It is an interesting, an excellent little book to place in the hands of young women going to service ; it reminds us of those admirable Repository Tracts by Hannah More, which, in their day, were a great instrument of good. Whilst we are speaking of the 'Widow Green and Her Three Nieces,' we may add our commendation of the cheap journal (the 'British Workman') in which the story first appeared ; in its getting up, and in the written matter of its columns, it is excellent."—*Athenæum.*

With an Engraving. Cloth, 1s.

## Voice from the Vintage;
or, the Force of Example.

BY AUTHOR OF "WIDOW GREEN."

"Too well and too widely known to need fresh commendation from us. The arguments contained in its pages are unanswerable, and the style compensates for any lack of brilliance by the tone of true piety and earnestness which constitutes the undercurrent of the whole."—*National Magazine.*

13

And may be had through any Bookseller.

**573** Straight edge and moulded garland border of leaves and small florets painted without regard for the moulding with leaves and tendrils in iron red and green, and a sepia-printed vignette of two hay- makers and the inscription: 'KIND ACTIONS NEGLECTED MAKES FRIENDSHIP SUSPECTED'. • Mark: L impressed • 6 ins. diam.
This is a reversed version of a vignette that appeared in *The Picture Book* (William Walker, Otley, circa 1815, reprinted in *The Oxford Book of Nursery Rhymes* by Iona and Peter Opie).

## STEAM AND WIND POWER

**574** Rococo edge with indistinctly moulded border of baskets of flowers and butterflies in tendrilled compartments, and a green print of a train coming out of a tunnel. • No mark • 7 ins. diam.
Probably William Smith, Stafford Pottery, Stockton-on-Tees, Yorkshire, circa 1825–1855.
The same print may be found on a plate with a swagged garland and medallion border, and on an alphabet bordered plate by Edge Malkin & Co.
This is a 2–2–2 passenger locomotive of the type used by a number of railways during the 1840s.
The print comes from the title-page of *The Train* 'A first-class magazine', published by Groombridge, London, 1856 – ? It was used again in *The Mother's Picture Alphabet* (S. W. Partridge, 1862): 'T begins Tunnel, through which went the Train/That brought Uncle Thomas and me back again.'

**575** Slightly wavy edge with moulded border of flowerheads and leaves alternating with pairs of cornucopias, painted in iron red, green, yellow and purple, and a sepia print (painted) of a coaching scene: 'DAMPF COACH VON LONDON NACH LIVERPOOL/Lohn der Fleissigkeit' (Steam coach from London to Liverpool – a reward for the diligent). • Mark: M painted; double footrim • 6½ ins. diam.
Probably Tyneside or Wearside.
Others in this vein, and made for the German market illustrate the steam coach from London to Bristol and London to Manchester.

**576** Rococo edge with moulded border of roses, tulips and asters painted red, blue, yellow and pale green, with a black print of 'THE OLD MILL'. • No mark • 7 ins. diam.

**577** Edge and border similar to 575 with the cornucopias replaced by iron red brush-strokes. The black print (painted) shows a paddle steamer: 'DAMPF SCHIFF VON LONDON NACH HAMBURG/Ein Geschenk fur meinon [sic] Lieben Jungen' (Steamship from London to Hamburg – a present for my dear child). • No mark; double footrim; base painted red • 6¼ ins. diam.
Probably Tyneside or Wearside.
A similar print and German inscription are recorded on an 8 ins. dog, fox and monkey bordered plate marked FELL.

**578** Rococo edge and moulded border of flowers and fruits in compartments, painted dark green, mauve and yellow, with a black print of shipping on a river. • No mark • 5 ins. diam.

**579** Rococo edge with indistinctly moulded border of flowers and leaves in compartments, painted green, red and black, with a manganese print of a 'STEAMBOAT'. • Mark: GOODWINS & HARRIS impressed; double footrim • 6 ins. diam.
Goodwins & Harris, Crown Works, Lane End, circa 1831–1838.
The same plate may be found with different painted and printed colours.

T begins Tunnel, through which went the Train
That brought Uncle Thomas and me back again.

574

575

576

577

578

579

**580** Cylindrical with plain loop handle and blue prints, 'GOING TO MARKET' on one side and a girl fetching water in a jug: 'FOR A GOOD GIRL' on the other. • No mark • 3 ins. ht.; 3 ins. diam.

**581** Cylindrical with loop handle and leaf terminals, pale green line to rim and a sepia print (painted) of a girl with a laden donkey: 'I rise before the break of day./And to the market haste away.' (see 552). • Mark: two green painted dashes • 2½ ins. ht.; 2½ ins. diam.
This and the following print are based on unidentified hand-coloured lithographs, probably cut from a picture sheet, that appeared in a 19th century scrap book (see page 152).

**582** As 581 with a copper lustre border and sepia print (painted) of a girl riding her donkey: 'Market's done my goods all sold./Come up Bess for I am cold.' (see 551). • Mark: a green painted X • 2⅜ ins. ht.; 2⅜ ins. diam.

**583** As 580 with green prints of 'HARVEST HOME' on one side, and 'CHERRIES RIPE' (see below) on the other. • No mark • 3 ins. ht.; 3 ins. diam.

**584** Cylindrical with plain loop handle and blue print of 'THRASHER/Progrefs of the LOAF.' (cf. 542 and 543). • No mark • 2½ ins. ht.; 2⅝ ins. diam.
This is an illustration in the *Progress of a Quartern Loaf* a poem by Mary (Belson) Elliott (William Darton, 1820).

**585*** Cylindrical with loop handle and leaf terminals, pink lustre lines and a sepia print of a girl and a boy looking at two beehives. • No mark • 2⅝ ins. ht.; 2⅜ ins. diam.
The same print appears on a plate illustrating one of Isaac Watts's verses (see 904).

**586*** Cylindrical with reeded loop handle, pink lustre rim and line on handle, and a manganese print of 'THE GLEANER'. • No mark • 2½ ins. ht.; 2⅜ ins. diam.
This print, in black, has been noted on a marked Davenport mug.

**587** As 581 with iron red line to rim and a sepia print (painted) of a milkmaid 'MILKING THE COW'. • No mark • 2½ ins. ht.; 2½ ins. diam.

**588** Cylindrical with flat-topped ear-shaped handle grooved at the sides, and a green print of a girl 'FEEDING POULTRY'. • No mark • 2½ ins. ht.; 2½ ins. diam.

**589** Porcelain cup and saucer, the cup with plain loop handle, turquoise rim and line to handle, and sepia prints (painted) of a boy holly picker on one side and a postman on the other. The saucer is decorated with the postman print. • No mark • 3 ins. ht.; 3¼ ins. diam. (top rim); diam. of saucer 5⅜ ins.

**590** Miniature saucer with iron red rim and a sepia print (painted) of 'THE HEN AND CHICKENS'. • No mark • 4¼ ins. diam.

**591** Shaped base and loop handle with a sepia print of two girls feeding poultry on one side and a girl with a begging dog on the other: 'A PRESENT FOR A GOOD GIRL'. • No mark • 2¾ ins. ht.; 2⅝ ins. diam. (See also 815.)

**592** Cylindrical with plain loop handle and green prints of an aproned man holding his hat out to a lady: 'THANK YOU MADAM' on one side, and 'THE TOP SPINNER' (see 261) on the other. • No mark • 3 ins. ht.; 3 ins. diam.

**593** As 592 with green prints of 'THE SAWYERS' on one side and 'GOOD EXERCISE' (see 272) on the other. • No mark • 2⅞ ins. ht.; 2⅞ ins. diam.

**594** As 592 with green prints of 'CHERRIES RIPE' on one side and 'THE GAME AT MARBLES' (see 258) on the other. • No mark • 2⅞ ins. ht.; 3 ins. diam.
This image is probably based on an illustration in *London Cries for Children* (Darton & Harvey, 1806) with the verse: 'Delicious to the taste are found/These tempting cherries, sound and round./Nowhere better will you meet,/For like sugar they are sweet;/But if you should incline to buy,/Be so kind first one to try.' [Reprinted in Andrew Tuer's *Old Fashioned Children's Books*, 1899–1900].

**595** Shaped base with reeded loop handle and a black print of a man carrying a stick hung with dead birds at one end and a basket of live chicks at the other, and a basket of eggs in his hand: 'A GIFT frOM A FRIEND'. • No mark • 2⅞ ins. ht.; 2¾ ins. diam.

GOING TO MARKET

HARVEST HOME

580　　　　　581　　　　　582　　　　　583

THRASHER
Progress of the LOAF

MILKING THE COW

584　　　　　585　　　　　586　　　　　587

FEEDING POULTRY

THE HEN AND CHICKENS

A GOOD GIRL

588　　　　　589　　　　　590　　　　　591

THANK YOU MADAM

THE SAWYERS

CHERRIES RIPE

A GIFT FROM A FRIEND

592　　　　　593　　　　　594　　　　　595

**596** Wavy feathered edge with flower moulded border crudely painted in dark green, blue and red, with a green print of a woman feeding poultry. • Mark: YMP impressed • 6¼ ins. diam.
Ynysmedw Pottery, Nr Swansea, circa 1850–1870.

**597** Wavy edge and well-moulded border of round-petalled blobbed daisies, and a poultry-feeding scene printed in colours. • Mark: W. S. & CO'S WEDGEWOOD impressed, and No 101 PASTIMES W S & Co printed in a cartouche. • 8 ins. diam.
William Smith & Co., Stafford Pottery, Stockton-on-Tees, Yorkshire, 1825–1855.
This is one of the series illustrated on page 68.

**598** As 596 with a green print of a man minding turkeys. • Mark: YMP impressed • 6¼ ins. diam.
Ynysmedw Pottery.

**599** Wavy edge and well-moulded blobbed daisy border with a red print of 'THE SHEPHERD BOY'. • Mark: SCOTT impressed • 6½ ins. diam.
Anthony Scott & Co., Southwick Pottery, Sunderland, 1838–1897.

**600** Straight edge and blobbed daisy border with a red print of 'THE MILK GIRL.' • No mark • 6¼ ins. diam.
Another plate in this series illustrates 'THE NURSE.'

**601** Straight edge and moulded shell border painted without regard for the moulding in iron red and pale green, with a black print (painted) of a girl pushing a wheelbarrow with a dog running behind. • No mark • 6½ ins. diam.

**602** Gadrooned edge and manganese-printed border of flower sprays with birds, and a central print of a shepherd. • No mark; double footrim • 4¾ ins. diam.

**603** Octagonal with rope-twist edge painted red, and dimpled floret border,

and a black print (painted) of a shepherdess. • No mark • 5½ ins. diam.
This print has been found, in blue, on a straight-edged plate with a fern and vertical sprig border, probably from Ynysmedw Pottery, Nr Swansea.

**604** Wavy edge and plain border with black lines, and a black print of a shepherdess carrying a lamb. • Mark: 2 impressed • 5 ins. diam.

**605** Straight edge and plain border with black lines, and a black print of 'THE WATER-CRESS GIRL.' • No mark; no footrim • 4¾ ins. diam.
The same print has been found on a plate with a blue sponged-pattern border and the impressed Bristol mark of Pountney & Co, August 1887.
This image may have been inspired by Wheatley's painting (and Bartolozzi's engraving) of *The Watercress Girl*, but it is not an exact copy.

THE HUSBANDMAN

Ye pamper'd great, who proudly ride
In gilded coaches, as ye glide
    Along the crowded street;
Scorn not the man who tills the fields
Who reaps the fruits which autumn yields,
    That rich and poor may eat.

Illustration from *The Rational Exhibition for Children*, Darton & Harvey 1800.

596

597

598

599

600 THE MILK GIRL

601

602

603

604

605 THE WATER-CRESS GIRL

**606** Straight edge with indistinctly moulded rose, thistle and shamrock border and a red print of a boy and a girl picking apples. • No mark • 6½ ins. diam.

**607** Rococo edge with moulded border of flowers and fruit, painted iron red, turquoise, green, orange and purple, with a black print (painted) of a milkmaid and her companion. • Mark: a painted squiggle • 7¼ ins. diam.

**608** As 606 with a red print of boy sowing seed. • No mark • 6½ ins. diam.

**609** Straight edge painted pink with a two-row border of blobbed daisies, and a green print (painted) of a 'FRUIT SELLER'. • No mark • 7¼ ins. diam.
This print is from an illustration entitled The French Melon Seller in Warne's *Holiday Album* 'A Book of Easy Reading for Children by Aunt Friendly' circa 1860. It was later used in the *Alphabet of Fruits*, one of Aunt Louisa's London Toy Books (Frederick Warne & Kronheim, 1875): 'M for the MELON the Frenchwoman sells,/By the arch within sound of the old Minster bells.'
For other prints from the same source see 172 and 518.

**610** Straight edge with moulded border of entwined dolphins and tridents, alternating with shell and seaweed motifs, painted green, iron red, mauve and yellow. The sepia print shows a haymaker and a little boy 'GOING HOME'. • No mark • 8½ ins. diam.

**611** As 609 with a sepia print (painted) of children 'BLACKBERRYING'. • No mark • 7¼ ins. diam.
This was one of the illustrations in the *Alphabet of Fruits* (see note to 609): 'B for the BLACKBERRY, open to all,/To the rich and the poor, to cottage and hall.'

**612** Slight rococo rim with moulded border of strapwork and cartouches, and a black print (painted) of a goat-herd in a landscape. • Mark: castle and anchor, impressed • 8 ins. diam.
W. H. & J. H. Ainsworth, Stockton Pottery, Stockton-on-Tees, Co. Durham, 1865–1901.
An unmarked plate with a similar border has a black print of a fisherman mending his nets outside his cottage.

**613** Rococo edge and moulded border of lambrequins and birds, with a green print of 'THE HAY MAKER'. • No mark • 7¼ ins. diam.

**614** Straight edge and blobbed daisy border with a black print of 'HOP PICKING'. • No mark; double footrim • 7½ ins. diam.
This is a different hop picking view to that on the Middlesbrough plates noted for 502.

**615** Straight edge and toothed rim with moulded border commemorating 'ALBERT EDWARD PRINCE OF WALES BORN Nov 9 1841', and a green print of a bird seller: 'COME BUY MY PRETTY BIRDS'. • Mark: a crown and POTTERY impressed • 7½ ins. diam.
Probably Swillington Bridge Pottery, Yorkshire, 1791-circa 1845.
The print is based on an unidentified hand-coloured lithograph, probably cut from a picture sheet (the same one as that of 551 and 552), that appeared in a 19th century scrap book.

**616** Octagonal with rope-twist edge painted yellow, and moulded border of dimpled florets, and a black print (painted) of 'THE BIRD MAN'. • No mark • 7 ins. diam.
This image is taken from the illustration of 'The Bird Catcher' in *The Daisy*; by Elizabeth Turner, first published in 1807, illustrated with wood engravings by Samuel Williams, (Darton & Clark, 21st edition, circa 1840).
The same print occurs, in blue, on a wavy edged plate with a feathery frond, floret, sprig and flower spray border.

**617** Vitruvian scroll and alphabet border, with a sepia print (painted) of a pedlar woman with a little girl. • No mark • 7¼ ins. diam.

Probably Edge Malkin, Newport and Middleport Potteries, Burslem, 1871–1903.
This illustration, entitled 'What will you buy my little dear?' was included at the end of the index to the bound volume of *The Child's Companion* for 1871. The engraving was signed J Robinson Sc. This is probably the artist and engraver John Henry Robinson (1796–1871).

**618** Straight edge and moulded border of swagged garlands, rose and honeysuckle sprays, painted iron red, two shades of green, and yellow, with a black print (painted) of a pottery seller with a basket of crockery on his back, and the Dutch inscription: 'Engelsch Steentug'. • Mark: an asterisk impressed and 87 painted • 7 ins. diam.

Probably Baker, Bevans & Irwin, Glamorgan Pottery, Swansea, 1813–1838. Similar images, of itinerant pottery sellers, are to be found on English delftware tiles of the 18th century.

**619** Octagonal with green grooved edge and plain border, and a black print of a pedlar man with a basket on his back and a dog at his side. • No mark • 5¾ ins. diam.

**620** Straight edge with dog, fox and monkey border, and an iron red print of 'THE FLOWER MAN'. • Mark: a painted X • 7½ ins. diam.
Possibly Tyneside or Wearside.

**621** Erratic edge and moulded border of feathery fronds, florets, posies of flowers and sprigs, painted green, blue, red and yellow, with a black print of a dentist 'Drawing a Tooth'. • Mark: a cross with triangular arms, impressed • 6 ins. diam.
This print is based on an illustration in *The Cowslip* by Elizabeth Turner first published 1811, this edition circa 1850, (Darton & Co.): 'Drawing Teeth./Miss Lucy Wright, though not so tall,/Was just the age of Sophy Ball: But I have always understood,/Miss Sophy was not half so good;/ For as they both had faded teeth,/Their teacher sent for Doctor Heath;/But Sophy made a dreadful rout,/And would not have hers taken out:/But Lucy Wright endur'd the pain,/Nor did she ever once complain;/Her teeth return'd quite sound and white,/While Sophy's ached both day and night.'

One cannot help sympathising with Sophy Ball: children (and adults) had to endure their teeth being drawn without anaesthetic until Edwardian times. The same plate may be found with this print in blue.

**622** Straight edge with border of moulded lines and an alphabet on a granular background, with a sepia print of 'THE NEWS BOY'. • No mark • 6¾ ins. diam.
This print was used by Edge Malkin, Burslem.
The source is an illustration in *The Mother's Picture Alphabet* with illustrations by Henry Anelay (S. W. Partridge, 1862): 'N begins News-boy, with papers to sell:/What a good thing it must be to learn to read well!/At Nine he leaves one at each customer's door;/And by Noon he will sell all he carries, and more.'

**623** Rococo edge and moulded border of rose sprays painted green, red and blue, with a black print of a man reading by a candle, signed T. Robson. • No mark • 5¾ ins. diam.
Middlesbrough, Yorkshire, 1834–1852.
This print is after Hogarth's painting *The Politician*, probably painted circa 1730 and etched by Sherwin, 1775.
For a note on Thomas Robson, see 111.

615

616

617

618

619

620

621

622

623

# Chapter 10 ENTERTAINMENT

This section includes all kinds of occupations involving an audience: some of them, like dancing, might also come under the heading of pastimes, but during (and before) the Victorian period dancing often took the form of a performance, which seems to justify the inclusion of such subjects as the polka here.

**624** Gadrooned edge painted red, and alphabet border, with a black print of 'THE ITALIAN SAVOYARD.' • No mark • 5 ins. diam.

**625** Vitruvian scroll and alphabet border, with a black line to the edge and a black print of 'THE ITALIAN BOY.' • No mark; double footrim • 6 ins. diam.
Probably Godwin, Burslem.
The source for this print is Harrison Weir's frontispiece to *Peter Parley's Annual* (Darton & Clark, 1846). This in turn may have come from an earlier picture sheet: the image appeared in hand-coloured lithographed form in a 19th century scrap book.

Another version of this print has been found, in green, on a 7½ ins. plate with a moulded border commemorating 'ALBERT EDWARD PRINCE OF WALES BORN Nov 9 1841', with the impressed crown mark of Swillington Bridge Pottery, Yorkshire.

**626** Rococo edge and moulded border of animals and birds, with two black lines, and a black print of 'THE FRENCH BOY./I am sorry those ladies staid with you so long./For, mamma, you have lost both a tune & a song./They have kept you, I think, but one moment too late,/For the boy with his organ has just left the gate.' • No mark • 5 ins. diam.
The print shows a peep show, or raree show, of the type commonly exhibited by travelling Savoyards.
Another plate, not shown here, has a print of an old lady and a child watching a boy with a large box-shaped peep-show suspended from a strap round his neck.

**627** Gadroon edge and alphabet border, with a black print of children watching 'THE ORGAN GRINDER'. • No mark • 6¾ ins. diam.

The same print was (later) used on alphabet bordered plates by Edge Malkin. The print is from one of Henry Anelay's illustrations for *The Mother's Picture Alphabet* (S. W. Partridge, 1862): 'O begins Organ: the tune is so gay,/The children could stand there and listen all day./Here, give the lad this, and let dear baby see: How he stares at the figures in wonder and glee!'

**628** Indistinctly moulded alphabet border, with a sepia print (painted) of a girl with a barrel organ and another with a tambourine. • Mark: EDGE MALKIN & Co • 7¼ ins. diam.
Edge Malkin & Co., Newport and Middleport Potteries, Burslem, 1871–1903.
This print is based on the illustration of The Little Tambourine Player in *Peter Parley's Annual* 1858 (Darton & Co.).

624

625

626

THE ITALIAN SAVOYARD.

THE ITALIAN BOY.

THE FRENCH BOY.

627

628

629

THE ORGAN GRINDER

THE BLIND PIPER.

630

631

632

LA POLKA

**629** Rococo edge and moulded border of florets and leaves in sections, painted dark green and maroon, with a black print of 'THE BLIND PIPER.' • Mark 6 (or 9) impressed • 6½ ins. diam.

**630** Rococo edge and moulded border of roses, tulips and asters, with a black print of a lady and gentleman dancing 'LA POLKA'. • Mark: SCOTT impressed • 6¼ ins. diam.
Anthony Scott, Southwick Pottery, Sunderland, circa 1800–1897.
The same plate may be found with a red print.
The Polka was introduced from Bohemia during the late 1830s, and became an extremely popular dance during the 1840s.
Similar prints appear on music covers of the time.

**631** Rococo edge with moulded border of tendrilled sprigs and a sepia print (painted) of a *pas de deux*. • No mark • 7½ ins. diam.
The same print has been found, in manganese, on a straight-edged plate with an indistinctly moulded tendrilled garland border.

**632** Straight edge painted red, and moulded border of rose sprays and rococo curlicues, and a sepia print of Harlequin and Columbine. • No mark • 6½ ins. diam.

**633** Toothed rim and alphabet border, with a sepia print (painted) of Punch & Judy. • No mark • 7½ ins. diam.
Probably Allerton, Longton, 1859–1942.
The source for this and the following Punch and Judy illustration is a series of unidentified 19th century hand-coloured prints.
Another version of this print, also in sepia but unpainted, occurs on a straight-edged plate with a moulded border of rose sprays and rococo curlicues.

**634** Slight rococo edge with moulded border of feathered fronds and florets

painted in pink lustre, iron red, blue, yellow and pale green, with a black print of 'Billy Button.' • No mark • 6½ ins. diam.
This print illustrates a popular early 19th century circus act.
The same print occurs on an 8 ins. plate with a moulded border of feathery fronds and flower sprays, and on a rococo-edged 5 ins. plate with a border of roses, tulips and asters.

**635*** As 633 with a sepia print illustrating a different stage in the Punch and Judy story. • No mark • 6¾ ins. diam.
Probably Allerton.

**636** Wavy edge and blobbed daisy border spotted in red, blue and pale green, with a green print of 'MISS ROSE in her GERMAN DRESS'. • No mark • 6½ ins. diam.
This print apparently shows Madame Vestris as The Broom Girl, an act later performed by John Liston; perhaps 'Miss Rose' was another female impersonator.

**637** As 636 with a sepia print of 'MISS ROSE in her ITALIAN DRESS'. • No mark • 5½ ins. diam.
This print also seems to show Madame Vestris in one of her roles.
Another plate in this series shows 'MISS ROSE in her GRECIAN DRESS'.

**638** Octagonal with pink-lustred rope-twist edge and border of dimpled florets and stars, with a sepia print (painted) of an unidentified theatrical performance in a 'Renaissance' setting. • Mark: a pink lustre X • 4½ ins. diam.

**639** Erratic edge and indistinctly moulded border of rose sprays and vertical fleurs de lys, splodged in pale green, red and blue, with a green print (painted) of 'JIM ALONG JOSEY/He get a long jim a long Josey/He get a long jim a long Joe.' • No mark • 6¼ ins. diam.
This was a negro minstrel song which became an American play-party game, in between a game and a dance, and innocent in the eyes of Quakers and puritans.

633

634

635

636

637

638

639

640

641

642

643

**640** Toy plate with straight edge and plain border, with a sepia print of 'THE ETHIOPIANS'. • No mark • 4 ins. diam.
The Ethiopians, or Ethiopian Opera, was a negro minstrel group which gave burlesque performances of Shakespeare and opera with negro melodies.

**641** Rococo edge with moulded border of birds and pendant lambrequins, splodged in yellow and blue, with a sepia print of 'JUMP JIM CROW/Wheel about and turn about and do Just so/Every time we wheel about we Jump Jim crow'. [sic] • No mark • 5½ ins. diam.
This print depicts one of the earliest negro minstrels, Thomas Dartmouth Rice, who appeared as Jim Crow at the Surrey Theatre in 1836. He was a white man 'blacked up' for the part, as were later imitators such as John Scott ('Little Scott'). The act was very popular and inspired other negro minstrel shows; they were regarded as suitable family entertainment and were given in halls as well as theatres. Negro minstrels were sometimes called 'Burnt Cork' minstrels when, as was often the case, the performers were burnt-cork-blackened white people. This particular image must have its origins in a print, but we have not traced it so far. However, it is known to have been worked on an alphabet sampler of the period.

**642** Rococo edge with moulded border of florets and leaves in compartments, painted pale green, iron red, pink and blue, and a black print (painted) of 'PAUL PRY'. • No mark; double footrim • 5½ ins. diam.
Paul Pry was a comedy by John Poole which first appeared in 1825. The meddlesome figure of the eponymous hero became one of John Liston's celebrated parts at Drury Lane. A similar figure to the one on this plate, carrying an umbrella, was used as a signature by the caricaturist William Heath (fl. 1820s).

**643** Octagonal with pink lustred ropetwist edge and dimpled floret border, with a black print of a negro performer: 'Me hab me regan gown – me hab me gingham coat./Hankecha tie me head, tanky massa, tie my troat,/An da warra mome wanty, me habme juka fan./Fe go da Berry Hill fego see Quaco Sam./Wid me ring ding ding etc.' • Mark: Manufactured for Mrs R. Brandon, Kingston, JAMAICA, printed in a decorative cartouche • 8 ins. diam.
*Private Collection.*

**644** Slightly tapered with plain loop handle and a green print of Punch in prison with the hangman arriving. • No mark • 2¾ ins. ht.; 2½ ins. diam.
This print is after one of George Cruikshank's illustrations to *Punch and Judy*, with text by J. P. Collier (S. Prowett, 1828).

**645** Round-rimmed base and loop handle with leaf terminals, and a sepia print (painted) of 'BILLY BUTTONS JOURNEY TO BRENTFORD'. • No mark • 2½ ins. ht.; 2¾ ins. diam.
(see note to 634).

**646*** Cylindrical with loop handle and leaf terminals, iron red rim and sepia print (painted) of a barrel organ player with his monkey: 'My Monkey's pranks and music's strains/Procure my daily little gains.' • No mark • 2⅜ ins. ht.; 2½ ins. diam.

This image is similar to the frontispiece of *Peter Parley's Annual* for 1846 (Darton & Clark).
(see note to 625).

**647** Shaped base and plain loop handle with a sepia print of a man putting a penny into a kneeling midget's hat: 'HERE IS A PENNY FOR YOU LITTLE MAN.' • No mark • 2⅝ ins. ht.; 2⅝ ins. diam.
This is an illustration of General Tom Thumb, the American dwarf (alias Charles Sherwood Stratton, 1838–1883).
(see also 701).

644              645              646              647

# Chapter 11 CARICATURE AND HUMOUR

William Combe's verses recounting *Dr Syntax's Tour in Search of the Picturesque* accompanied a series of humorous illustrations by Thomas Rowlandson and were published from 1810 by Ackermann, in instalments. These 'poetical peregrinations' were such 'a capital hit' that *Dr Syntax's Tour in Search of Consolation* and *Dr Syntax in Search of a Wife* were encouraged to follow. The Dr Syntax craze has many parallels in modern popular cartoon characters. Glimpses of Dr Syntax, 'an old clergyman and schoolmaster, who felt, or fancied himself, in love with the fine arts', appear on many moulded-bordered plates: not all are traceable to Rowlandson.

**648** Cylindrical with plain loop handle and a green print of pig stealers with an old woman at a stile: 'You aint seen a little bit of Pig have yer Gentlemen:/Pig no Do you take us for a couple of Pigstealers good homan.' • No mark • 2½ ins. ht.; 2⅜ ins. diam.

**649** Round-rimmed base with reeded loop handle and leaf terminals, a black line inside the top rim and a blue print of two sparring men 'Breaking down the Bridge of an Enemy' (see 686). • No mark • 2⅝ ins. ht.; 2⅝ ins. diam.

**650** Slightly tapered, with plain loop handle and a black print of a negro punching a boy outside a school: 'LOVE & LIBERTY'. • No mark • 2⅜ ins. ht.; 2 ins. diam.

**651** Shaped base with plain loop handle and a blue print of an astonished man sitting on a rock in a stream, with two men apparently fighting in the background: 'ISOLATED'. • Mark: underglaze blue blobs • 2¾ ins. ht.; 2½ ins. diam.

## DR. SYNTAX

**652** Straight edge with unpainted rose, honeysuckle and swagged garland border, and a black print of Dr Syntax on horseback with a lady. • No mark • 6¾ ins. diam.
This print seems close to 'Dr Syntax Losing his Way' but in the original there is no lady on the back of the horse.

**653** Straight edge with unpainted dog, fox and monkey border and a blue print of 'DR SYNTAX PURSUED BY A BULL'. • No mark • 5 ins. diam.
*Private Collection.*

**654** Straight edge painted blue with rose spray and rococo curlicue border and a sepia print painted in Pratt colours, of 'DR SYNTAX RETURNED FROM HIS TOUR.' • No mark • 6½ ins. diam.
*Private Collection.*

DR SYNTAX PURSUED BY A BULL.

DR SYNTAX RETURNED FROM HIS TOUR.

These two illustrations are taken from *Dr. Syntax's tour in search of the Picturesque.*

648        649        650        651

652          653         654

## HOBBY RIDING

The plates on this page poke fun at the craze of hobby horse riding. Steerable two-wheeled 'horses' or velocipedes propelled by the feet became a fashionable craze for women as well as men, from 1818 when Baron von Diais of Paris took out a patent for such a vehicle, described as a Draisena or Dandy-horse in Ackermann's *Repository* (February 1819). Hobby horse riding schools flourished for the next few years. The 'Lady's Accelerator' appears to be a three-wheeled version of the hobby horse. The hobby riding craze was a popular subject with contemporary caricaturists, but we have yet to find the source of the Brough examples illustrated here.

**655\*** Straight edge with narrow moulded border of flowers and leaves in a close-packed garland, and a blue print of 'THE REAL DANDY HOBBY'. • Mark: BROUGH impressed • 6½ ins. diam.
Thomas Brough, Lane End, circa 1818–1822.
Prints in this series may also appear on plates with garland and spotty floret borders.

**656** As 655 with a blue print of 'THE SAILORS HOBBY'. • Mark: BROUGH impressed • 6½ ins. diam.

**657** As 655 etc with a blue print of 'JOHN BULLS HOBBY'. • Mark: BROUGH impressed • 6½ ins. diam.

**658** As 655 etc with a blue print of 'THE JEWS HOBBY'. • Mark: BROUGH impressed • 6½ ins. diam.
This print has also been found on a vitruvian scroll and alphabet bordered plate of a later period.

**659\*** As 655 etc with a blue print of 'THE ALDERMANS HOBBY'. • Mark: BROUGH impressed • 6½ ins. diam.

**660** As 655 etc with a blue print of 'THE DOCTORS HOBBY'. • Mark: BROUGH impressed • 6½ ins. diam.

**661\*** Straight edge with red line and indistinctly moulded blobbed daisy border with a black print (painted) of a woman on a velocipede: 'THE SUMMER STYLE'. • No mark • 6½ ins. diam.

**662\*** Straight edge and moulded border of continuous flowers and stems, with a black print (painted) of a woman on a tricycle: 'THE LADYS ACCELERATOR/ WONDERS WILL NEVER CEASE'. • No mark; no footrim • 7 ins. diam.
Similar prints have been found on a plate with a continuous garland border of small florets and leaves, and on one with a swagged garland, rose and honeysuckle border (Baker Bevans & Irwin, Swansea). Robert Cruikshank illustrated *The Lady's Accelerator* (1819) as a satire on 'the latest craze in locomotion, the cumbersome and short-lived velocipede'. This plate is not identical to Cruikshank's illustration but is based on the same idea.

**663** Straight edge with indistinctly moulded border of florets and a sepia print of a man on a hobby horse trying to avoid geese: 'A COUNTRY PARTY'. • No mark • 6¾ ins. diam.

THE VELOCIMANIPEDE.
Invented by Mr. BIRCH, Coach Maker, 72, Gr.ᵗ Queen Street, Lincolns Inn Fields.
Exhibited before their ROYAL HIGHNESSES THE DUKE & DUCHESS of KENT in Kensington Gardens.
Now to be seen at Wigley's Rooms Spring Gardens.

Illustration from an early 19th century scrapbook.

655    THE REAL DANDY HOBBY

656    THE SAILORS HOBBY

657    JOHN BULLS HOBBY

658    THE JEWS HOBBY

659    THE ALDERMANS HOBBY

660    THE DOCTORS HOBBY

661    THE SUMMER STYLE

662    THE LADYS ACCELERATOR WONDERS WILL NEVER CEASE

663    A COUNTRY PART

## SYMPTOMS

The prints illustrated here all parody new forms of locomotion and the uses of steam power; we have been unable to discover their precise sources, but have come across other prints based on some of the same ideas. Many were published during the 1820s. *Locomotion* by Richard Seymour (Shortshanks) published by Thomas McLean circa 1828 is one example, and *Shaving by Steam* also by Richard Seymour (published by E. King, 1828) is another.

**664** Octagonal with rope-twist edge and line-petalled daisy border, with a black print illustrating 'SYMPTOMS of GOING it in STYLE.' • No mark • 5½ ins. diam.

**665** Octagonal with dimpled floret border and a red print illustrating 'SYMPTONS [sic] OF WHOLESALE TRADE.' • No mark • 6 ins. diam.

**666** As 664 with a black print of 'SYMPTOMS of WHOLESALE TRADE' (similar to 665). • No mark • 5½ ins. diam.

Another version of this print has been found on a plate with a lustred rococo edge and a moulded bird and butterfly border.

**667** Straight edge and moulded border of rose, thistle, shamrock, harp and flower sprays, painted pale green, yellow and red, with a black print of 'SYMPTONS [sic] OF GOING IT IN STYLE.' • No mark • 5½ ins. diam.

**668** As 664 etc with a black print of 'SYMPTOMS of ANGLING.' • No mark • 6½ ins. diam.

**669** Rococo edge and moulded border of florets and leaves in compartments, painted blue, red and black, with a black print of 'SYMPTOMS of PLOUGHING.' • No mark; double footrim • 5½ ins. diam. Possibly Goodwins & Harris, Crown Works, Lane End, circa 1831–1838.

This print may be found on octagonal plates with dimpled floret borders as 665, and on rococo-edged plates with moulded and painted rose, tulip and aster borders.

**670** Rococo edge with a single row of indistinctly moulded daisies in the border, and painted flower sprigs. The sepia print illustrates 'SYMPTOMS of WALKING made EASY.' • No mark; double footrim • 5¾ ins. diam.

**671** Rococo edge and moulded rope-twist, flower and curlicue border, painted in turquoise, iron red, purple and blue, with a black print (slightly painted) illustrating 'SYMPTOMS of WALKING made EASY.' • No mark • 6½ ins. diam.

**672** As 670 with a green print illustrating 'SYMPTOMS OF GRAVE-DIGGING.' • No mark; double footrim • 5¾ ins. diam.

This print also occurs on rococo-edged plates with moulded and painted rose, tulip and aster borders. In these, SYMTOMS is spelled without a P.

664

665

666

667

668

669

670

671

672

## LIMERICKS AND TIM BOBBIN

**673** Finely potted, with straight beaded edge and continuous vine border. The blue print illustrates the limerick: 'There was an Old Woman of Gloster/Whose Parrot two Game as it cost her/But his tongue never ceasing/Was vastly displeasing/To the talkative Woman of Glos'ter.' • Mark: CLEWS WARRANTED STAFFORDSHIRE in a circle round a crown, impressed • 5½ ins. diam.
James and Ralph Clews, Cobridge Works, Cobridge, Staffordshire, 1818–1834.
This and the following three prints are from *The History of Sixteen Wonderful old Women, illustrated by as many engravings, exhibiting their principal eccentricities and amusements* published by John Harris, London, 1820. These are the first known limericks, and may have provided the inspiration for Edward Lear. Besides those illustrated here, the 16 comprised an Old Woman named Towl; an Old Woman of Ealing; an Old Woman of Norwich; an Old Woman of Croydon; an Old Woman of Leith; an Old Woman from France; an Old Woman in Surrey; an Old Woman of Exeter; an Old Woman of Bath ('as thin as a lath'); an Old Woman in Spain; an Old Woman at Leeds, and an Old Woman of Devon.

**674** As 673 with a blue print illustrating the limerick: 'There was an Old Woman of Gosport/And she was one of the cross sort/When she dress'd for the Ball/Her wig was too small/Which enrag'd this Old Lady of Gosport'. • Mark: CLEWS WARRANTED STAFFORDSHIRE in a circle round a crown, impressed • 4 ins. diam.

**675** As 673 etc with a sepia print illustrating the limerick: 'There was an Old Woman of Harrow/Who visited in a Wheel barrow/And her servent [sic] before,/Knock loud at each door/To announce the Old Woman of Harrow'. • Mark: CLEWS WARRANTED STAFFORDSHIRE in a circle round a crown, impressed • 4¾ ins. diam.
This print has also been found in blue.

**676** As 673 etc with a sepia print illustrating the limerick: 'There lived an Old Woman at Lynn/Whose nose very near touch'd her chin/You may easy supose [sic] She had plenty of Beaux/This charming Old Woman Lynn'. • Mark: CLEWS WARRANTED STAFFORDSHIRE • 6¼ ins. diam.

**677** Erratic edge painted blue, with a moulded border of flower sprays and vertical sprigs painted green, red, yellow and blue. The sepia print (painted) illustrates a verse from 'TIM BOBBIN/The court and country here depicted are,/One's fat and jolly, t'other's poor and bare./Plenty sits smiling on the courtier's brow/Whilst meagre want the country's

face doth shew.' • No mark • 8 ins. diam.
This, and 679, 680 and 681, are all from *The Human Passions Delineated*, a series of illustrated, but not very childish, verses satirising the contrasts between rich town folk and poor country dwellers, by the Lancashire writer John Collier, alias Tim Bobbin, first published in 1773.
Several of the prints also appeared on Herculaneum pottery, Derby porcelain and tin-glazed tiles.

**678** Edge and border similar to 677 and a sepia print (painted) of a man quizzing a woman with his glass: 'A Fine Woman pon Honor!/How the Gentlemen look at me!' • No mark; double footrim • 7 ins. diam.
This print has also been noted on mugs.

**679\*** Edge and border as 678 with a sepia print (painted) illustrating a verse from 'TIM BOBBIN/Old squint ey'd Nan, who, by the paultry [sic] trade/Of selling wooden spoons and ladles made/A shift to live, and get tobacco too/And call'd sometimes where folks good ale did brew.' • No mark • 7 ins. diam.

181

*A Soldier maimed and in the Beggars List.*
*Bul thus relieved by a wellfed Pluralist.*

**680** Edge and border as 678 etc, with a red print illustrating a verse from 'TIM BOBBIN/But let me not, in House, or Lane, or Street,/These treble-pension'd Parsons ever meet;/And when I die, may I still number'd be/With the rough Soldier, to Eternity.' • Mark: a painted squiggle • 5¾ ins. diam.
This image, *The Pluralist and Old Soldier*, was used earlier on English tin-glazed tiles of the Sadler & Green type.

**681** As 678 etc with a black print (painted) illustrating a verse from 'TIM BOBBIN/Behold ye worldlings whence true pleasure springs/Not from much wealth, or from the smiles of kings./A single bottle sets our minds at rest./'Tis not full bags, contentment makes the feast.' • No mark • 5¾ ins. diam.
*Private Collection.*

**682** Wavy edge with moulded border of florets alternating with dotted lines in semicircles and vertical rows, and a black print of a violinist: 'One Scraper at a Door enough'. • The print bears the initials [?] W B; no mark on underside • 5¾ ins. diam.

**683** As 682 with black print of a pick-pocket: 'Drawing from the Life.' • No mark • 5¾ ins. diam.

**684** As 682 etc with a black print of a fat beadle accosting a man: 'Giving up the Ghost'. • No mark • 5¾ ins. diam.

**685** Octagonal with rope-twist edge and dimpled floret border, with a sepia print of two men illustrating 'HODGES' FELICITY/Now Hodges tell me what is Felicity/Why Zur I think it's summet inside oth Pig.' • No mark; double footrim • 5¼ ins. diam.
Hodge was a contemptuous name for a farm labourer or peasant.

**686** As 685 with a black print of two men sparring: 'Breaking down the Bridge of an Enemy.' • No mark • 5¼ ins. diam. (see 649)

**687** As 685 etc with a sepia print of 'POT BOYS/Cant even have a day to one self – up at 6 in the morning . . . apprentice – Vy at my. . . ation I went to bed when . . . . like a place.' [indistinct inscription] • No mark; double footrim • 6 ins. diam.

**688** Octagonal with rope-twist edge and blobbed daisy border, with a sepia print of a boy chasing a dog with a kite in his mouth: 'RUN MY LAD WITH ALL YOUR MIGHT/OR ELSE THE DOG WILL SPOIL YOURE KITE.' • No mark • 5¾ ins. diam.
This print also occurs on a cylinder-shaped mug.

**689** As 687 with a sepia print of two veterans with peg legs and hook arms: 'COMPANIONS IN ARMS/Joe my riglar give us yr hand: come wot may we'll never take to our Heels while we have got a leg to stand upon.' • No mark; double footrim • 6 ins. diam.
Another plate in this series has a sepia print of a man and a boy at a table and the title 'TOO MUCH OF A GOOD THING./ What be e crying for Boy?/Because I can't eat any more.'

**690** Rococo edge with moulded border of pendant roses, thistles and shamrock, painted red, green and blue, with a sepia print of two men on a ship: 'Ar'nt you well Sir . . Not wery.' • Mark: the print is signed W. Brown del; no mark on underside • 5 ins. diam.

**691** As 685 with a manganese print of two men: 'DYERS/It's impossible for any man to Dye upon such Terms, we can hardly live as it is'. • No mark; double footrim • 5¼ ins. diam.

**692** Rococo edge with moulded border of roses, fuchsia and vertical columnar sprays, and a sepia print of a boy on a goat: 'JACK'S GALLOPING FAST ACROSS THE MEAD/. . . CERTAINLY ON A FUNNY STEED.' • No mark • 5 ins. diam.
This print is probably based on a Bewick vignette.

**693** Octagonal with rope-twist edge and indistinctly moulded border of blobbed daisies, spotted with green, blue and red, and a manganese print of two men by a fishmonger's stall with a dog being bitten by a lobster: 'Un homard a bas pris/A cheap Lobster.' • No mark; double footrim • 7¼ ins. diam.

**694** As 693 with a black print of a man fishing: 'La Savate/The old Shoe' • No mark; double footrim • 7¼ ins. diam.

**695** As 693 with a manganese print of duelling monkeys: 'Satisfaction/Satisfaction.' • No mark; double footrim • 7¼ ins. diam.
Another in this series shows a fat man and a boy outside a lawyer's office, illustrating 'Mon fils Monsieur/My Son Sir'.

**696** Octagonal with wide moulded border of lambrequins, florets and fleurs de lys on a lattice background, with a black print (painted) of an old woman sailing a tub: 'The wind that blows, the ship that goes, & the lass that loves a sailor.' • No mark • 8¾ ins. diam.
Probably Tyneside or Wearside, circa 1840.

**697** As 693 etc, with a black print of a man missing his coach: 'Je suis retarde/I am too late'. • No mark; double footrim • 8¼ ins. diam.

**698** As 696 with a sepia print of boys after a fight, one having a nosebleed: 'Flow thou regal purple stream'. • No mark • 8½ ins. diam.
Probably Tyneside or Wearside, circa 1840.
Another in this series shows two goats with the inscription 'Nanny will thou gang wi' me.'

**699** Slightly wavy edge with indistinctly moulded border of blobbed daisies and a sepia print of a man in a footbath and two others in tubs behind: 'A LECTURE ON THE COLD WATER CURE.' • Mark: asterisk, impressed; double footrim • 7 ins. diam.

A version of this print, with negro figures, has been found on an 8 ins. vitruvian scroll and alphabet bordered plate. It is a companion to the Lecture on Arithmetic and the other humorous mathematics plates on page 119.

**700** Octagonal with dimpled floret border and a black print of soap box orators and a Punch and Judy show: 'Two of a Trade can never agree.' • No mark • 7¼ ins. diam.

**701** Straight edge and moulded border of florets and leaves painted green, blue, red and yellow, with a blue print of a woman dancing with a midget: 'NAPOLEON POLKA.' • Mark: DIXON PHILLIPS & Co in a semicircle round an anchor, impressed • 6½ ins. diam.
Dixon Phillips, Garrison Pottery, Sunderland, 1840–1865.
This print shows the polka, newly fashionable in the 1840s, being danced by 'General Tom Thumb' the American dwarf see note to 647.

693

694

695

696

697

698

699

700

701

**702** Vitruvian scroll and alphabet border with red lines, and a green print of a foppish soldier: 'I'M sure in all the Army List, There's not a nattier or a brisker/And where's the female to resist; Such a redundancy of whisker?' • No mark • 7 ins. diam.

**703** Wavy edge and indistinctly moulded border of blobbed daisies, with a black print of a uniformed man on a horse taking a letter to a woman sitting by an open window, with the inscription, 'LACKEY'. • No mark • 7¼ ins. diam.
This is probably not a military uniform but a footman's, or 'lackey'.

**704** Indistinctly moulded alphabet border with a black transfer of a seated soldier with two men, one drawing a caricature of his profile on the wall behind. • No mark • 7¼ ins. diam.
Possibly Elsmore & Son, Clayhills Pottery, Tunstall, Staffordshire, 1872–1897 (a marked example is recorded).
This subject calls to mind an illustration from *The Good Boy's Soliloquy* (Darton, 1811) which is captioned by the verse: 'I must not ugly faces scrawl/With charcoal on a whitewashed wall.'

**705** Straight edge and flat border with a sepia print (painted) of a man on a vegetable-sprouting donkey. • Mark: Z impressed • 6 ins. diam.

**706** Straight edge and moulded border of swagged garlands, rose and honeysuckle sprays, sponged in grey, red and yellow, with a black print of a dandy and his lady: 'Who Binds himself till almost dead/And with a wig adorns his head/And looks like a complete Blockhead/The Dandy'. • No mark • 7½ ins. diam.
The same print occurs in blue on a garland-bordered plate marked with an impressed crown (possibly for Clews of Cobridge).
George Cruikshank illustrated *Monstrosities* in 1816, 1824 and 1825 etc, alias 'London Dandies' (and 'Dandisettes', as female dandies were known). The ladies were characterised by huge hats, short skirts, overflowing bosoms and bulging tummies, while their companion men had narrow waists and exaggerated trouser shapes, sometimes topped by preposterous hats to match the ladies'. There was even a print of *Juvenile Monstrosities* in 1826.

**707** Straight edge painted black with garland and medallion moulded border, and a sepia print (with a painted rose spray below) of a lady 'QUIZZING'. • No mark • 6 ins. diam.

**708** Vitruvian scroll and alphabet border, with a sepia print (and painted rose spray) of a gentleman 'SPYING'. • Mark: THOs GODWIN BURSLEM STONE CHINA, printed; double footrim • 5¼ ins. diam.
Thomas Godwin, Canal Works, Navigation Road, Burslem, 1834–1854.

**709** As 708 with a black print of 'LAUGHING'. • No mark • 5 ins. diam.
Probably Godwin, Burslem.
*Private Collection.*

**710** As 708 etc with a black print of 'SNUFFING'. • No mark • 5 ins. diam.
Probably Godwin, Burslem.
Another print in this series is 'GAPEING'.
*Private Collection.*

702

703

704

705

706

707

708

709

710

187

**711** Straight edge and indistinctly moulded border of blobbed daisies, and a green print (painted) of two children in a go-cart pulled by a dog chasing a rabbit. • No mark • 7 ins. diam.
This plate may be found with a sepia print, and in different sizes.

**712** Straight edge with purple line and moulded border of rose sprays and rococo curlicues, with a manganese print of an apple poacher suspended from the tree by his smock. • No mark • 6½ ins. diam.

**713** Indistinctly moulded alphabet border with a sepia print of a boy climbing over a wall after stealing apples. • No mark • 7¼ ins. diam.
Probably Allerton, Park Works, Longton, 1859–1942.

**714** Toothed edge and alphabet border with a manganese print (painted) of children and their overturned go-cart, with the dog eating the rabbit. • No mark • 7 ins. diam.
Probably Allerton.
This print is the sequel to that of 711; it may also be found in sepia on alphabet bordered plates like this.

**715** As 713 with a sepia print (painted) of two men carrying a donkey over a wooden bridge. • No mark • 6¾ ins. diam.
Probably Allerton.

**716** As 713 etc with a sepia print (painted) of a couple by a river, oblivious of the charging bull behind them. • No mark • 7¾ ins.
Probably Allerton.

**717** As 713 etc with five sepia-printed (and painted) hunting scenes. • Mark: C. A. & Sons ENGLAND printed • 7 ins. diam.
Charles Allerton, Park Works, Longton, circa 1890.

**718** Straight edge and segmented border of alternating sprigs and scallop pattern, with a sepia print of a wild-looking boy and a pig: 'IRELAND'. • No mark • 5¾ ins. diam.

**719** As 713 with five sepia-printed (and painted) hunting scenes. • No mark • 7 ins. diam.
Probably Allerton.

# Chapter 12 FLORA AND FAUNA

In this section we include children with their pets when these are an important theme in the picture, rather than incidental, as well as wild animals and birds. Not included here are hunted or working farm animals.

**720** Octagonal with rope-twist edge and moulded border of florets (in the corners) and stars, painted red, light green, blue and yellow. The black print shows visitors to the ostrich house at the London Zoo: 'ZOOLOGICAL GARDENS/THE OSTRICH'. • Marks: DAVENPORT in a semicircle above an anchor with 4 4 on either side of it, impressed and DAVENPORT printed in black • 5¾ ins. diam.
Davenport, Longport, Staffordshire, 1844.
The London Zoo was first opened in 1828 and books for children were soon being illustrated with appropriate engravings. Among them were *A Visit to the Zoological Gardens* by Mrs. Markham (1829), and a *Zoological Keepsake* by an anonymous author (1830). The same ostrich house as that on our plate can be seen in *Henry and*

*Emma's Visit to the Zoological Gardens in the Regent's Park with an Account of what they saw there*, by Mr. J. Bishop (1829).

**721** Straight edge and flat border with brown-printed alphabet around a central square enclosing a kangaroo and her baby (painted green and brown): 'Wild Animals/The Kangaroo'. • Mark: diamond registration mark for 1882 and B.P. Co, printed • 6¼ ins. diam.
Brownhills Pottery, Tunstall, Staffordshire.
This is one of a series of Wild Animal plates; others included 'The Elephant', 'Bear with Cubs'. 'The Tiger', 'The Stag', 'The Leopard' and 'The Lion'.
This print appeared among the 4,000-odd wood engravings in *Knight's Pictorial Museum of Animated Nature*. Undated, but circa 1850.

**722** As 720 with a pink lustre line to the edge and iron red and light green painting to the border florets and stars. The purple print shows visitors to London Zoo: 'ZOOLOGICAL GARDENS/MONKEY HOUSE'. • Marks: as 720 • 5¾ ins. diam.
Davenport, Longport, Staffordshire, 1844.

The illustration shows the first monkey house in the zoo; it was in use from 1829–1839.

**723** Lobe edge with moulded border of florets in segments, green lines to border and yellow dots to the florets. The central manganese print shows a 'TIGER'. • No mark • 6½ ins. diam.
The same tiger print is used on the jug illustrated on page 9.

**724** Wavy edge with moulded border of three rows of blobbed round-petalled daisies and an inner row of sprigs. The black print is of 'A SLY FOX'. • No mark • 7¼ ins. diam.

**725** Straight edge with rose, thistle and shamrock border and a black print of a 'GOAT'. • No mark • 5 ins. diam.
This plate is part of a series which also includes 'DEER' and 'HARE'.

**726** Straight edge with dog, fox and monkey border and a black print of 'THE GREAT PERFORMER OF THE ADELPHI'. • No mark • 4¾ ins. diam.
This was the Elephant of Siam who first performed at the Adelphi Theatre in 1829 and later appeared in Wombwell's Menagerie. Her career and manifold talents are recounted in *The Victorian Staffordshire Figure* by Anthony Oliver.
*Private Collection.*

**727** Straight edge with rose, honeysuckle and swagged garland border painted in iron red, light green, purple and yellow without regard for the moulding. The black print (painted) shows a man riding a zebra. • No mark • 6¼ ins. diam.

**728** Wavy edge with feathered frond and floret border painted in pink lustre, blue, yellow, light green and iron red, with a black print of a boy paying a 'Visit to the Zebra'. • No mark • 6¾ ins. diam.

720

721

722

723

724

725

726

727

728

**729\*** Rococo edge with border of flower sprigs in compartments, painted in Pratt colours. The blue print shows a boy grooming his pony: 'As Morning breaks I rise from bed/And by strong inclination led/Hasten to see well clean'd and fed/MY PRETTY PONY'. • No mark • 6 ins. diam. The text and illustration are from *My Pony* by J. Baker (William Darton, 1812).

**730\*** Straight edge with well-moulded continuous flowery garland border and a blue print of a boy thrown from his pony: 'Once ere my pony I could well restrain/He threw me off and dragg'd me by the rein./But for this vicious trick I'll never feign/MY GRATITUDE!' • Mark: a crown impressed • 6 ins. diam.
Possibly James & Ralph Clews, Cobridge, Staffordshire, 1818–1834.

**731\*** Straight edge with border of flowers and leaves in a continuous garland painted in orange, light green and yellow, with a blue print of a boy on his pony: 'Yet steady are thy motions all/I never knew thee slip or Fall/So gentle to the pat or call/Art thou my PONY'. • No mark • 5¾ ins. diam.
Text and illustration from *My Pony*.

**732** Straight edge with segmented border of alternating sprigs and scallop pattern, and a red print of 'GENTLEMAN & BOY RIDING./To Brighton or Worthing and all with full speed,/Which way are you going so mightily fast?/Take care of the reins for your mettlesome steed/Might stumble and lay you too low at the last.' • No mark • 5¾ ins. diam.

**733\*** Straight edge with moulded border of flowers and leaves in a continuous garland and a black print (painted in Pratt colours) of a boy leading his pony: 'Thy limbs are formed in beauty's mould./To me thou'rt worth thy weight in gold,/Thy skin is white as driven snow,/Thy pace is not too quick or slow./MY NOBLE PONY.' • Mark: J impressed • 7 ins. diam.
The illustration and (abridged) verse are from *My Pony*.

**734\*** Straight edge with leafy wreath border lustred purple and painted red, with a sepia print of the boy on his pony as 731. • Mark: lustred squiggle; double footrim • 5¼ ins. diam.

**735** Octagonal with border of roses, thistles and shamrock, alternating with tendrils, painted pink, light green and yellow. The black print shows a horse standing in the desert, with pyramids in the distance. • Mark: four blobs in a square, impressed • 5¼ ins. diam.

**736** Straight edge with moulded border of alternate Arabic and Roman numerals, and a blue print of a Shetland pony. • No mark • 4¾ ins. diam. (see 790).

**737** Straight edge with rose, thistle and shamrock border painted red, light green and yellow, with a black print of the boy on his pony as 731 and 734. • No mark • 4¾ ins. diam.

729

730

731

732

733

734

735

736

737

**738** Vitruvian scroll and alphabet border with red line to edge and black (painted) print of a child on a pony: 'FROLICS OF YOUTH/SEE HOW I RIDE'. • No mark • 7½ ins. diam.
This print was also used for commemoratives of The Prince of Wales (see 1191).

**739** Indented edge with sectioned border of moulded leafy curlicues and sprays of roses and pansies. The black print shows a woman on horseback with a falcon, 'TAKING A RIDE'. • No mark; triple footrim • 6½ ins. diam.

**740** Virtually straight edge, reeded and feathered, with moulded border of vertical sprigs, blobbed green, red and light blue. The sepia print (painted) shows THE BOY & HIS PONY/Oh James what a beautiful pony you have got/I'll ask Papa to buy me one that I will'. • No mark • 7¼ ins. diam.

**741** Straight edge with radiating grooved border and a black (painted) print of a girl riding a pony with a dog running alongside. • Mark: DAWSON and (beneath) 5 impressed • 5¾ ins. diam.
John Dawson & Co., South Hylton and Ford Potteries, Sunderland, circa 1799–1864.
Other plates in the same series include the mounted Nubian print as 1153.

**742** Rococo edge with moulded daisy garland border painted with a green line. The black print shows a little boy leading a pony with a little girl riding: 'TAKING A RIDE'. • No mark; double footrim • 7 ins. diam.

**743** Vitruvian scroll and alphabet border with (painted) sepia print of a woman riding side-saddle through a farmyard. • Mark: EDGE MALKIN & CO impressed • 7¼ ins. diam.
Edge Malkin & Co., Newport and Middleport Potteries, Burslem, circa 1871–1903.
This print is based on an illustration by T. Robinson entitled *Ride over the Farm*. It appeared in a section of 'Country Pictures'

in the *Picture Scrap Book* or *Happy Hours at Home* (Religious Tract Society, circa 1860).

**744** Straight edge and indistinctly moulded blobbed daisy border, and a black print of 'HORSE & GROOM'. • No mark • 6¼ ins. diam.

**745** Edge and border as 742 with painting in pale green, light blue and red, and a blue print of a boy on a pony watched by another. • No mark; double footrim • 7 ins. diam.
The same image occurs on a plate with a moulded border of flower sprays and fleurs de lys, and on the mug 1019. The print is from *Peter Parley's Annual 1862*.

**746** Wavy edge with indistinctly moulded border of three rows of blobbed daisies and a black print of a boy on a pony with a companion and a groom: 'READY FOR A RIDE'. • Mark: LONDON impressed in a fan shape over an anchor • 6 ins. diam.
This mark could denote one of five factories (see note for 16).

738

739

740

741

742

743

744

745

746

**747** Rococo edge with moulded border of roses, tulips and asters and a sepia print of a girl feeding a sheep: 'EMMA'S PETT' [sic]. • No mark • 6 ins. diam.
Probably Scott, Southwick Pottery, Sunderland, circa 1800–1897.

**748** Elaborately shaped rococo edge painted black, with moulded border panels and green and red painted sprigs. The blue transfer shows a little boy driving a goat cart with a little girl behind: 'THE YOUNG CHARIOTEER.' • No mark • 8¼ ins. diam.
The print is based on a lithograph by Gunthorpe, *Sprigs of Nobility*, published in *The Star* magazine, circa 1830.

**749** Straight edge with moulded basket-work border and a black print of 'MY LITTLE NAN'. • No mark • 6 ins. diam.
The same print has been found in sepia on a plate with a reeded and feathered edge and border of vertical sprigs.

**750** Straight edge and crisply moulded dog, fox and monkey border painted iron red, green, pink, yellow and brown, with a sepia print (painted) of two girls with sheep in a garden. • No mark; double footrim • 7½ ins. diam.
Probably Tyneside or Wearside.

**751*** Octagonal, with moulded border of florets, sketchily painted in red, green and blue, and a red transfer of a donkey standing in an oval box: 'My Ass in a Bandbox'. • Mark: green painted blob • 4¾ ins. diam.
A similar donkey to this appears among examples of 19th century printers' stock blocks, illustrated in *Wm. Davison's New Specimens of Cast-metal Ornaments and Wood Types* by Peter Isaac (Printing Historical Society, 1990), but without the container. A band box was originally a small oval box in which a clergyman's collar bands would be kept; later the term was used for larger oval-shaped boxes used as general containers, especially for millinery. In 19th century America, the making of decorative bandboxes was a well-known commercial activity. The significance of this particular image, perhaps a pun, has so far escaped us.

**752** Straight edge with alphabet border against a granular background, and a sea-green print of a donkey in a stable. • No mark • 7¼ ins. diam.

**753** Rococo edge with feathered frond and floret border painted red, blue, green and yellow, with a red print of a man on a donkey outside a cottage, with people looking on: 'Come up Donkey'. • Mark: undecipherable printed mark; double footrim • 5¾ ins. diam.

**754** Toy plate with rococo edge and green-printed garland border, with a green print of girls decorating a sheep with a garland. • No mark • 4¼ ins. diam (see 791).
Other sheep subjects include 'FEEDING THE LAMB', a blue print of a girl with a lamb in a garden, on an unmarked wavy-edged, daisy-bordered plate.

**755** Toy plate with rococo edge and sea-green-printed lacy border, and a sea-green print of a girl playing with a goat on a lead. • Mark: GOAT and CE&M printed • 5 ins. diam.
Cork, Edge & Malkin, Newport Pottery, Burslem, 1860–1871.
The same print can be found in red, manganese and in black, and on 4 ins. plates.

**756** Straight edge with moulded border of roses, thistles and shamrock and a black print of children decorating a donkey: 'THIS IS JACK'S BIRTHDAY'. • No mark • 5¾ ins. diam.
The same plate has been found with an orange lustred border and a green print, and the same print, in black, occurs on a plate with a border of sprigs painted red and green.

747

748

749

750

751

752

753

754

755

756

**757\*** Vitruvian scroll and alphabet border with red lines, and a black print of a boy leaning on a drum, asleep, with his dog on watch: 'THE SENTINEL'. • Mark: T&B GODWIN NEW WHARF impressed • 5¼ ins. diam.
Thomas & Benjamin Godwin, New Wharf and New Basin Potteries, Burslem, Circa 1809–1834.

**758\*** As 757 with a red print of a child riding a large dog: 'THE LITTLE JOCKEY'. • Mark: T&B GODWIN NEW WHARF impressed • 5¼ ins. diam.
The same print is to be found on rococo-edged plates with rose, tulip and aster borders.

**759\*** As 757 with a black print of a boy with a dog: 'THE PLAYFELLOWS'. • Mark: T&B GODWIN NEW WHARF impressed • 5¼ ins. diam.
A version of this print occurs on a straight-edged plate with a moulded border bearing the inscription 'ALBERT EDWARD PRINCE OF WALES BORN Nov 9 1841' and marked with an impressed crown, possibly for Swillington Bridge Pottery, Yorkshire.

**760** Straight edge with moulded border of roses, thistles and shamrock, lustred orange, and a green print of a little girl riding on a dog, helped by a boy. • No mark • 6¾ ins. diam.
This image is based on a lithograph that appeared in an issue of *The Saturday Magazine* circa 1830.

**761** Rococo edge with moulded border of roses, tulips and asters painted yellow, purple, blue and green, with a black print of a dog tied to a kennel, barking at retreating burglars: 'When night enveloped all in shade/Who checked the lawless Robbers Trade/And roused us by the noise he made. MY TIPPOO./Still share my cake, my crust of bread,/Still let me gently pat thy head/Till I am old, and thou art dead. MY TIPPOO.' • Mark: four green painted blobs; double footrim • 6 ins. diam.

The text is from the poem, *My Tippoo* by J. Baker, one of several early 19th century poems about dogs called Tippoo.

**762** Reeded and feathered edge with vertical sprig border, and a black (painted) print of a boy riding on the back of a large dog. • No mark • 6½ ins. diam.
The source for this print is an illustration by Harrison Weir, 1864, which was used in *The Children's Friend*, February 1865, with the caption 'Barry, the St Bernard Dog.'

**763** Rococo edge with moulded border of roses, fuchsia and vertical columnar sprays, and a sepia print of a boy with a large dog outside a kennel. • No mark • 6 ins. diam.

The print is based on an engraving in *The Child's Companion*, October 1845.
Another version appears in purple on an indistinctly moulded daisy-bordered plate with a straight edge; a companion plate shows a dog begging and holding a hat towards a small boy with a lady.

**764** Octagonal with rope-twist edge painted green and moulded border of dimpled florets, with a sepia print of a boy and a girl giving a baby a ride on a large dog: 'DOCILITY'. • No mark • 6 ins. diam.
The same print occurs on wide-bordered octagonal plates by Bailey & Ball with painting in various colours.

**765\*** Straight edge and garland border painted in Pratt colours, with a blue print (painted) of a boy riding a large dog: 'Behold me mounted on my Noble Tray/ I'm sure he'd carry me the live long day/ And not one Grumbling word would say/ MY NOBLE DOG'. • No mark • 6½ ins. diam.
See note for 777.
*Private Collection.*

757

758

759

760

761

762

763

764

765

**766** Rococo edge and moulded border of roses, tulips and asters, painted red, green and blue, with a black print of a boy with a dog on a lead and a girl with her doll: 'MY POMPEY'. • No mark; triple footrim • 6¼ ins. diam.
The popularity of Pompey as a dog's name may have been connected with patriotic feeling around the time of Nelson, whose naval base, Portsmouth, was (and is) nicknamed Pompey. Equally it may have been engendered by Francis Conventry's popular work *Pompey the Little* (1751).

**767** Wavy edge with moulded border of three graduated rows of blobbed, round-petalled daisies and a blue print of a girl on an ottoman stretching her hand towards a dog: 'POMPEY'. • No mark; double footrim; • 6 ins. diam.

**768** Straight edge and moulded border of florets and leaves in a continuous tendrilly garland, the florets painted red, blue and yellow, and a black print of children with a begging dog: 'SIT UP POMPEY.' • Mark: POWELL & BISHOP impressed within an oval • 6¼ ins. diam.
Powell & Bishop, Hanley, 1876–1878.
The same plate is to be found in a larger size.

**769** Rococo edge and moulded border of roses, tulips and asters, and a red print of a little girl with a hawk on a string, and a large dog. • No mark • 6 ins. diam.

**770** Wavy edge with moulded border of blobbed daisies and inner row of sprigs, with a black print, as 767, within a decorated circle, entitled 'Childhood'. • Mark: MOORE & CO impressed • 7½ ins. diam.
(Samuel) Moore & Co., Wear Pottery, Southwick, Sunderland, 1803–1874.

**771** Rococo edge and moulded border of butterflies and flower sprays painted blue, green, red and yellow, against a background pattern of impressed dots. The blue print shows a boy and his dog beside a river: 'SEIZE 'EM POMPEY.' • Mark: P&C impressed • 7 ins. diam.
Probably Procter & Collingwood, Staffordshire, circa 1850.

**772** Slightly rococo edge with feathered frond and floret border painted in pink lustre, blue, green, yellow and iron red, with a black print of two boys playing with two dogs: 'Carlo swimming.' • Mark: lustre X • 6½ ins. diam.
The same print may be found in sepia, painted, on octagonal daisy-bordered plates with lustred edges.
The name Carlo for a dog was almost certainly popularised by *The Life of Carlo – The Famous Dog of Drury Lane Theatre* (Tabart, 1806) whose seafaring and subsequent theatrical adventures included rescuing a drowning child – a part Carlo managed 'with zeal and sagacity'. His story was recounted in autobiographical form, a device adopted for another popular children's book, the *Memoirs of Dick, the little Poney*: 'supposed to be written by himself; and published for the instruction and amusement of little masters and misses' (Tabart, 1806).

**773** Rococo edge and moulded border of flower sprays and single florets, painted red, purple, green and yellow, with a red print of a reclining lady holding a bird out to a girl, with a dog leaping to get it. • No mark; triple footrim • 8 ins. diam.

**774** Edge and border similar to 769, with a sepia print of a little girl with a dog lying down: 'TIRED OF PLAY'. • No mark • 6 ins. diam.
Probably Scott, Southwick Pottery, Sunderland.
This plate may be found in a smaller size.

766

767

768

769

770

771

772

773

774

**775** Rococo edge with moulded border of alternating swags and posies of flowers, with two black lines. The black print shows a girl with a begging dog: 'THE BEGGARS PETITION.' • No mark • 6½ ins. diam.
This print has also been noted on a vitruvian scroll and alphabet bordered plate. *The Beggar's Petition* was a well-known pious poem by Moss; here its title has been adopted for a much more frivolous idea.

**776** Octagonal with rope-twist edge and moulded border of dimpled daisies, with larger florets in the corners. The black print shows a girl in a garden with a begging dog. • No mark; double footrim • 6¾ ins. diam.

**777** Indented edge and moulded border of rococo curlicues alternating with flower sprays, painted red, pale green and yellow, and a sepia print of a girl 'TEACHING TRAY TO DANCE'. • No mark • 6½ ins. diam.
The popularity of Tray as a dog's name may originate from the nursery rhyme *Old Mother Hubbard*: in some early editions her dog is called Tray.

**778** Straight edge painted green with a blobbed daisy border and a black print of two girls playing with a dog. • Mark: D impressed; double footrim • 5 ins. diam.
Possibly Bovey Tracey Pottery, Devon, 1842–1894.

**779** Straight edge and crisply moulded border of flowers and leaves in a repeating garland, and pink lustre lines. The black print shows two children with a dancing dog; the girl plays a hurdy-gurdy. • Mark: ELLIOT & CO impressed above an asterisk • 8½ ins. diam.
This mark seems to be unrecorded, and is possibly a retailer's mark. The print, *Dancing Dog*, was used on a Don Pottery plate circa 1820–1834 and a saucer by Sewell & Donkin, St. Anthony's Pottery, Newcastle, circa 1821–1852.

**780** As 778 with a black print of a boy with his dog. • No mark; double footrim • 5 ins. diam.
Possibly Bovey Tracey Pottery, Devon.

**781** Edge and border as 777 with dark brown line to edge and a sepia print of a boy in a landscape with a begging, pipe-smoking dog. • No mark • 7½ ins. diam.

**782** Rococo edge with moulded rose and jasmine border, painted green, red and dark blue, with a black print of a cottage interior with a woman and boy watching a begging dog. The print is signed T Robson. • No mark • 5¾ ins. diam.
Middlesborough Pottery, 1834–1844; see 111 for a note on Thomas Robson.

**783** Straight edge with moulded and orange lustred border of roses, thistles and shamrock, with a black print of a boy with a begging, pipe-smoking dog, another version of the image in 781. • No mark • 7½ ins. diam.

775

776

777

778

779

780

781

782

783

**784*** Vitruvian scroll and alphabet border with a black (painted) print of a dog fetching a stick in a lily pond. • No mark; double footrim • 6¼ ins. diam.
Possibly Godwin, Burslem.
This print was probably based on an illustration by Harrison Weir, dated 1862, of which an engraving appeared in the *Band of Hope Review*, 1 February, 1867 (S. W. Partridge).

**785** Slight rococo edge with moulded border of roses, fuchsia and vertical columnar sprays, and a black print of a child with an alphabet book sitting beside a dog in a kennel: 'THE PLAYMATES'. • No mark • 6 ins. diam.
This print also appears on vitruvian scroll and alphabet bordered plates.

**786** Rococo edge with feathered frond and floret border painted in pink lustre, blue, yellow, green and iron red, with a black print of a little boy hugging a dog while another looks on. • Mark: two impressed blobs, and two lustre blobs • 6¾ ins. diam.

**787** Straight edge with moulded border of flower sprays centred on a floret, and a black print showing a cat with its paw in a goldfish bowl. • No mark • 6¾ ins. diam.
Possibly William Smith, Stockton, circa 1825–1855.

**788** Rococo edge with continuous daisy garland border painted blue, red and green, with a black print of 'THE CAT'S CONCERT./Music hath charms to sooth [sic] the savage breast.' • No mark • 6¾ ins. diam.
The same print appears on a rococo-edged plate with a moulded scroll and curlicue border.

**789** Straight edge with moulded border of elongated florets, and a black print showing 'THE KITTENS IN THE PANTRY'. • No mark • 6¼ ins. diam.

**790** Straight edge and moulded border of alternating Arabic and Roman numerals, with a blue print of a dog outside a barrel-shaped kennel. • No mark • 4¾ ins. diam.
This is a companion plate to 736.

**791** Toy plate with rococo edge, green-printed garland border and a green print of children and dogs playing with a wheelbarrow. • No mark • 4½ ins. diam.
This is a companion plate to 754.

**792** Rococo edge and moulded border of florets and leaves in sections, painted dark blue and green, with a black print of 'THE DOG.' • No mark • 4½ ins. diam.

**793*** Vitruvian scroll and alphabet border with red lines, and a manganese print of 'CAT AND KITTENS'. • Mark: T&B GODWIN NEW WHARF • 5 ins. diam.
Thomas & Benjamin Godwin, New Wharf and New Basin Potteries, Burslem.
The source of this print is a lithograph published by Engelmann Graf Coindet & Co., Dean Street, London 1828.
The same plate may be found in a larger size and with a black print.

784

785

786

87

788

789

790

791

792

793

**794*** Octagonal with rope-twist edge painted green and moulded border of line-petalled blobbed daisies. The black (painted) print shows a girl with a cat: 'THE FAVOURITE'. • No mark • 5¼ ins. diam.
Versions of this print appear on an octagonal plate with a dimpled daisy border and on an erratic edged toy plate with a border of flower sprays, the latter marked with an impressed anchor.

**795*** Rococo edge and moulded border of roses, tulips and asters painted green, red, blue and yellow, with a black print of a boy with a cat looking into a mouse cage: 'WOULDN'T YOU LIKE TO CATCH HIM'. • No mark • 6 ins. diam.
Possibly John Carr, Low Lights Pottery, North Shields, Northumberland, circa 1845–1900.

**796*** Octagonal with floret border painted pink, blue and yellow, and a black (painted) print of a girl teaching a cat from an alphabet book: 'Come Pussy will you learn to read/I've got a pritty [sic] book.' • No mark • 4¾ ins. diam.

The source for this print is the illustration from the frontispiece of *Rhymes for the Nursery* 'by the authors of Original Poems' (Darton, 17th edition, 1825).

**797** Straight edge with greyhounds, goat and butterfly border, and a black print of a little girl with a cat watching a bird: 'THE FAVOURITE.' • No mark • 6¾ ins. diam.

**798** Rococo edge with moulded dots and blue line, and moulded sprigs of rose, thistle and shamrock. The black print shows a little girl holding a cat: 'INNOCENCE/DO YOU SEE MY LITTLE TOMMY'. • No mark • 8 ins. diam.

**799** Rococo edge painted red, with moulded border of tendrilly flower sprigs and a sepia print of a girl with a kitten: 'LITTLE TITTY.' • No mark • 7¼ ins. diam.
A similar print, entitled 'OUR EARLY DAYS' has been noted on a straight-edged plate with a moulded border of scallops and florets.

**800** Erratic edge painted with a black line and flat border with three painted sprigs, and a green print of a little girl feeding a wrapped cat on her lap: 'THE YOUNG NURSE'. • Mark: STONEWARE in a semi-circle above B&T impressed • 6 ins. diam.
This could come from Bettany and Tomlinson, Lane End, 1843–1844; Barker & Till, Burslem, 1846–1850, or Barrow & Taylor, Hanley, 1859.
Unmarked versions of this plate, with sepia prints, are also known, and the same print was used on daisy-bordered plates from the Middlesbrough Pottery Co.

**801*** Straight edge with dog, fox and monkey border (unpainted) with a green print of 'TABBY.' • Mark: TG in underglaze blue script • 5 ins. diam.
Possibly Tyneside or Wearside.

**802** Rococo edge with border of florets clumsily painted in blue, yellow, red and green, with a green print of children

playing with a cat: 'JUMP TOM JUMP'. • Mark: MIDDLESBRO POTTERY in a semi-circle around an anchor and surmounted by 2, impressed, and a green-printed 12. • 6¼ ins. diam.
Middlesbrough Pottery Co., Yorkshire, 1834–1844.
A version of this print can be found on straight-edged plates with rose, thistle and shamrock borders.

794

795

796

797

798

799

800

801

802

**803** Shaped base and plain loop handle with a green print of a boy riding a pony: 'AH! TROT AWAY JACK YOU SOON WILL GET BACK/TO YOUR HOME NOW SCHOOL HOURS ARE OVER:/AS SOON AS YOU'RE ABLE PUT BOB IN THE STABLE/AND PRAY GIVE HIM PLENTY OF CLOVER.' • No mark • 2¾ ins. ht.; 2¾ ins. diam.

**804\*** Reeded base and round-moulded rim, with plain loop handle, silver lustre to the rim, base and handle, and a finely printed scene of a man on a horse and a boy on a pony, with a spired church and a pottery with smoking bottle ovens in the background. • No mark • 2¾ ins. ht.; 2⅝ ins. diam.
Enoch Wood & Sons, Burslem, 1818–1846. The background shows a view of the Fountain Place pottery.

**805** Toy teabowl with iron red rim and sepia prints (painted) of a child on a pony 'LEARNING TO RIDE' on one side and 'A FISHING PARTY' on the other. • No mark • 1¾ ins. ht.; 2¾ ins. diam of top.

**806** Shaped base and loop handle with leaf terminals, and a black print of a boy with his horse and a dog. • No mark • 2¾ ins. ht.; 2¾ ins. diam.

**807** Cylindrical with pointed ear-shaped handle and black-printed borders, and prints of children with sheep (the same print on both sides). • No mark • 3⅝ ins. ht.; 3⅞ ins. diam.

**808** Cylindrical with plain loop handle and a black print of 'NEDDY AND ME'. • No mark • 2⅞ ins. ht.; 3 ins. diam.

**809** Shaped base and plain loop handle with sepia prints of 'OLD JACK THE DONKEY AND HIS MASTER JOE' on one side, and 'THE MILK-FETCHING DOG' on the other. • No mark • 3⅝ ins. ht.; 3¾ ins. diam.

**810** Porcelain with shaped base and rim, spurred loop handle and gold lines, with a finely printed scene of a boy playing his pipe to three dancing pigs on one side and a dancing couple on the other. • Mark: a printed squiggle and COPELAND, and a diamond registration mark for 28 October 1867 • 2½ ins. ht.; 3 ins. diam.
Copeland, Spode Works, Stoke-on-Trent.

G is for *Gratitude*, which we should show
Towards all who assist us as onward we go
In this chequered way, which indeed would be drear,—
Did we not meet with friends who are kind and sincere!

**811** Shaped base and plain loop handle, with a black print of Androcles and the Lion in the cave. • No mark • 2¾ ins. ht.; 2⅝ ins. diam.
This is an illustration from *The Alphabet of Virtues* (Darton, London, circa 1856): 'G is for *Gratitude*, which we should show/Towards all who assist us as onward we go/In this chequered way, which indeed would be drear,/Did we not meet with friends who are kind and sincere.'

**812** Round-rimmed base with plain loop handle and a green print of a 'GOAT'. • No mark • 2⅝ ins. ht.; 2⅝ ins. diam.

**813** Drab-coloured, cylindrical, with plain loop handle and a black print of a child riding in a goat-cart, watched by a man. On the opposite side is the verse: 'THE PLEASANT RIDE./A pretty goat, with horns so long,/With coat so rough, and legs so strong;/Drew Mary in her chaise so gay,/To ride about when fine the day;'. • No mark • 2½ ins. ht.; 2½ ins. diam.

**814** Shaped base and plain loop handle, with a black print of a child in a 'DOG CART.' • No mark • 2⅝ ins. ht.; 3 ins. diam.

**809** The opposite side.

**815** The opposite side of 591.

Two Enoch Wood mugs with silver lustre borders, from the Geoffrey Godden Collection, are similar to 804 but 3½ ins. ht. Another mug from the same series, with a canary yellow ground, is illustrated on the front cover, whilst another is in the Willett Collection, Brighton.

803          804          805          806

807          808          809

810          811          812          813

814          809          815

**816** Narrow rim to base, and plain loop handle, with red-printed borders and scenes, of a boy with a begging dog on one side and boy with a large dog sitting down on the other, with 'ELIZABETH' printed in black in the middle. • No mark • 2⅜ ins. ht.; 2½ ins. diam.
This mug may be found in varying colours and with different names.

**817** Cylindrical with loop handle and leaf terminals, and a black print of a girl with a hoop 'PLAYING WITH POMPEY'. • No mark • 2⅜ ins. ht.; 2½ ins. diam.

**818** Round-rimmed base, with plain loop handle, copper lustre to base, rim and handle, pink lustre inside rim, and an iron red print of a child riding a dog: 'THE LITTLE JOCKEY' (see 758). • No mark • 2¼ ins. ht.; 2½ ins. diam.

**818A** Toy plate with wavy edge and a green monochrome print of CRIBB, possibly named after the famous boxer. • No mark • 3¾ ins. diam.

**819** Round-rimmed base and gadroon-moulded rim, with pointed ear-shaped handle and black prints (washed over in buff/grey) of two puppies playing with a turkey's foot (the same print on each side). • No mark • 2⅝ ins. ht.; 3 ins. diam.

**820** Porcelain with shaped base and moulded rim, with a spurred loop handle, gilded lines and a finely printed group of four dogs. • No mark • 2¾ ins. ht.; 3⅛ ins. diam.

**821** Porcelain, tapered, with moulded rim, pointed ear-shaped handle and a sepia print (slightly painted) of a bulldog. • No mark • 2¾ ins. ht.; 2½ ins. diam.

**822** Porcelain with round-rimmed and reeded base, beaded rim and spurred ear-shaped handle, with applied mouldings of greyhounds, blue with lustre spots. • No mark • 3 ins. ht.; 2⅞ ins. diam.

**823** Cylindrical with plain loop handle and a black print of two men with 'DANCING DOGS'. • No mark • 2⅝ ins. ht.; 2½ ins. diam.

**824** Cylindrical with loop handle and leaf terminals, and a red print of three geese looking at 'TOBY THE SHOW DOG'. • No mark • 2⅞ ins. ht.; 2¾ ins. diam.

**825** As 824 with a red print of four dogs 'RACING FOR A PRIZE'. • No mark • 3 ins. ht.; 2⅝ ins. diam.

**826** Shaped base and loop handle with leaf terminals, and green prints of a girl with a leaping dog on one side, a boy with a bubble pipe (as on plate 207) on the other and 'A PRESENT FOR A GOOD GIRL' in the middle. • No mark • 2¾ ins. ht.; 2¾ ins. diam.

**827** Cylindrical with two ear-shaped handles and sepia prints (painted) illustrating the Fox and the Grapes ('THE GRAPES ARE SOUR') on one side, and the story of the Fox and the Crow ('LISTEN TO MY PRETTY VOICE') on the other. • No mark • 3¼ ins. ht.; 3¼ ins. diam.
Both illustrations are to the well-known Aesop fables.

**828** Similar to 827 with sepia prints (lustred in orange) of a dog carrying a dead pheasant on one side and two greyhounds with a dead hare on the other. • Mark: FIELD SPORTS printed on a garter enclosing No 2 and E. M. & Co B beneath • 3½ ins. ht.; 3¼ ins. diam.
Edge Malkin & Co., Newport and Middleport Potteries, Burslem, 1871–1903.

**827** The opposite side.

**828** The opposite side.

828

827

816

817

818

818a

819

820

821

822

823

824

825

826

827

828

## MONKEY BUSINESS

The monkey tricks on this page belong to the long-favoured European tradition of *singeries*: these delicate and temperamental representatives of distant and exotic lands were incorporated into artistic decoration, often in humorous and humanised form, from the late 17th century onwards, and continued to fascinate the Victorians, both as artistic subject matter and as part of the stock-in-trade of itinerant showmen.

**829** Rococo edge with feathered frond and floret border painted in pink lustre, blue, yellow, green and iron red, and a sepia print of a monkey sitting on a table looking into a mirror, with a man peering round the door and two children looking through the window: 'Shave for a Penny.' • Mark: two lustre blobs • 6 ins. diam.
Larger versions of this plate exist, some with black prints.
The idea is reminiscent of an engraving in Bewick's *History of Quadrupeds*, illustrating 'The MONKEY kind . . . full of frolic and grimace, greatly addicted to thieving, and extremely fond of imitating human actions, but always with a mischievous intention.'

**830** Straight edge and moulded garland border of narcissus florets and leaves, with a green print of a monkey teasing a chained dog with its tail: 'DONT YOU WISH YOU MAY GET IT'. • No mark • 5½ ins. diam.

**831** Edge and border as 829 with a black print of 'Pig Race'. • No mark • 6 ins. diam.

**832** Straight edge painted with a green line and border with moulded stems of wheat, tulip and bluebell. The black (painted) print shows a monkey teasing a cat by pulling her tail: 'TAKE YOUR TIME MISS LUCY'. • Mark: J&G MEAKIN impressed • 7¼ ins. diam.
J. & G. Meakin, Eagle Pottery and Eastwood Works, Hanley, 1851 onwards.

**833** Straight edge, painted black, and moulded border of rococo curlicues alternating with flower sprays, and a black print of dogs round a table, a large poodle presiding. • No mark; double footrim • 6½ ins. diam.
This transfer is based on the painting by Edwin Landseer, *Laying Down the Law* (also called *Trial by Jury*) now in the Devonshire Collection, Chatsworth. It was etched by Thomas Landseer (the artist's brother) circa 1841–1842. *Source picture courtesy of the Trustees of the Chatsworth House Trust.*

**834** Edge and border as 832 with black (painted) print as 830. • Mark: J & G Meakin as 832. • 7¼ ins. diam.

**835** Vitruvian scroll and alphabet border with a sepia print of ducks using bathing machines. • No mark • 7¼ ins. diam. *Private Collection.*

**836** Straight edge with border of radiating lines and a red print of anthropomorphic ducks; 'SAILORS THREE, LOOK TO SEA;/IF IT BLOWS A GALE THERE'LL BE.' • No mark • 7¼ ins. diam.

**837** Edge and border as 835 with a sepia print of anthropomorphic ducks drilling. • No mark • 7¼ ins. diam.
These two plates come from an alphabet bordered series which also includes a girl in a kennel, pulling a dog; two girls with a pony in a meadow; children donkey riding on a beach; a child in a large bonnet lying in a meadow, and ducks holding school. Some have the printed mark H A & Co, probably for Henry Alcock & Co., Elder Pottery, Cobridge, Staffordshire, 1861–1910. *Private Collection.*

829 Shave for a Penny.

830 DONT YOU WISH YOU MAY GET IT.

831 Pig Race.

832 TAKE YOUR TIME MISS LUCY

833

834 DONT YOU WISH YOU MAY GET IT

835

836 SAILORS THREE, LOOK TO SEA. IF IT BLOWS, A GALE THERE'LL BE.

837

**838** Toothed edge and greyhound, goat and butterfly border crudely painted in black, light green and red, with a black print of a girl feeding rabbits: 'THE FAVOURITE RABBITS/Their cell to store with clover sweet/How joyous at each sunshine hour. I haunted evry [sic]/green retreat Of forest, garden, heath & bower.'
• No mark • 5¾ ins. diam.

**839** Octagonal with rope-twist edge and blobbed daisy border, and a green print of a boy showing a guinea pig to a girl: 'JUVENILE COMPANIONS'. • No mark • 6½ ins. diam.
Versions of this print can be found on miniature plates with straight edges and flat borders and on plates with indented edges and borders of alternating rococo curlicues and flower sprays.

**840** Vitruvian scroll and alphabet border with a black (painted) print of 'WILLIE AND HIS RABBIT'. • No mark • 6 ins. diam. Probably Staffordshire.
The same plate can be found in a smaller size.

**841** Rococo edge with feathery frond and floret border painted in pink lustre, blue, green, yellow and iron red, with a black print of a boy and a girl with rabbits.
• Mark: a lustre blob • 6¾ ins. diam.

**842** Octagonal with rope-twist edge and dimpled floret border, with a black (painted) print of children with rabbits as 841. • No mark • 5½ ins. diam.

**843** Vitruvian scroll and alphabet border with a sepia print (painted) of a little girl with rabbits. • Mark: EDGE MALKIN & CO impressed • 7 ins. diam.
Edge Malkin & Co., Newport and Middleport Potteries, Burslem, circa 1871–1903.
The print comes from an illustration by Henry Anelay in *The Mother's Picture Alphabet* (S. W. Partridge, 1862): 'R begins Rosa: how pleased she appears,/To watch those plump Rabbits with long silky ears!'

**844** Cylindrical with loop handle and leaf terminals, and black prints, 'FEEDING THE RABBIT' on one side, and 'ROBERT' on the other. • No mark • 2⅜ ins. ht.; 2¼ ins. diam.
This print has also been found on a marked Davenport mug.

**845** Cylindrical with plain loop handle and a black print of a boy sitting on a garden seat feeding birds. • No mark • 2⅝ ins. ht.; 2½ ins. diam.

**846** Round-rimmed base with plain loop handle and a black print of a boy with a bird and a cage. • Mark: 36 and 4 impressed • 2⅜ ins. ht.; 2¾ ins. diam.

**847** The opposite side of the mug 259 showing 'MY PRETTY BIRD'. (cf. plates overleaf).

838       839       840

841       842       843

844       845       846       847

**848\*** Wavy-edged octagonal, with deep border of moulded patterns, painted with blue lines, and a black print (painted) of a girl feeding poultry: 'HEN & CHICKENS'. • Mark: Diamond registration mark for Bailey & Ball, Longton, 1847. • 6 ins. diam.

**849** Rococo edge with crisply moulded border of roses, tulips and asters and a sepia print of a girl with a bird cage and a cat: 'PUSS YOU MUST NOT HURT MY PRETTY BIRD'. • Mark: a crown and POTTERY impressed; triple footrim • 6½ ins. diam.
Swillington Bridge Pottery, Yorkshire, 1791-circa 1845.
The same plate may be found in a larger size.

**850** As 848 with red lines to border, and a sepia print (painted) of a girl with 'THE DOVES'. • Mark: Diamond registration mark for Bailey and Ball, Longton, 1847. • 6 ins. diam.

**851\*** Rococo edge and border of roses, tulips and asters painted red, green and blue, with a black print of a girl holding a bird: 'MY PRETTY BIRD'. • No mark; triple footrim • 7½ ins. diam.

**852** A toy plate with a similar print to 849 in black. • No mark • 3¾ ins. diam.

**853** Toy plate with a black print of a girl with a bird cage on a table. • No mark • 4 ins. diam.
The same plate may be found with a manganese print, while another version of the print occurs on wavy-edged, daisy-bordered plates entitled 'MY BIRD'.

**854** Straight edge with flat border printed with feathers and tendrilly sprigs in manganese, and a black central print of a girl with a bird. • No mark; double footrim • 6¾ ins. diam.
A version of this print was used on marked Brameld teapots and other wares, circa 1820.

**855** Straight edge and concave border with black lines, and a black print of a girl with a bird: 'MY FAVOURITE BIRD'. • No mark • 5¾ ins. diam.

**856** Rococo edge with moulded animal border and a sepia print of a little girl with a bird beside its cage: 'MY PRETTY BIRD'. • No mark • 6¾ ins. diam.
*Private Collection.*

**857\*** Rococo edge with moulded border of flowers and leaves in compartments, painted iron red, light green and yellow, with a blue print of TOM AND HIS PIGEONS'. • No mark; double footrim • 5½ ins. diam.

**858** Rococo edge with continuous daisy garland border painted iron red, pale green and blue, with a dark red print (painted) of two ladies and a boy with doves in front of a Chinese house and landscape. • Mark: 8 impressed • 6 ins. diam.
Prints of this nature were used by Hilditch of Lane End, 1822–1830.

848

849

850

851

852

853

854

855

856

857

858

**859** Straight edge and flat border with a black-printed pattern of vitruvian scrolls, Greek keys, grapes and vine-leaves, painted green and blue, with a black print of a guinea fowl painted green and yellow, 'Pintado'. • No mark • 5¼ ins. diam.

**860** Irregularly wavy blue grooved edge and flat border, with a blue transfer of 'Cock'. • No mark • 6½ ins. diam.

**861** Straight edge with lambrequin and elongated alphabet border and a black print of 'EAGLE AND NEST'. • No mark • 6½ ins. diam.

**862** Straight edge with rose, thistle and shamrock border, and a black print of 'EAGLE'. • No mark • 4¾ ins. diam.

**863** Octagonal toy plate with rope-twist edge and moulded floret border with a black print of 'SWAN'. • No mark • 3¾ ins. diam.

**864** Straight edge with gadrooned and alphabet border, painted red, and a sepia print of pheasants. • No mark • 5 ins. diam.

**865** As 862 with a green print of 'TITMOUSE'. • No mark • 4¾ ins. diam.

**865a** Round rimmed base, plain loop handle, and a sepia print of THE GOLDFINCH below a pink lustre border. • No mark • 2⅜ ins. ht.; 2½ ins. diam.

**866** Erratic edge with moulded border of scrolls, leaf sprigs and crowns flanked by royal busts, clumsily painted in pink lustre, green, blue, brown and yellow, with a sepia print (painted) of 'THE HEN IN THE FLOWER GARDEN'. • Mark: a brown painted squiggle; double footrim • 7½ ins. diam.
*Private Collection.*

**867** Rococo edge with moulded border of florets and leaves in sections, painted dark green and red, with a blue print of a woman holding a dove, with an eagle flying towards her: 'DEATH OF THE DOVE'. • No mark • 5¾ ins. diam.

Illustration from *Mother Goose's Melodies* 1833, (Munroe & Francis). Reproduced in Les Livres de l'Enfance.

859

860

861

862

863

864

865

865a

866

867

**868** Twelve-sided with iron red edge and moulded border of large and small dimpled florets painted iron red, pale green, yellow and pink, with a black print, vividly painted, of a woodpecker on a tree trunk. • No mark; double footrim • 6½ ins. diam.
The source is probably Thomas Bewick's illustration of the Black Woodpecker in *British Birds* (1797 and subsequently).

**869** Straight edge with dog, fox and monkey border painted in iron red, purple, yellow and green, with a black (painted) transfer of birds in a flowering tree. • Mark: asterisk, impressed • 5¾ ins. diam.
Probably Baker, Bevans & Irwin, Glamorgan Pottery, Swansea (1813–1838).

**870\*** As 868 with a painted print of a bird with a nest of eggs, on a branch. • No mark • 6½ ins. diam.
This is from Bewick's illustration of the Coal Titmouse (ibid).

**871** Wavy edge with moulded border of three rows of blobbed daisies and a black (painted) print of a bird and a dragonfly among flowers. • No mark • 7¾ ins. diam.

**872** Bright yellow glazed plate with border as 869 and transfers of birds on branches, clumsily painted. • No mark • 7½ ins diam.
Probably Tyneside or Wearside.
Another yellow glazed plate, with the same border, is printed in sepia (and painted) with three boys 'PLAYING AT SOLDIERS'.

**873** Rococo edge and moulded border of eagles and flower posies in compartments, and a manganese print of 'THE PARTRIDGE'. • No mark • 7¼ ins. diam.
Probably Cambrian Pottery, Swansea, 1824–1831.

**874** Wavy edge with three rows of blobbed daisies and a black (painted) print of a parrot among flowers. • No mark • 5¾ ins. diam.

**875** Reeded and feathered edge with vertical sprig border and a sepia print of 'CHAFFINCH With warble sweet'. • No mark • 6¼ ins. diam.

**876\*** Lobed edge and moulded border of birds and stags, with a red print (painted) of 'THE PARTRIDGE' as 873. • No mark; double footrim. • 6½ ins. diam.

868

869

870

871

872

873

874

875

876

**877\*** Straight edge with moulded dog, fox and monkey border, painted iron red, brown, pale green and yellow, with a sepia print (painted) of a bird on a basket of fruit. • Mark: BAKER, BEVANS & IRWIN impressed in a semicircle around 3 with additional blue-printed and painted marks • 4½ ins. diam.
Baker, Bevans & Irwin, Glamorgan Pottery, Swansea, 1813–1838.

**878** Scallop edge with moulded garland border painted iron red, light greens, yellow and pale blue, with a sepia print (painted) of a basket of flowers. • No mark; double footrim • 6½ ins. diam.

**879** As 877 with a sepia print (painted) of flowers and leaves. • Mark: BAKER BEVANS & IRWIN impressed in a semicircle round 3 impressed, with a printed 3 and a painted squiggle • 4½ ins. diam.

**880** Straight edge with moulded flower border, painted in two shades of pink lustre and pale green and yellow, around a plain centre. • No mark; no footrim • 4¾ ins. diam.

**881** Straight edge with rose, honeysuckle and swagged garland border painted iron red, green and yellow, and a black print (painted) of a bird among flowers. • Mark: impressed asterisk • 6 ins. diam.
Probably Baker, Bevans & Irwin.

**882** Straight edge painted red, with garland and medallion border and a black (painted) print of fruit, leaves and wheat. • No mark • 5¼ ins. diam.
The same print occurs on an octagonal plate with red painted edge and blobbed daisy border.

**883\*** Rococo edge with continuous daisy garland border painted iron red, green, yellow and blue, with a sepia print (painted) of 'Tom tit in a Cherry tree'. • Mark: C gouged in glaze • 7¼ ins. diam.
This and 885 are companion plates to 15.

**884** Gilded wavy edge with three graduated rows of blobbed daisies and a single daisy in the centre, surrounded by a gilded circle with feather moulding. • Mark: DILLWYN & Co in a semicircle; triple footrim • 5¾ ins. diam.
Dillwyn & Co., Cambrian Pottery, Swansea, circa 1811–1850.
Daisy plates of a similar type, with or without gilding or painting, may be found, both marked and unmarked; they were probably produced by a number of different factories.

**885** As 883 with a sepia print (painted) of a vase of flowers and the inscription 'Every Leaf & Flower/Shews GODS Power.' • Mark: C gouged in glaze • 7¼ ins. diam.

877

878

879

880

881

882

883

884

885

Tom tit
in a Cherry tree.

Every Leaf
Shews          Flower
Power

223

# Chapter 13 CHINOISERIE

The plates shown here are part of the long-continued decorative pre-occupation with the Orient; some are obviously of childish interest while others seem to be of more general ornamental intent. As well as the examples illustrated, chinoiserie subjects have been found on rococo-edged plates with daisy borders; small rococo-edged plates with borders of continuous daisy garlands, and octagonal plates with garland and medallion borders.

**886** Rococo edge with moulded border of flower sprays and eagles in sections, painted green, blue and maroon, with a sepia print of a Chinese child with a bird on a stand: 'CHINESE AMUSEMENT/MY PRETTY PHEASANT'. • No mark • 7½ ins. diam.
Probably Cambrian Pottery, Swansea, 1824–1831.
Others in the Chinese Amusement series include 'KILLING THE DRAGON', 'THE FAVOURITE BIRD', and 'JUMPING THE ROPE'.

**887** Rococo edge with moulded border of flowers and fruits in sections, painted in iron red, green, turquoise, purple and orange, with a black print (painted) of two Chinamen, one with a spear, in a landscape with a wild boar in the background. • Mark: a painted squiggle • 7¼ ins. diam.

**888** Straight edge and plain border with a black print of Chinese children playing. • No mark • 7 ins. diam.
This print has also been found, in manganese, on a plate with a plain border painted with red lines.

**889** Straight edge with swagged garland, rose and honeysuckle border painted iron red, pale green, turquoise, yellow and purple, with a black print (painted) of a chinoiserie group. • Mark: 18 painted • 7½ ins. diam.
Baker, Bevans & Irwin, Glamorgan Pottery, Swansea, 1813–1838.
The same plate has been found in 6¾ ins. size.

**890** Rococo edge with moulded border of feathered fronds and florets, some painted maroon, green and yellow, with a green print of 'The Ropeskipper.' • No mark • 8 ins. diam.
This print has also been found, in black, on a plain-bordered plate painted with a pink lustre line.

**891** Erratic edge and moulded border of blobbed daisies, with two black lines, and a green print of a Chinese bird seller. • No mark • 7¼ ins. diam.
The same print appears on a daisy-bordered plate marked for the Tyneside firm of Maling, 1850s.
Another plate in this series has a green print of a Chinese musician.

**892** Octagonal with pink lustred rope twist edge and border of florets and stars, with a black print (painted) of 'CHINESE MUSICIANS'. • No mark • 5½ ins. diam.

**893** Straight edge with continuous garland border of leaves and florets, painted in pale green and red dots without regard for the moulding. The blue print (painted) shows two Chinese figures in a flowery bower. • Mark: L impressed • 6 ins. diam.

**894** As 892 with a black print (painted) of a 'CHINESE VILLA'. • No mark • 5½ ins. diam.

886

887

888

889

890

*The Rope dancer*

891

892

CHINESE MUSICIANS

893

894

CHINESE VILLA

# Chapter 14 PIETY AND VIRTUE

Victorian religiosity is most powerfully represented in children's wares, from the simple Sunday school prize mugs and commemoratives to the sentimental recommendations to such virtues as meekness, good humour, loyalty and innocence in the Flowers that Never Fade series.

The severity of some of the inscriptions is a salutary reminder of an age when the fear of God was put into children as often as a feeling of love and warmth towards an all-forgiving father: 'Commit not offences for the day of retribution will come'; 'Many employ the first of their years to make their last miserable', and so on. Fear of retribution, divine or parental, was a much-exploited means of developing a child's conscience in an age unencumbered with doubts about inculcating a sense of guilt.

The many plates inscribed with Isaac Watts's poems represent a gentler vision of childhood piety, but the religious path was still a straight and narrow one, in which children of an idle, squabbling, disobedient, vain or untruthful disposition were likely to lay up for themselves trouble on earth as well as in heaven. The reality of death, which stalked child and adult alike, is reflected in many an inscription, as well as the images of orphan children (see 517 and 527).

While it may or may not be of significance that scenes of the death of Christ on the cross outnumber nativities in this collection (perhaps nativity scenes were more subject to breakage), it is remarkable that so few popular Old Testament images appear: Joseph and his Brothers make a disproportionately big splash with the poor quality examples showing Elijah, and David with Goliath's head, while the most obvious candidates for children's wares, Adam & Eve and Noah's Ark, are virtually non-existent.

Another pervasive social influence of the period was poverty, and the privileged in all communities were encouraged to dispense charity to those less fortunate than themselves. Such kindness was in turn expected to call forth one of the most highly-esteemed 19th century virtues, that of gratitude, from those so patronised.

Being good on its own was not enough: 'To be happy without being holy is impossible' was a stark affirmation and, as is clear from the illustrations in the first section as well as this one, even ceramics were used as an encouragement to childish piety.

**895** Wavy edge with border of moulded flowers and leaves, painted in light, bright colours and a central cartouche inscribed 'FRIENDS IN NEED ARE FRIENDS IN DEED.' • Mark: black painted A • 5½ ins. diam.

**896** Lobe edge with moulded border of flowers, leaves and tendrils in a continuous garland, painted iron red, greens and yellow, with the inscription: 'MY HEART IS FIX'D/I CANNOT RANGE/I LIKE MY CHOICE/TOO WELL/TO CHANGE'. • No mark; double footrim • 6½ ins. diam.

**897** Slightly wavy edge and border of horizontal flower sprays and vertical posies, painted in light, bright colours with the inscription: 'He that learned/Wise and good wou'd/be, Must first begin/his work at ABC.' • Mark: red painted squiggle and three dots; double footrim • 5½ ins. diam.

**898** Edge and border as 896 with a black print (painted) of an angel suspending the inscription: 'AND THE RIGHTEOUS/ SHALL BE HAD/IN EVERLASTING/ REMEMBRANCE'. • No mark; double footrim • 6½ ins. diam.
This print is also to be found on plates of different sizes with other moulded floral borders.

**899** Straight edge with rose, honeysuckle and swagged garland border painted in iron red, greens and yellow, and a black print (painted) of a figure beside a tomb inscribed 'There is Rest in Heaven'. • Mark: black painted Y • 7 ins. diam.
Probably Baker, Bevans & Irwin.
Smaller versions of this plate are known.

**900** Lobe edge with border of leaves, tendrils, strawberries and. wheatears, painted iron red, greens and yellow, and a sepia print (painted) of an angel holding a crown: 'THE REWARD OF THE RIGHTEOUS IS A CROWN OF GLORY'. • No mark; double footrim • 6½ ins. diam.

**901** Edge and border as 900 with the printed inscription: 'My son give ear to/the instruction of thy/Father. And despise not/ the counsel of thy/Mother.' • No mark; double footrim • 4½ ins. diam.
The inscription is from Proverbs VI 20.

**902** Rococo edge with border of flower sprigs and florets, painted in iron red, pink, green and yellow, and the inscription: 'Virtue the chiefest/beauty of the mind/ The noblest ornament/of Human kind.' • Mark: two parallel lines with three dots between; double footrim • 5 ins. diam.

**903** Edge and border as 896 with the inscription: 'To be Happy/Without being Holy/is impossible.' • Mark: a dot within a circle; double footrim • 4½ ins. diam.
Other inscriptions on similar plates include 'HONOUR AND OBEY THY PARENTS' and 'A REWARD FOR INNOCENCE AND TRUTH'.

895

896

897

898

899

900

901

902

903

## ISAAC WATTS

Isaac Watts (1674–1748) was a non-conformist divine whose efforts to purvey Christian morality and good behaviour in a child-oriented and memorable form were revolutionary in their time and enduring in their appeal to later generations. His *Divine Songs attempted in Easy Language for the Use of Children* were first published in 1715, and their straightforward ideas and lilting metre ensured that children were familiar with them for the next two centuries. Innumerable editions of the *Divine Songs* were published, particularly after their copyright expired in 1772, and Lewis Carroll's parodies gave them a new lease of life a century later. The following two pages of illustrations are evidence of Watts's central place in the 19th century child's upbringing.

**904** Pearlware with straight edge and continuous moulded border of flowering shamrock, and a blue print of a boy and a girl looking at two beehives, with the inscription: 'In works of labor [sic] or of skill/I would be busy too:/For Satan finds some mischief still/For idle hands to do'. • No mark • 4½ ins. diam.
The verse is from *Divine Songs for Children* by Isaac Watts (1674–1748) – Against Evil Company.

**905** Straight edge with dog, fox and monkey border painted in iron red, sepia, green and yellow, with a sepia print (painted) of a woman with two children beside a beehive and the verse: 'How doth the little busy bee/Improve each shining hour/And gather honey all the day/From every opening flower'. • Mark: 14 impressed, and a painted squiggle • 4½ ins. diam.
Probably Baker, Bevans & Irwin, Swansea, 1813–1838.
The verse is from *Divine Songs for Children* – Against Idleness and Mischief.

**906** As 904 with a blue print of a beggar holding his hat towards a boy and a girl, and the verse: 'Not more than others I deserve,/Yet God hath given me more:/For I have food while others starve/Or beg from door to door.' • No mark • 4½ ins. diam.
The verse is from *Divine Songs for Children* – Praise for Mercies Spiritual and Temporal.

**907** Octagonal with irregularly wavy sides and blue grooved edge, and the verse: 'When we devote our youth to God/'Tis pleasing in his eyes./A flower when offered in the bud/Is no vain sacrifice.' • No mark • 6¼ ins. diam.
The verse is from *Divine Songs for Children* – The Advantages of Early Religion. The same verse has been noted on a similar plate with a brown edge and transfer; another brown example has the verse: 'Whatever brawls disturb the street/There should be peace at home./Where sisters dwell and brothers meet/Quarrels should never come.' (*Divine Songs*, Love between Brothers and Sisters).

**908** Irregular wavy edge and border of three rows of round-petalled blobbed daisies, and a central printed garland (slightly painted) enclosing two verses: 'AGAINST IDLENESS/In works of labor [sic] or of skill/I would be busy too:/For Satan finds some mischief still/For idle hands to do./In books, or works, or healthful play/Let my first years be past./That I may give for ev'ry day,/Some good account at last.' • No mark • 5¾ ins. diam.
From *Divine Songs for Children* – Against Idleness and Mischief.

**909*** Octagonal with rope-twist edge and moulded border of two rows of dimpled florets blobbed in dark blue, green and red, and another row round the central red-printed garland enclosing the verses: 'EVENING SONG/I lay my body down to sleep/Let angels guard my head/And through the hours of darkness keep/Their watch around my bed./With cheerful heart I close mine eyes/Since thou will not remove/And in the morning let me rise/Rejoicing in thy love.' • Mark: 6/32 impressed (probably the date, June 1832). • Double footrim; 6¼ ins. diam.
The verses are from *An Evening Song* by Isaac Watts.

**910** Rococo edge and continuous daisy garland border, with green line to rim, and a central sepia-printed garland (slightly painted) enclosing the verses: 'EARLY PIETY/What bless'd examples do I find/Writ in the word of truth,/Of children that began to mind/Religion in their youth./Jesus, who reigns above the sky/And keeps the world in awe/Was once a child as young as I/And kept his father's law.' • No mark; double footrim • 4½ ins. diam.
The verses are from *Divine Songs for Children* – Examples of Early Piety.

**911** As 910 with a sepia print: 'OBEDIENCE TO PARENTS/Children that would fear the Lord/Hear what their teachers say/With reverence meet their parents word/And with delight obey./Have you not heard what awful plagues/Are threaten'd by the Lord/To him that breaks his father's law/Or mocks his mother's word.' • No mark; double footrim • 4½ ins. diam.
The verses are from *Divine Songs for Children* – Obedience to Parents.

**912** As 910 and 911 with unpainted border and the black-printed verses: 'AGAINST LYING/O 'Tis a lovely thing for youth/To walk betimes in wisdom's way/To fear a lie, to speak the truth,/That we may trust to all they say/But liars we can never trust,/Tho' they should speak the thing thats true/For he who does one fault at first/And lies to hide it, makes it two.' • No mark; double footrim • 4½ ins. diam.
The verses are from *Divine Songs for Children* – Against Lying.

**913\*** Octagonal with border of roses, thistles and shamrock alternating with tendrilled sprigs, painted in iron red, green, and yellow. The central black print (unpainted) shows a boy and a girl with tulips and a butterfly and the verse: 'The tulip and the butterfly/Appear in gayer coats than I./Let me be dress'd fine as I will/Flies, worms and flowers exceed me still.' • No mark • 6½ ins. diam.

The verse is from *Divine Songs for Children* by Isaac Watts – Against Pride in Clothes, and the illustation is from the title page to the Charles Tilt edition of 1832, which was probably illustrated by John Thomson. The copy in the National Art Library at the Victoria & Albert Museum is inscribed on the flyleaf by the painter John Constable: 'Emily Constable, a birthday present from her dear Papa, By whom the pictures were painted on purpose for her 1833'.

The same print occurs on daisy-bordered plates with the impressed K mark (as 916) and on round-petalled daisy-bordered plates.

The following six prints come from the same edition of Isaac Watts's *Divine Songs*.

**914** Straight edge with green line to rim and moulded border of wheat, tulip and bluebell. The central black print (painted) shows the young Christ in the Temple with the verse: 'At twelve years old he talk'd with men:/The Jews all wondering stand:/Yet he obey'd his mother then/And came at her command'. • Mark: J & G Meakin, impressed • 6½ ins. diam.

J. & G. Meakin, Eagle Pottery and Eastwood Works, Hanley, 1851– present day. This plate circa 1860. *Divine Songs* – Examples of Early Piety.

The same print was used on daisy-bordered plates with impressed K mark (as 916) and on a plate with an arcaded border of roses, thistles and shamrock.

**915** Straight edge with moulded border of rose, tulip and aster sprigs, painted iron red, pale green and yellow, with a central black print of a mother rocking a cradle and the verse: 'Hush my dear lie still and slumber/Holy angels guard thy bed./Heavenly blessings without number/Gently falling on thy head.' • No mark • 6¼ ins. diam.

*Divine Songs* – A Cradle Hymn.

The same print was used on daisy-bordered plates with the impressed K mark (as 916), and on alphabet bordered plates by J. & G. Meakin.

**916** Wavy edge with border of three rows of pointed-petalled blobbed daisies and a sepia print (painted) of a child on a couch watched by angels, and the verse: 'I lay my body down to sleep/Let angels guard my head/And through the hours of darkness keep/Their watch around my bed.' • Mark: K impressed • 7½ ins. diam.

*Divine Songs* – An Evening Song.

A version of this print was used by J. & G. Meakin.

**917** Straight edge with swag and ribbon moulded border and a black transfer (painted red and blue) of a child praying, overlooked by angels with harps, and the verse: 'How glorious is our heavenly King/Who reigns above the sky/How shall a child presume to sing/His dreadful majesty'. • Mark: large impressed 1 • 7 ins. diam.

*Divine Songs* – A General Song of Praise to God.

The same print was used on a plate with moulded border (as 915).

913

914

915

916

917

918

919

920

921

231

**918** Wavy edge with border of round-petalled blobbed daisies, and a central sepia print (painted) of Christ rising from the tomb with the verse: 'Behold him rising from the grave:/Behold him rais'd on high:/He pleads his merit there to save/Transgressors doom'd to die.' • No mark • 6¾ ins. diam.

This illustration from Tilt's 1832 edition of Watts's *Divine Songs* – Praise to God for our Redemption, is in turn derived from Piero della Francesca's *Resurrection* fresco in Borgo San Sepolcro.

The same print is to be found on daisy-bordered plates with the impressed K mark (as 916), on a plate with an arcaded border of roses, thistles and shamrock, and on a plain bordered plate with painted sprigs.

**919** Wavy edge with moulded floral border and basket weave inner border, and a black print of a man with a little boy, the name Henry, and the verse: 'Let children that would fear the Lord/Hear what their teachers say/With rev'rence meet their Parents word/And with delight obey.' • No mark • 8¼ ins. diam.
Verse from Isaac Watts, *Divine Songs* – Obedience to Parents.

**920** As 919 with a print of a bird flying down to nestlings, the name Anne, and the verse: 'Birds in their little nests agree/And 'tis a shameful sight/When children of one family/Fall out and chide and fight'. • No mark • 8¼ ins. diam.
Verse from Isaac Watts, *Divine Songs* – Love between Brothers and Sisters.

**921** As 919 and 920 with a black print of a mother and daughter at a table under a tree, the name Sarah, and the verse: 'Twill save us from a thousand snares/To mind religion young./Grace will preserve our following years/And make our virtue strong.' • No mark • 8¼ ins. diam.
Verse from Isaac Watts, *Divine Songs* – The Advantages of Early Religion.
The source for this print is the illustration to *My Daughter* by Richard Gregory (see 68 and 69).
Others in this series include a print of a full church and preacher and the verse; 'Lord how delightful 'tis to see/A whole assembly worship thee/At once they sing at once they pray/They hear of heaven and learn the way' (Isaac Watts, *Divine Songs* – For the Lord's Day Evening), and a print of Ananias being struck down and the verse: 'Have we not or heard or read/How God abhors deceit and wrong/How Ananias was struck dead/Catch'd with a lie upon his tongue.' (*Divine Songs* – Against Lying).

**922** Pearlware with wavy edge and moulded border of fleurs de lys alternating with grooved arches; the blue transfer-printed 'GRACE before MEAT' and 'GRACE after MEAT' is surrounded by a decorated circle. • No mark • 4¾ ins. diam.
(See 937).

**923** Straight edge with dog, fox and monkey border painted in iron red, manganese, yellow and green. The circular black print is also painted: 'Be ye to/Others kind and true/As you'd have/others be to you/And neither say nor/do to them/Whate'er you would not/take again'. • Marks: asterisk, impressed and 8 painted • 5¾ ins. diam.
Probably Baker, Bevans & Irwin, Glamorgan Pottery, Swansea, 1813–1838.
The verse is by Isaac Watts: *Our Saviour's Golden Rule*.

**924** As 922 with blue-printed 'PRAYER/on entering the Church' and 'PRAYER on leaving the CHURCH'. • No mark • 4¾ ins. diam.

**925** Rococo-edged plate with moulded border of flower sprays and florets alternating with birds in compartments, painted iron red, green and blue, with a central iron red print of 'THE TREAD MILL/Terror to evil-doers'. • No mark; triple footrim • 5½ ins. diam.
Probably Cambrian Pottery, Swansea, 1824–1831.
Coldbath Fields Prison, in London (on the site of the present Mount Pleasant Post Office) was among several that had a treadwheel in the 19th century. This was in line with the period's drift towards punitive prison life in contrast to the sociable nature of such institutions in the 18th century. [Information from *Ackermann's Illustrated London* by Fiona St Aubyn.]

**926** Edge and border as 925, painted in dark blue, maroon and olive green, with a central manganese inscription within a decorative circular border: 'Children learn to fear the Lord/And that your days be long/Let not a false or spiteful word/Be found upon your tongue'. • No mark • 5¾ ins. diam.
Swansea Pottery, circa 1824–1831.
A companion plate to this is illustrated in E. Morton Nance's *Swansea and Nantgarw* with the verse 'The child that longs to see my face/Is sure my love to gain/And thos' that early seek my face/Shall never seek in vain'.

**927** Erratic edge with moulded border of flowers and leaves in compartments, badly painted iron red, olive green and manganese, and a central transfer-printed inscription within a decorative cartouche: 'My life's a narrow span,/A short uncertain day/And if I reach the age of man/It soon will pass away'. • No mark • 5½ ins. diam.

**928** Straight edge with toothed rim and greyhounds, goat and butterfly border clumsily painted in black, green and maroon, with a green print of a mother and child and the inscription: 'THE SERIOUS BOY/How kind in all his work & ways/Must our Creator be: I learn a lesson of his

**922**

GRACE before MEAT.
Bless O Lord these thy good
creatures to our use and us for
thy service through Jesus Christ
our Lord   Amen.

GRACE after MEAT.
BLESSED and praised be thy
holy name, O Lord, for these
and all thy other blessings
bestowed upon us, through
Jesus Christ our Lord
Amen.

**923**

Be ye to
others kind and true
As you'd have
others be to you
And neither say nor
do to them
Whate'er you would not
take again

**924**

PRAYER
on entering the Church
Let the words of my mouth,
and the meditation of my heart
be acceptable in thy sight O LORD,
my strength and my Redeemer.
Amen.
PRAYER on leaving the CHURCH.
Blessed and praised be thy Holy
Name O Lord, for this and all other
opportunities of attending thee
in thy house and service; make
me I pray thee a doer of thy
word, and not a hearer only
through Jesus Christ
our Lord Amen.

**925**

THE TREAD-MILL.

Terror to evil-doers.

**926**

Children learn to fear the Lord,
And that your days be long
Let not a false or spiteful word
Be found upon your tongue.

**927**

My life's a narrow span,
A short uncertain day,
And if I reach the age of man,
It soon will pass away.

**928**

THE SERIOUS BOY.
How kind in all his works & ways
Most our Creator be; Learn a
of his praise From every thing.

**929**

FEAR GOD
HONOUR THE
KING.

**930**

AN ONLY SON
And can so kind a Father frown
Will he who stoops to care For little
sparrows falling ... an infant's prayer.

praise From ev'rything I [see] . . .' • Mark: 1 impressed • 4¾ ins. diam.
This print and An Only Son (930) were used on alphabet bordered plates marked Wedgewood & Co.
The verse is from *Hymns for Infant Minds* by Jane and Ann Taylor, 1812.

**929** Edge and border as 923 with the rectangular inscription: 'FEAR GOD/ HONOUR THE /KING.' • Mark: 0 impressed • 4¾ ins. diam.
Probably Baker, Bevans & Irwin.
*Private Collection.*

**930** As 928 with a green print of a child sitting on mother's lap and the inscription: 'AN ONLY SON/And can so kind a Father frown/Will he who stoops to care For little/sparrows falling [down Ignore] . . . an infant's prayer'. • Mark: blob impressed • 4¾ ins. diam.
The verse if from *Hymns for Infant Minds* by Jane and Ann Taylor, 1812.

**931** Heavy alphabet-bordered plate with vitruvian scroll edge, wavy line round inner rim, and blue painted line round base of scrolled edge. The central black and slightly painted print shows a child praying: 'THE LORD'S PRAYER/Our Father, which art in Heaven.' • No mark • 7½ ins. diam.
Probably Staffordshire.

**932** As 931 with a print of an old lady and two girls: 'THE LORD'S PRAYER/Hallowed be thy name.'

**933** As 931 etc with a print of children giving broth to a poor man: 'THE LORD'S PRAYER/Give us this day our daily bread.'

**934** Straight edge with flattish border, black line to rim and a dark brown print of a woman in a cap with a praying child: 'EVENING PRAYER'. • No mark • 7¼ ins. diam.
The illustration is from *The Mother's Picture Alphabet* (S. W. Partridge, 1862): 'P

begins Prayer, such as dear little Ned/ Beside Mamma prayed before going to bed.'

**935** As 931 etc with a print of a woman praying at a sick child's bedside: 'THE LORD'S PRAYER/Thy kingdom come Thy will be done in earth as it is in heaven.'

**936** Vitruvian scroll and alphabet border with painted line to edge and a black (slightly painted) print of a woman and two girls in church: 'THE LORD'S PRAYER/ For thine is the kingdom & the power & the glory for ever & ever. Amen.' • No mark • 6¼ ins. diam.
Probably Staffordshire.

**937\*** Pearlware plate with wavy edge and moulded border of arches and fleurs de lys (as 922 and 924) and a blue print of 'LORD'S PRAYER'. • No mark • 4¾ ins. diam.
The Lord's Prayer, printed in blue, also appears on a straight-edged pearlware

plate with a moulded border of continuous leaves and acorns, probably Brameld, circa 1820.

**938** Wavy edge with three rows of blobbed daisies diminishing in size towards the central black print of a family round a table: 'FAMILY PRAYER'. • Mark: LONDON in a fan shape, above an anchor, impressed • 6 ins. diam.
(See note to 16).

931

932

933

934

935

936

937

938

**939** Straight edge with rose, honeysuckle and swagged garland border, painted iron red, green and yellow, with a black-printed (and painted) inscription within a decorative square: 'O may I still from sin depart/ Have a wise and understanding heart/ Jesus to me be given/And let me through the spirit know/To glorify my GOD below/ And find my way to heaven'. • Mark: three dashes impressed • 6 ins. diam.
Probably Baker, Bevans & Irwin, Glamorgan Pottery, Swansea, 1813–1838.
Similar plates, with slight variations in painted colouring are known.

**940** Rococo edge and moulded border of fruits and flowers in compartments, painted in reds, green and yellow, and a central black-printed inscription within a decorative printed (and painted) square: 'Art thou not dear/unto my Heart/Oh search that Heart/and see/And from my bosom/tear the part/that beats not true/to thee.' • No mark • 7¼ ins. diam.

**941** As 939 with a blue-printed decorative square (painted) enclosing Christ on the cross and the inscription: 'JESUS WHEN HE HAD CRIED AGAIN WITH A LOUD VOICE YEILDED [sic] UP THE GHOST'.
• Mark: asterisk, impressed and black painted 11 • 6 ins. diam.
Probably Baker, Bevans & Irwin.
Similar plates with different colouring of transfer and painting are known.

**942** As 939 etc with a black print (painted) illustrating 'St LUKE CHAP. VII. V14. the Widow's Son raif'd to life'. • No mark • 7 ins. diam.
Probably Baker, Bevans & Irwin.

**943*** Lobe-edged dish with moulded border of birds and butterflies painted in reds and green, and a nativity scene printed (and painted) within a wreath, with the encircling inscription: 'Where is he that is born king of the Jews for we have seen his star in the east'. • Mark: three brown painted dots; double footrim • 6½ ins. diam.

**944** As 942 etc with a black print (painted) illustrating 'The Miracle of the Five Loaves & 2 Fifhes'. • Mark: black painted squiggle • 5½ ins. diam.
Probably Baker, Bevans & Irwin.

**945** Straight edge with swagged garland and medallion border, and a black print illustrating 'INCIDENTS IN THE LIFE OF OUR BLESSED SAVIOUR./And all that heard him were astonished at his/ understanding and answers. Luke 11. 47.'
• No mark • 6½ ins. diam.

**946** Rococo edge with moulded border of flowers and leaves in compartments, painted green, turquoise, blue and iron red, with a painted print of 'Christ Crucified/John 19 Ch Verse 34' within a red circle. • Mark: V impressed and X painted black • 7¼ ins. diam.
Similar plates illustrate a mother and a child praying: 'The ORDER of Morning and Evening PRAYER'; and people receiving Communion in both kinds: 'the ORDER of the LORDS Supper or Holy Communion.'

**947** As 945 with a green print illustrating 'HISTORY OF OUR SAVIOUR/JESUS BLESSING LITTLE CHILDREN'. • No mark • 7¼ ins. diam.

Illustration from an early 19th century scrapbook.

939

*O may I still from sin depart*
*Have a wise and understanding heart*
*Jesus to me be given*
*And let me through the spirit know*
*To glorify my GOD below*
*And find my way to heaven*

940

*Art thou not dear*
*unto my Heart*
*Oh search that Heart*
*and see*
*And from my bosom*
*tear the part*
*that beats not true*
*to thee.*

941

INRI

JESUS WITH A
WHEN LOUD
HE HAD VOICE
CRIED YEILDED UP
AGAIN THE GHOST

942

St LUKE CHAP VII.V.14 the Widow's Son restored to life.

943

944

The Miracle of the Five Loaves JOHN 6.9

945

INCIDENTS IN THE LIFE OF OUR BLESSED SAVIOUR.

*And all that heard him were astonished at his*
*understanding and answers Luke 2.47*

946

Christ Crucified.

John 19 Ch. Verse 34

947

HISTORY OF OUR SAVIOUR

JESUS BLESSING LITTLE CHILDREN

**948\*** Straight edge with rose, honey-suckle and swagged garland border painted iron red, green and yellow, with iron red line to edge, and a black print (painted) of 'FAITH' in the centre. • Mark: black painted V and dot • 6¾ ins. diam.
Probably Baker, Bevans & Irwin, Glamorgan Pottery, Swansea, 1813–1838.

**949\*** As 948 with a black print (painted) of 'HOPE' within a decorative circle. • Mark: -- impressed • 6¾ ins. diam.
Probably Baker, Bevans & Irwin.

**950\*** As 948 with a central print (painted) of 'CHARITY' • Mark: circle impressed • 6¾ ins. diam.
Probably Baker, Bevans & Irwin.

**951** As 948 etc with a black print (painted) of 'FAITH HOPE CHARITY'. Mark: -- impressed and black painted squiggle • 6¼ ins. diam.
Probably Baker, Bevans & Irwin.

**952** Erratic edge and moulded border of flower sprays and vertical sprigs, painted (chipped) in red, green, yellow, blue and turquoise, and an iron red transfer of 'CHARITY'. • No mark; double footrim • 8 ins. diam.

**953** Rope edge with moulded border of flowers and leaves in compartments, painted iron red, green, yellow and sepia, with a sepia print (painted) of 'CHARITY'. • No mark • 6¾ ins. diam.

**954** Straight edge and moulded border of flowers, leaves and swags, clumsily painted in green, yellow, iron red and blue, and a black (painted) print of 'FAITH'. • No mark; double footrim • 5¾ ins. diam.
A similar figure of Faith has been noted on Swansea copper lustred wares.

**955** Octagonal with grooved edge painted green, and a black print of Faith holding her cross. • No mark • 5¾ ins. diam.

**956** As 954 with a print of 'HOPE'. • No mark; double footrim • 5¾ ins. diam.

948        949        950

951        952        953

954        955        956

**957** Straight edge with curlicue moulded border and a black print of the 'SACRED HISTORY of JOSEPH and his BRETHREN/ JUDAH refigning himself and BRETHREN into the hands of JOSEPH.' • No mark • 6¼ ins. diam.

**958** Reeded and feathered edge painted blue with vertical sprig border blobbed in green and red, and a blue-black illustration of the 'SACRED HISTORY of JOSEPH and his BRETHREN/JOSEPH interpreting the DREAMS of PHARAOHs Chief BUTLER and BAKER.' • No mark • 7½ ins. diam.
The same print is to be found in brown on a plate with a moulded border of blobbed pointed-petalled daisies, and on a Middlesbrough marked plate with a rose and jasmine border.

**959** Rococo edge with rose and jasmine border and a black print illustrating the 'SACRED HISTORY of JOSEPH and his BRETHREN/POTIPHAH'S WIFE falfely accufing JOSEPH.' • No mark • 7½ ins. diam.
Probably Middlesbrough Pottery, 1834–1844.

**960** Straight edge with swagged garland and medallion border and a manganese print illustrating the 'HISTORY OF JOSEPH/JOSEPH PUT INTO PRISON IN EGYPT.' • No mark; triple footrim • 6½ ins. diam.
Another in this series illustrates 'THE BROTHERS PUTTING JOSEPH INTO THE PIT.'

**961** Edge and (unpainted) border as 958 with a black print illustrating the 'HISTORY OF JOSEPH/JOSEPH PRESENTING HIS AGED FATHER TO THE KING OF EGYPT'. • No mark • 6½ ins. diam.

**962** Edge and border as 959 with a black print illustrating the 'SACRED HISTORY of JOSEPH and his BRETHREN/JOSEPH'S FIRST DREAM'. • No mark • 6½ ins. diam.
Probably Middlesbrough.

**963** Wavy edge with moulded border of beads, florets and curlicues, and a black print illustrating the 'SACRED HISTORY of JOSEPH and his BRETHREN/JOSEPH'S SECOND DREAM.' • No mark; double footrim • 7¼ ins. diam.
This print also occurs on a straight-edged plate with continuous floret border.

**964** Octagonal with rope-twist edge and moulded border of dimpled florets and (smaller) stars, painted in pink lustre, blue, yellow and green, with a black print of 'JOSEPH'S TWO DREAMS.' • Mark: lustred 10 • 6¼ ins. diam.
The same print (sometimes painted) occurs on similar plates with unpainted borders (some with blobbed florets and some with dimpled florets and stars) with a lustred line to the edge, and (in purple) on an octagonal garland-and-medallion bordered plate with red line to edge.

THE SABBATH MORNING HYMN.

Illustration from a children's periodical of 1861.

957

958

959

960

961

962

963

964

**965** Rococo edge with moulded border of flower sprays and insects in curlicue frames alternating with baskets of flowers, blobbed in blue, green, red and yellow, with a black print of 'HISTORY OF JOSEPH/ JOSEPH SOLD TO THE MERCHANTS'. • No mark • 7 ins. diam.
Probably William Smith, Stafford Pottery, Stockton-on-Tees, Yorkshire, circa 1825–1855.

**966** As 965 with a print of 'HISTORY OF JOSEPH/PHAROAH PUTTING THE GOLD CHAIN ON JOSEPH'S NECK'. • No mark • 7 ins. diam.
Another plate in this series is illustrated with 'JOSEPH PRESENTING HIS AGED FATHER TO THE KING OF EGYPT'.

**967** As 965 etc with a black print of 'HISTORY OF JOSEPH/THE BROTHERS PUTTING JOSEPH INTO THE PIT'. • No mark • 7 ins. diam.

**968** Slightly wavy edge with border of three rows of blobbed daisies, and a black print of 'THE GOOD SAMARITAN'. • Mark: garter and initials GFS & Co, impressed • 7½ ins. diam.
George F. Smith, North Shore Pottery, Stockton-on-Tees, circa 1855–1860.

**969** Reeded and feathered edge with vertical sprig border blobbed in green, red and blue, and a sepia print of a man going

for another with an axe: 'THE COMMANDMENTS/Thou shalt do no murder'. • No mark • 7½ ins. diam.
A similar image, in reverse, appears on a Liverpool tin-glazed earthenware tile of 1740–1760, allegedly depicting Cain slaying Abel.
Another 'COMMANDMENTS' print, on an octagonal daisy-bordered plate, shows a parson haranguing three children playing marbles on a tomb: 'Thou shalt not take the Name of the Lord thy God in vain.'

**970** Edge and border as 968 with a black print of St. Paul's shipwreck with the inscription: 'A NIGHT AND A DAY HAVE I BEEN IN THE DEEP 2 Cor. XI 25'. • Mark: a garter and initials GFS & Co, impressed • 7½ ins. diam.
George Smith, Stockton.

**971** Rococo edge with moulded border of roses, tulips and asters in segments and a smudgy blue-black print of 'DAVID WITH THE HEAD OF GOLIATH'. • No mark • 6¾ ins. diam.
This border is of a similar pattern to one used by Dillwyn & Co., Swansea and Scott, Southwick Pottery, Sunderland.

**972** Wavy edge and moulded border of stars and dotted lines, painted in red, blue, yellow and green, with a black print of 'ELIJAH FED BY RAVENS'. • No mark • 6¾ ins. diam.

A similar image appears on a Bristol tin-glazed tile of 1725–1750.

**973** Rococo edge and moulded border of trailing strawberries, leaves and tendrils, and a red print of 'DANIEL IN THE LION'S DEN/HE TRUSTED IN GOD'. • No mark • 7 ins. diam.
*Private Collection.*

965

966

967

968

969

970

971

972

973

**974** Erratic edge with feathered frond and floret border painted in pink lustre, blue, green, red and yellow, with a black-printed decorative cartouche and inscription: 'To Err is Human/to Forgive Devine'. [sic] • No mark • 6 ins. diam.

The quotation is from Alexander Pope (1688–1744), *An Essay on Criticism*.

**975** Pearlware with straight raised rim and moulded spray borders painted in Pratt colours, and a blue (slightly painted) print of a negro on one knee holding his arms heavenwards: 'MY BIBLE/May ignorance no longer reign/Henceforth the Heathen shall proclaim/His Makers love – and bless the name of/BIBLE'. • No mark • 7½ ins. diam.

This print also appears in blue on a plate with a garland and spotted floret border painted in Pratt colours.

The illustration comes from a colour sheet, *My Bible*, by William Jolly, published by William Darton junior, 1812.

**976** Nearly straight edge and moulded border of lambrequins painted red, green and yellow, and birds on rococo swirls, and a central blue-printed cartouche and inscription: 'IF EVERY ONE WOULD MEND/ONE/ALL WOULD BE AMENDED.' • No mark • 5¼ ins. diam.

A similar cartouche and the inscription 'Hear Counsel & receive Instruction' has been noted on a plate with a continuous moulded floret border.

**977** Rococo edge with moulded border of flowers and leaves in compartments, painted green, blue and yellow, with a central red print of 'SAINT ANDREW' with his cross. • No mark; double footrim • 5½ ins. diam.

Probably Goodwins & Harris, Lane End.

A plate with the same transfer and similarly moulded border is marked GOODWINS & HARRIS impressed.

**978** Wavy-edged octagonal with wide border of moulded patterns painted with two black lines. The central black and slightly painted print shows a man preaching to people of different races: 'PREACH THE GOSPEL TO EVERY CREATURE/MISSIONARY'. • Mark: printed registration mark for March 1847 • 7¾ ins. diam.

Bailey & Ball, Longton.

This plate occurs in smaller sizes and with sepia prints and painted lines of different colours.

**979** Slightly indented edge and flat border with pink lustre line, and a central black print of 'The Missionary'. • No mark; double footrim • 6¾ ins. diam.

The same print occurs on a 7½ ins. plate with edge and border as 974.

**980** Wavy edge with moulded border of flowers and leaves in a continuous garland, painted iron red, light green and blue, with a black print (painted) of a beehive surrounded by a garland: 'INDUSTRY/LEARN TO LIVE.' • Mark: a crown impressed • 6½ ins. diam.

**981** Straight edge with toothed rim painted green, and greyhound, goat and butterfly border crudely painted in brown, green and yellow, and a central sepia print as 980. • No mark • 7¾ ins. diam.

**982\*** Octagonal with rope-twist edge painted blue and dimpled daisy border, and a black print (painted) of a boy and a girl looking at a beehive: 'INDUSTRY'. • No mark • 5¾ ins. diam.

The same print may be found on octagonal wavy-edged plates with deep borders of patterns by Bailey & Ball.

Illustration from an early 19th century scrapbook.

974

975

976

977

978

979

980

981

982

## WESLEY AND METHODISM

The Potteries were an important stronghold of Methodism during the 19th century, but children's plates with moulded borders and Wesley subjects were produced also in Swansea and in the North-East, particularly in Sunderland and Newcastle (the initials J&P for Jackson & Patterson, Sheriff Hill Pottery, Newcastle-upon-Tyne, 1830–1845, appear on some examples). Many pieces were produced for the centenary of the Wesleyan Methodist Society in 1839.

**983** Straight edge with rose, honeysuckle and swagged garland border painted iron red, green and yellow, with a black (painted) print of 'THE REVEREND JOHN WESLEY' in a circle flanked by figures of 'HOPE' and 'CHARITY' with an all-seeing eye above and the inscription: 'I Trust in the Lord I also myself shall Come shortly'. • Mark: –– impressed • 6 ins. diam.
Probably Baker, Bevans & Irwin, Glamorgan Pottery, Swansea, 1813–1838.

**984** As 983 with slightly different palette. • Mark: a grid of 12 squares impressed, and a black painted squiggle • 6¾ ins. diam.
Probably Baker, Bevans & Irwin.

**985** As 983 etc with a (painted) print of Wesley preaching in a church: 'WESLEY speaks from Amos Chap. IV. v. 12/Prepare to meet thy GOD'. • Mark: a squiggle as on 984 • 5½ ins. diam.
Probably Baker, Bevans & Irwin.

**986** Octagonal with rope-twist edge and dimpled floret border with a black print of 'CENTENARY HALL 1839/LONDON'. • No mark • 5½ ins. diam.
The same print occurs on wavy-edged plates with moulded floret borders painted and lustred.
The Centenary Hall and Mission House was in Bishopgate, London, but is now demolished. This was among the pieces made to mark the Wesleyan centenary of 1839.

**987** Octagonal with rope-twist edge and border of dimpled florets and stars painted in pink lustre, blue, yellow and green, and a black print of 'REVd J. FLETCHER'. • No mark • 6¼ ins. diam.
This was probably John William Fletcher, or De La Flechère (1729–1785), a Swiss-born theologian who came to England in 1750, was ordained in the Church of England in 1757 and became vicar of Madeley in Shropshire in 1760. He was a close friend and colleague of John Wesley and was regarded as an outstandingly holy man.

**988** Octagonal with pink lustre rope-twist edge and dimpled floret border, with a black print (painted) of an open Bible on a cushion and the inscription 'REVd J. WESLEY BORN JUNE 1703 DIED MAR 2nd 1791.' • No mark • 5 ins. diam.
*Private Collection.*

983

984

985

986

987

988

## SUNDAY SCHOOL

The Sunday School movement, developed in the late 18th century by such figures as Robert Raikes, Sarah Trimmer and Hannah More, gained momentum during the 19th century, particularly in urban areas. The wares illustrated on this page and the next are typical of those given to children as prizes for good attendance and achievement at Sunday School.

**989** Large cylinder-shaped mug with loop handle and a black print of a boy and a girl holding a banner inscribed 'WESLEYAN/ SUNDAY SCHOOL/CROSS BANK/BATLEY. • No mark • 3¾ ins. ht.; 3½ ins. diam.

**990** Octagonal plate with rope-twist edge and blobbed daisy border, with a blue print of a boy and a girl holding a scroll with the inscription 'THE FEAR OF THE LORD IS THE BEGINING [sic] OF WISDOM'. • No mark • 6½ ins. diam.
This print illustrates the use of a stock block with a cut-out central section allowing different inscriptions to be inserted. This image occurs on many plates and mugs, with varying words. Another example reads: 'SUFFER LITTLE CHILDREN TO COME UNTO ME'.

**991** Mug with shaped base and loop handle, and blue prints, as 990, with the inscription 'HONOUR THY FATHER AND THY MOTHER' on one side and 'TRAIN UP A CHILD IN THE WAY HE SHOULD GO' on the other. • No mark • 3⅜ ins. ht.; 3⅝ ins. diam.

**992** Cup [and saucer] with spurred ring handle and an all-over blue-printed pattern of squares and crosses and the (black) inscription 'SAINT JOHN'S BACUP SUNDAY SCHOOL'. • Mark: B impressed (on cup) • top of cup 3⅞ ins. diam (2⅜ ins. ht.); top of saucer 5¾ ins. diam.

**993** Mug with shaped base and loop handle and a blue transfer print as 990 with the inscription 'REMEMBER NOW THY CREATOR IN THE DAYS OF THY YOUTH'. • No mark • 2¾ ins. ht.; 2⅞ ins. diam.

**994** As 993 with a black print and the inscription 'TRAIN UP A CHILD IN THE WAY HE SHOULD GO'. • No mark • 2¾ ins. ht.; 2¾ ins. diam.
A similar mug has the inscription 'THE FEAR OF THE LORD IS THE BEGINING OF WISDOM' in sepia.

**995** Cup with spurred ring handle and fine black print of a small school building: 'TAUNTON SUNDAY SCHOOL 1895/ FOUNDED 1820'. • No mark • 3½ ins. diam (top); 2 ins. (base); 3⅛ ins. ht.

**996** Cylinder mug with loop handle and green-printed inscription within a decorated surround: 'It is less painful to/LEARN IN YOUTH/than to be ignorant/IN OLD AGE'. • No mark • 2½ ins. ht.; 2½ ins. diam.

**997** Cylinder mug with shaped base, loop handle and black transfer pattern to handle and rim, and a coat of arms with the motto 'BE JUST & FEAR NOT' on either side of the central inscription: 'CARLISLE SUNDAY SCHOOLS/PRESENTED/BY/ W. MAXWELL. ESQ/MAYOR/1887/QUEEN'S JUBILEE YEAR.' • No mark • 3¼ ins. ht.; 2⅞ ins. diam.

**998** Cylinder mug with loop handle and red prints of figures on a background of clouds, with semicircular superscriptions: on one side 'THY WORK IS A LAMP UNTO MY FEET' and on the other 'MY FATHER, THOU ART THE GUIDE OF MY YOUTH'. • No mark • 2¾ ins. ht.; 2⅝ ins. diam.

989

990

THE FEAR
OF THE LORD IS
THE BEGINING
OF WISDOM

991

WESLEYAN
SUNDAY SCHOOL
CROSS.BANK
BATLEY.

HONOUR THY
FATHER AND
THY MOTHER

992

SAINT·JOHNS
BACUP
SUNDAY SCHOOL

993

REMEMBER NOW
THY CREATOR
IN THE DAYS OF
THY YOUTH

994

TRAIN UP A CHILD
IN THE WAY
HE SHOULD GO

995

TAUNTON SUNDAY SCHOOL 1835
FOUNDED 820

996

It is less painful to
LEARN in YOUTH,
then to be ignorant
IN OLD AGE.

997

CARLISLE SUNDAY SCHOOLS
PRESENTED
BY
W. MAXWELL. Esqe
MAYOR
1887
QUEEN'S JUBILEE YEAR

998

THY WORD IS A LAMP UNTO MY FEET

**999** Straight edge with beaded line and alphabet border, and a central black inscription within a decorated rectangular cartouche: 'Commit not offences/for the day of/retribution will come'. • Mark: N impressed • 5½ ins. diam.
Others in this series include 'Frugality is a/fortune & industry/a good estate' within a cartouche, and 'Conscience is a terror/to the wicked but a/comfort to good men' within a lily of the valley garland.

**1000** Wavy edge and indistinctly moulded blobbed daisy border (spotted in blue and red), and the black-printed inscription 'A GOOD CONSCIENCE/and a Table well furnished/with Plenty of good/Provisions/WHAT IS BETTER THAN THAT'. • No mark; indented line round underside of rim. • 5½ ins. diam.
A favourite verse of the period, in the same vein, was inscribed on jugs and mugs and, in particular, on a ten-sided plate with a garland and medallion border: 'Let the wealthy and great/Roll in splendour and state/I envy them not I declare it/I eat my own Lamb/My own Chickens and Ham/I shear my own fleece and I wear it.'

**1001** Straight edge with border of two rows of blobbed daisies and a red-printed inscription within a garland of lily of the valley: 'Experience keeps/a dear school but/Fools will learn in/no other.' • No mark • 5¼ ins. diam.
This is one of Benjamin Franklin's maxims (see page 272).
Other plates with the same border include the inscription 'For age & want/save while you may/no morning sun/lasts all the day' (Benjamin Franklin) within a lily of the valley garland, and 'He that betrays/his trust will never have confidence/reposed in him' within a rectangular decorated cartouche.

**1002** Edge and border as 999 with a black-printed inscription in a decorated surround 'GOOD THOUGHTS/should always be encouraged/to prevent/BAD ACTIONS.' • Mark: four squares, impressed • 6½ ins. diam.

Another in this series is inscribed 'REASON/should guide our Actions/RELIGION/our THOUGHTS, and/REFLECTION/our expressions'.

**1003** Wavy edge with border of three rows of indistinctly blobbed round-petalled daisies and a black inscription within a wreath: 'THOU/GOD/SEEST ME/Gen XVI. 13'. • No mark • 7½ ins. diam.

**1004** Straight edge with border of two rows of indistinctly moulded round-petalled blobbed daisies and a central green inscription within a decorated border: 'REASON/should guide our Actions/RELIGION/our THOUGHTS, and/REFLECTION/our expressions'. • Mark: a cross, impressed • 7¼ ins. diam.

**1005** Straight edge with vitruvian scroll and alphabet border painted with a yellow line. The black-printed inscription is surrounded by a slightly painted decorative garland: 'Many employ the first/OF THEIR YEARS/to make/THEIR LAST MISERABLE.' • No mark; double footrim • 7½ ins. diam.
Others in this series include the inscriptions: 'Conscience is the rewarder/OF VIRTUE/and the avenger/OF CRIME'; 'It is less painful to/LEARN in YOUTH/than to be ignorant/IN OLD AGE', and 'Be as careful/OF WHAT YOU SAY/as of what/YOU DO'.

**1006** Octagonal with garland and medallion border and a black inscription within a decorated circular border: 'Let your passions/be govern'd by reason/and your wishes/by Moderation'. • No mark • 6¼ ins. diam.
Others in this series include the inscriptions 'A GOOD MAN/passeth by an Offence/and a/NOBLE SPIRIT/scorneth revenge' (6¼ ins. diam); 'Look not into/GOD'S DECREES/but into/his commands' (7 ins.); 'Be upright in/principle/Pure in morals/and sincere/in Religion' (8 ins.); 'GOOD THOUGHTS/should always be encouraged/to prevent/BAD ACTIONS' (8 ins); 'From the experience of others/do thou learn wisdom/and from their failings/correct thine own faults' (8 ins.), and 'Let your passions/be govern'd by reason/and your wishes/by Moderation' (8 ins.), and 'DRUNKENNESS revenges the madness of the hour, with the sad repentance of many.'

**1007** As 1002 with a red painted inscription 'Look not into/GOD'S DECREES/but into/his commands'. • No mark • 7¼ ins. diam.

999

Commit no offences
for the day of
retribution will come

1000

A GOOD CONSCIENCE
and a Table well furnished,
with Plenty of good
Provisions
WHAT IS BETTER THAN THAT

1001

Experience keeps
a dear school but
Fools will learn in
no other.

1002

GOOD THOUGHTS
should always be nourished
to prevent
BAD ACTIONS

1003

THOU
GOD
SEEST ME
Gen XVI., 13.

1004

REASON
should guide our actions
RELIGION
our THOUGHTS and
REFLECTION
our expressions

1005

Many employ the first
OF THEIR YEARS
to make
THEIR LAST MISERABLE

1006

Let your passions
be governed by reason,
and your wishes
by Moderation.

1007

Look not into
GOD'S DECREES
but into
his commands

## FLOWERS THAT NEVER FADE

The 'flowers of virtue' illustrated on this page and the next highlight the qualities most admired in the 19th century, as well as the period's patterns of gender stamping.

**1008** Straight edge with indistinctly moulded bead and alphabet border painted with two green lines, and a black print splodged in green, red and dark blue, of a boy and a girl in a landscape: 'INNOCENCE/In every grove the linnets sing./To welcome the return of spring: The smiling/fields once more look green. In ev'ry hedge a flow'r is seen.' • No mark • 7¼ ins. diam.

**1009\*** Rococo edge with moulded border of roses, tulips and asters painted green, pink, yellow and blue, with a black print of children in a landscape: 'GENEROSITY/However poor however plain On this you may depend,/The kind the generous and the good Will never want a friend.' • Mark: 11/39 (for November 1839); double footrim • 8 ins. diam.

**1010** As 1008 with a print of children looking at a one-legged man on crutches: 'LOYALTY/I love my country & my king./their glory is my pride. That urged to/arm when fighting by my comrades. side by side.' • No mark • 7¼ ins. diam.
The same print appears on a plate with a moulded border of lambrequins and birds.

**1011** As 1008 etc with a print of two children looking at potted plants: 'CONTEMPLATION/Lord what is life? – 'Tis like a flow'r/That blossoms & is gone! We see it/flourish for an hour. With all its beauty on.' • No mark • 7¼ ins. diam.

**1012** As 1008 etc with brown lines to border and a print of children in a landscape: 'EARLY RISING/The sun is up, we'll brush the dew/To hear the huntsmen's gay halloo & hark/the dog's enliv'ning cry. Now see! the horsemen gallop by.' • No mark • 7¼ ins. diam.

**1013\*** Erratic edge and flat border striped red and a red print of a woman, three children and a dog: 'CHEERFULNESS/A cheerful voice & smiling eyes/By every one are loved. While sulky/looks & sullen tones. By all are disapproved.' • Mark: B impressed • 4¾ ins. diam.

**1014** Wavy-edged plate with moulded border of leaves and curlicues and a red print of children with a begging negro: 'PIETY/While God regards the wise & fair./The noble & the brave. He listens to the beggar's prayer & the poor Negro slave.' • Mark: Z impressed; double footrim • 5 ins. diam.

**1015** As 1013 with a print of two girls looking at sheep: 'MEEKNESS/In a modest, humble mind,/God himself will take delight, But the/proud & haughty find They are hateful in his sight.' • Mark: B impressed • 4¾ ins. diam.
The verse is from Jane & Ann Taylor, *Hymns for Infant Minds*, 1812.
Others in this series include 'GOOD HUMOUR/Good humour is the greatest charm/That children can possess; It makes/them happy & whats more It gives them power to bless'; 'GENEROSITY' as 1009, and 'ATTENTION/And when I learn my hymns to say/And work & read & spell I will not/think about my play, But try to do it well' (*Hymns for Infant Minds*). All are marked K impressed. 'Attention', 'Meekness' and 'Politeness' ('If little boys & girls were wise/They'd always be polite,/For sweet behaviour in a child/Is a delightful sight') are recorded on plates from Fairbairns Pottery, Newbottle, circa 1830–1840; an example of 'Politeness' in the V&A collection (currently on loan to Sunderland Museum) is inscribed in the border moulding: 'TEMPERANCE – A TRIFLE FOR MY CHILD'; another has the border inscription: 'KEEP HOLY THE SABBATH DAY,' and a third has moulded roses, tulips and asters.

1008

1009

1010

1011

1012

1013

1014

1015

**1016** Shaped base and plain loop handle with pink lustre lines to rim, base and handle, and a green print of a family at the dining table: 'The Grace.' • No mark • 2½ ins. ht.; 2½ ins. diam.

**1017** As 1016 with a black print of a family at 'Evening Prayer.' • No mark • 2½ ins. ht.; 2⅜ ins. diam.

**1018** Cylindrical with loop handle and leaf terminals, and brown lines to rim and handle, with a sepia print of two girls in a bedroom kneeling against a chair saying their prayers beneath a portrait of a cleric. • No mark • 2⅝ ins. ht.; 2⅝ ins. diam.
The same image, entitled 'THE EVENING DUTY' has been noted on a rococo-edged plate with a moulded flower garland and curlicue border.

**1019** Shaped base and plain loop handle, with pink lustre lines round base and inside top rim. The black prints, on one side a house in a landscape with a sailing boat on a lake and on the other, a boy on a donkey with another, illustrate 'FLOWERS THAT NEVER FADE/KINDNESS/Oh look! brother look! at my dear little Neddy/How good humour'd he seems, so quiet and steady!/Ill-natur'd and spiteful how many you see/To donkeys which always astonishes me.' • No mark • 2⅞ ins. ht.; 3⅛ ins. diam.
The source for this print is *Peter Parley's Annual* 1862 (see 745).

**1020** Shaped base and plain loop handle, with sepia prints (painted), on one side a

family group in front of a cottage, and on the other a landscape with a turret by a lake with a sailing boat, illustrating 'THE REMEMBRANCE OF HOME/ATTACHMENT./Brothers & sisters hand in hand/Our lips together move/Then smile upon this little bnd [?band]/And join our hearts in lov'. • No mark • 2½ ins. ht.; 2½ ins. diam.

**1021** As 1020 with green prints (painted) of two girls looking at sheep on one side (cf 1015), and a landscape with a house near a lake with a sailing boat on the other, illustrating 'THE DELIGHTS OF HOME/MEEKNESS/In a modest, humble mind/God himself will take delight/But the proud & haughty find/They are hateful in his sight.' • No mark • 2¾ ins. ht.; 2¾ ins. diam.

**1022** As 1020 etc with black prints (painted) of a girl and a boy in a landscape on one side and a castle by a lake with swans on the other, illustrating 'THE DELIGHTS OF HOME/INNOCENCE./In every grove the linnets sing./To welcome the return of spring./The smiling fields once more look green./In ev'ry hedge a flow'r is seen.' See 1008. • No mark • 2⅝ ins. ht.; 2¾ ins. diam.

**1023** Cylindrical with reeded handle and black prints, on one side a similar landscape view to 1019, and on the other a beggar with his dog looking hopefully towards two girls, illustrating 'FLOWERS THAT NEVER FADE/CHARITY/Oh thank you dear ladies, for trying to cheer,/A heart that can only reply by a tear/God reward you & yours for the comforts you give,/And the prayers of an old man be yours while I live'. • No mark • 2¾ ins. ht.; 2¾ ins. diam.

**1024** Rounded base rim and plain loop handle with black prints of thatched cottages in a landscape on one side, and a little girl talking to a lady with a parasol on the other (see 1025), illustrating 'FLOWERS THAT NEVER FADE./GOOD HUMOUR./Good humour is the greatest charm/That children can possess;/It makes them

happy, and what's more,/It gives them power to bless.' • No mark • 2¾ ins. ht.; 2¾ ins. diam.

**1019** The opposite side of the mug shown above.

**1023** The opposite side.

**1025** Shaped base and profiled handle with black prints and inscriptions as 1024. • No mark • 3⅛ ins. ht.; 3¼ ins. diam.

**1020** The opposite side.

**1021** The opposite side.

**1022** The opposite side (cf. 1008).

The Grace.

Evening Prayer.

NEVER FADE

1016              1017              1018              1019

THE REMEM

THE DELI

THE DELIG

FLOWERS T

1020              1021              1022              1023

FLOWERS T

FLOWERS T

NEVER FADE

NEVER FADE.

1024              1019              1023              1025

CE OF HOME

OF HOME

S OF HOME

1020              1021              1022

**1026** Rococo edge with moulded border of flower sprays and insects in curlicue frames alternating with baskets of flowers, painted in pink, blue, green and yellow, and a sepia print of children in a garden: 'Die Verbejung' (the reading lesson); 'Was ein Hakchen werden will das Krummt sich bei zeiten' (to be successful you yourself must work). • Mark: WS & Co's QUEEN'S WARE STOCKTON impressed • 6¼ ins. diam.
William Smith & Co., Stafford Pottery, Stockton-on-Tees, Yorkshire, circa 1825–1855.
The same print has been noted on a 9 ins. daisy-bordered plate from William Smith, Stockton.
These plates, and the subsequent examples with German inscriptions, were among the many produced at William Smith's factory for export during the middle years of the 19th century.

**1027** As 1026 with a manganese print of a boy and a girl in a landscape: 'Der blinde Wilhelm' (blind William); 'Freunde in der Noth gehen viele auf ein Loth' (friends in need are friends indeed). • Mark: WS & Co's QUEEN'S WARE STOCKTON impressed • 6¾ ins. diam.

**1028** As 1026 etc with a manganese print of a child with a hoop and a dog in a landscape with a suspension bridge in the background: 'Der Fleiss' (industry); 'Ein gutes Wort findet eine gute Statt' (a good word finds a good place). • Mark: WS & Co's QUEEN'S WARE STOCKTON impressed • 6¼ ins. diam.

**1029** As 1026 etc with a manganese print of three children with a basket of cherries in a landscape with a train in the background: 'Die Frucht Schnittern' (the fruit pickers); 'Zu geschehenen Sachen muss das Beste reden (when something has happened you must always say the best you can). • Mark: WS & Co's QUEEN'S WARE STOCKTON impressed, and 13 printed • 8 ins. diam.
The locomotive in the background is similar to the Stockton and Darlington

Railway 0-6-0 locomotive *Derwent* of 1845. This had a characteristic tender both in front and behind the locomotive. The coaching stock is circa 1850.

**1030** Straight edge with moulded border of horizontal stylised sprays painted in green, pink and blue, with a black print of children in a garden beside a lake: 'Das jugendlich Vergnugen' (youthful pleasure); 'Das hanschen nicht lernt, wird hans nicht wissen' (what a boy does not learn, a man will not know). • Mark: John Wilkinson, Wedgewood Pottery Stafford August 10th 1836, scratched in the glaze • 7¾ ins. diam.
William Smith & Co., Stockton-on-Tees.
A smaller plate with the same border pattern and a green print of De blinde Wilhelm (as 1027) is marked WS & Co's WEDGEWOOD impressed. Both these plates and the next one date from before 1848 when Wedgwood's successful court action prevented Smith from using that firm's name (see note for 234).
Another in the same series (and with the same marks) has a black print of a boy reading a book under a tree and the inscription 'Der fleifsige knabe/Bald weils ich meine Lexion!' (The diligent boy/Soon I'll know my reading).

**1031** As 1026 etc with a red print of a woman and two children at a dining table: 'Das Tischoebet' (grace); 'Wer das Gluck hat, der fuhrt die Braut heim' (with luck you will bring home the bread). • Mark: WS

& Co's WEDGEWOOD impressed • 8 ins. diam.
Plates in this series may be found in 8 ins. or 6¼ ins. sizes with prints of differing colours and with either Smith's WEDGEWOOD or QUEEN'S WARE mark.

**1032** Reeded edge and alphabet border on a granular background, and a blue print of two men in an office: 'IMPORTANCE OF PUNCTUALITY/Indeed Sir you are punctual/Servants & Children/Must be punctual when their Leader is so/Appointments indeed become Debts.' • No mark • 6½ ins. diam.
Another in this series has a green print of a man, woman and boy: 'You are behind time Sir the Mail is gone/Punctuality is Important/Because it subserves the peace/And good temper of a Family'.

**1033** Octagonal with green edges and moulded border of basket-weave, lambrequins, fleurs de lys and florets, with a black print of a boy handing a purse to a man and woman in the street: 'AVARICE/Riches should be admitted into our Houses but not into our/Hearts we may take them into our possession/but not into our affections./HONESTY'. • No mark • 7½ ins. diam.
Another in this series is printed with a scene in which a woman throws a teapot at a man in a chair (her husband?): 'PROMISES/Take heed what you promise see that it be just & honest/& what is in your power to perform & when you/have so promised be true to your word./PASSION'.

**1034** Straight edge with moulded border of roses, tulips and asters painted red, green, yellow and blue, with a pink lustred line to edge, and a black print of two men beside a coach: 'IMPORTANCE OF PUNCTUALITY/Well here we are in good time./METHOD/Is the very hinge of business/And there is no method without Punctuality.' • Mark: DAVENPORT with 6 above and an anchor below, impressed, and DAVENPORT printed in black • 5½ ins. diam.

1026

1027

1028

1029

1030

1031

1032

1033

1034

257

**1035** Straight edge with blue sponged border and a black print of a ragged boy and girl begging from a person looking over a wall: 'BEGGING ALMS'. • No mark • 6½ ins. diam.

**1036** Straight edge with moulded border of feathery fronds with posies of roses, pansies and leaves in sections, and a red print of a beggar with four girls: 'WHAT LITTLE GIRLS CAN DO'. • No mark • 7½ ins. diam.

**1037** Erratic edge and moulded border of three rows of blobbed daisies, and a black print of a peg-legged man with crutches holding his hat out to a lady and gentleman: 'Benevolence is commendable in all persons/Begin to be good in time it cannot be too soon.' • No mark • 6 ins. diam.

**1038** Reeded and feathered edge with vertical sprig border and a manganese print of 'THE POOR BOY AND THE LOAF'. • Mark: MOORE & CO impressed • 6¼ ins. diam.
Samuel Moore & Co., Wear Pottery, Sunderland, 1802–1874.
This illustration appeared in *The Child's Companion*, October 1854.
It was also printed in black on an unmarked plate with a straight edge and unmoulded border painted with two red lines.

**1039** Straight edge with moulded border of elongated florets and a black print of a man on crutches with two children: 'BLIND MAN./To kindest pity now inclined,/See these children wish to give/A trifle to the poor and blind,/Thus assisting him to live.' • No mark • 6½ ins. diam.
The illustration comes from *A present for infants; or, Pictures for the nursery* (Darton, Harvey & Darton, 1819).

**1040** As 1038 with a sepia print of 'THE BEGGAR BOY'. • No mark • 6¼ ins. diam.

**1041** Erratic edge and moulded sprig border clumsily painted in light green, pink, blue and yellow, with a red print of a woman with a child and a parrot; 'A GOOD GIRL.' • No mark • 7¼ ins. diam.

**1042** As 1041 with well-moulded but unpainted border and a sepia print illustrating 'OBEDIENCE TO PARENTS'. • No mark • 5½ ins. diam.

**1043** Straight edge with rose, honeysuckle and swagged garland border painted iron red, green and yellow, with a black (painted) print of a woman with children, and a church in the background: 'SET GOOD EXAMPLES.' • Mark: black painted 18 • 7½ ins. diam.
Probably Baker, Bevans & Irwin, Glamorgan Pottery, Swansea, 1813–1838.

1035

1036

1037

1038

1039

1040

1041

1042

1043

# Chapter 15 THE TEMPERANCE MOVEMENT

General attacks on drunkenness began to be focussed into an organised temperance movement during the 1820s, at a time when friendly and co-operative societies, mechanics institutes and other associations aimed at the betterment of the working man were also burgeoning.

There were plenty of reasons for the problem of drunkenness in the early 19th century. To begin with there were very few 'safe' non-alcoholic thirst-quenchers: drinking water was scarce and often dangerously contaminated; while tea, coffee and chocolate were getting cheaper they were still more expensive and less accessible than gin or beer; fresh milk was not generally available in towns, and soft drinks and cordials were as yet undeveloped. Alcoholic drinks were widely held to provide extra energy for physical labour.

The position of the drinking place – inn, tavern or alehouse – in the social life, particularly of working class districts (where there were more licensed drinking places per head of population than in richer areas) was another major factor. As well as providing centres for meeting and recreation, drinking places offered levels of heat and light unheard of in most poor homes; there were newspapers, comfortable chairs and even lavatories.

The scarcity of parks or open spaces accessible to working people in towns, and the lack of public libraries and assembly halls also conspired to make the drinking place a focus for all kinds of social gatherings: the yards and large rooms of inns were used for sporting, dramatic and musical events, for political and educational meetings, for trading and auctions, and even for inquests. Publicans were often entrusted with the money collected in savings funds or burial clubs for their patrons, and in some cases they acted as registrars of births and deaths.

It was not until the mid-19th century that libraries, museums, music halls and public parks began to provide alternative recreational places to the public house. Drinks like coffee, chocolate and most especially tea, were greatly increasing in popularity, while non-alcoholic cold drinks like ginger beer, lemonade and soda water were being sold in vast quantities, and by publicans too. Most important were improvements in housing and in water supplies.

The temperance movement appealed to the 'respectable' poor – those who identified with the middle-class values of clean living, self-help and prudence – who saw such an association as a means of bettering themselves and resisting the temptation that was all around them. Its other aim was to reach out to the habitual drunkard who lacked the self-discipline and motivation to clamber out of his downward spiral of poverty and deprivation.

It was a strongly non-conformist, Liberal movement, based mainly in the urban areas of the north of England. It also had divisions within it between those who advocated abstinence from spirits but not beers, and the teetotallers.

The anti-spirits movement of the 1830s included many brewers – always prominent in evangelical and philanthropic circles – and was supported by free traders who hoped to curb the power of the magistrates (and therefore of the Government) by the introduction of free licensing. Not for them the interference of Government control, advocated by the American-inspired Prohibitionists of the 1850s. Other groups with vested interests in the early temperance movement were doctors who had by this time realised the harmful effects of alcohol on health and were beginning to curb their earlier habit of prescribing it for practically every complaint; coffee and tea traders for obvious reasons; industrialists who needed sober workers to man their machines; evangelicals and Quakers who for generations had eschewed spirits in favour of beer.

The first English temperance society was established in 1830 in Bradford by Henry Forbes, a Scottish worsted manufacturer; it was followed by societies in Warrington, Manchester and Leeds and a year later by the London Temperance Society, later renamed the British and Foreign Temperance Society.

It was not long before the obvious became clear – that an anti-spirits campaign did nothing to combat drunkenness in predominantly beer-drinking areas, and pressure began to build up for a campaign against all intoxicating liquors. This more radical form of the temperance movement gave rise to a new social world, of temperance hotels, friendly societies, public halls, periodicals and even entertainment 'to enable teetotallers to survive in a drink-ridden society.' One teetotal friendly society, The Rechabites, founded in 1835, had 13,000 members by 1868.

The most powerful of all the early teetotal groups was the Preston Temperance Society, one of whose 'missionaries', James Teare, is commemorated on a children's plate. The Preston Society was among many that introduced the 'long' pledge, which forbade the offering of intoxicants to others, as well as (the 'short' pledge) entry to drinking places. Preston's most prominent teetotaller was Joseph Livesey, whose *Malt Lecture* summed up the whole movement's philosophy and helped to promote teetotalism throughout the north of England. Another, Richard Turner, is said to have been the

1044     1045     1046

first to apply the word 'teetotal' to abstinence from spirits, wines and beer – by accident, so legend goes, on account of his stutter (try saying 'total' with a stuttering T). The first national teetotal society was the British Association for the Promotion of Temperance, which splintered from the British and Foreign Temperance Society over the long and short pledge.

Those who signed the pledge needed courage, not only to change their whole way of life, but often to brave the taunts of neighbours and workmates. There were anti-teetotal demonstrations instigated by publicans, and opposition from conservatives who saw political (Chartist) dangers in such radical enthusiasms. Whereas the anti-spirits campaign had been supported by the middle and upper classes, these groups were almost entirely absent from the more extreme teetotal movement whose

support came mainly from working class radicals and non-conformists. In spite of its anti-sectarian beginnings, teetotalism had become irrevocably linked with denominational religiosity by the 1860s.

One of the few Roman Catholic teetotal campaigners was Father Mathew, also immortalised on children's plates, whose missionary work during the 1840s was especially influential in Ireland and upon Irish immigrants with their traditional susceptibility to the evils of drunkenness.

**1044** Octagonal with rope-twist edge and dimpled floret border, and a black print (painted) of 'FATHER MATTHEW/ ADMINISTERING THE TOTAL ABSTINENCE PLEDGE.' • No mark • 6¼ ins. diam.
Similar plates may be found with variations in the daisy borders and slight differences in the transfer prints.

**1045** Wavy-edged octagonal with wide border of moulded patterns and a sepia print (painted) of Father Mathew preaching (as 1044); 'MAY GOD BLESS YOU AND GRANT YOU STRENGTH AND GRACE TO KEEP YOUR PROMISE.' • Mark: printed diamond registration mark for 1847 • 8 ins. diam.
Bailey & Ball, Longton, Staffordshire.

**1046** Rococo edge and moulded border of roses, tulips and asters. The central black print is a portrait of 'JAMES TEARE [of] PRESTON/The indefatigable advocate of Total Abstinence from all intoxicating Liquors.' • Mark: Dillwyn & Co and a cross impressed • 6¼ ins. diam.
Swansea Pottery, Wales, 1830–1840.
Teare is known to have lectured in Swansea on Temperance and the Maine Law (Prohibitionism) during the 1850s.

## MOTTOES AND INSIGNIA

The prints on the following five plates were probably taken from 'stock blocks'; similar images appear in printers and typefounders sample books of the 19th century.

**1047** Octagonal with lustred rope-twist edge and dimpled floret border; the black print (painted) shows a temperance coat of arms with supporters representing Sobriety and Domestic Comfort and the inscription 'BE THOU FAITHFUL UNTO DEATH'. • Mark: lustred S and three green painted blobs • 6¼ ins. diam.
Larger plates with the same border and painted in the same palette, with variations in the print, are to be found.

**1048** Straight edge and plain border with printed zig-zag pattern to rim, and a brown transfer of Sobriety and Temperance figures supporting a coat of arms and mottoes. • Mark: anchor impressed • 7 ins. diam.

**1049** Octagonal with rope-twist edge painted black and blobbed daisy border, and a sepia print (painted) of a man and a woman supporting temperance mottoes and trophies. • Mark: South Wales Pottery and 8 impressed • 6 ins. diam.
South Wales Pottery, Llanelly, circa 1850.

**1050** Rococo edge and continuous daisy garland border painted red, blue, green and yellow, with a black-printed inscription: TEMPERANCE IS THE PARENT OF SOBRIETY, HEALTH, PROSPERITY, INDUSTRY, MODESTY, PRUDENCE, HUMILITY, CHEERFULNESS, TRANQUIL-LITY, CONTENTMENT, PIETY, DOMESTIC HAPPINESS.' • No mark; double footrim • 6¼ ins. diam.

**1051** As 1050 with a sepia print of a temperance coat of arms and supporters. • No mark; double footrim • 7¼ ins. diam.

**1052** Rococo edge with border of flowers and leaves in compartments, and a black-printed coat of arms with supporters representing the Rechabites Order. • No mark • 5½ ins. diam.
Probably Goodwins & Harris.
The Independent Order of Rechabites was a teetotal friendly society founded in 1835 and named after Rechab who 'enjoined his family to abstain from wine and to dwell in tents' [Brewer's *Dictionary of Phrase and Fable*; – Jeremiah XXXV 6, 7]. Cecil Torr, in *Small Talk at Wreyland* [OUP 1979, p. 581], mentions the Rationals and Rechabites in his Devon village: 'for many years the Rationals had a church-parade upon Whit-Sunday and a fete upon Whit-Monday. In 1908 they decided not to have their fete that year: so the Rechabites announced a fete upon Whit-Monday, and then the Rationals announced their fete as usual, fearing that their rivals would annex Whit-Monday permanently. So there were two fetes going on together in fields not far apart, and each had a big brass band. This little dispute gave rise to an incredible display of hatred and malice between the two societies.'

**1053** Straight edge with a red line and border of garlanded rose sprays. A manganese print, clumsily painted, shows an angel holding a cartouche inscribed 'Intemperance is Ireland's bane, England's curse and Scotland's woe'; an all-seeing eye looks down from above, a pair of tablets representing the Ten Commandments stands beside the angel and 'THE DRUNKARD SHALL NOT ENTER THE KINGDOM OF GOD' is written below. • No mark • 6¾ ins. diam.
The same print (and palette) have been noted on octagonal plates with moulded garland and medallion borders, and in sepia on one side of a jug, with the same image as 1047 on the other. • No mark • 5¾ ins. diam.

**1054** Erratic edge and border of moulded flower sprays alternating with vertical sprigs, clumsily painted in maroon, green, blue and yellow. The circular blue-printed inscription sets out the Pledge: 'I PROMISE TO ABSTAIN FROM ALL INTOXICATING LIQUERS [sic] AS LONG AS I LIVE, EXCEPT FOR MEDICINAL OR SACRAMENTAL PURPOSES, AND TO DISCOURAGE THE CAUSE AND PRACTICE OF INTEMPER-ANCE.' • No mark • 8 ins. diam.

Printer's Ornament from a catalogue of Vincent Figgins Type Foundry, mid 19th century.

1047

1048

1049

1050

1051

1052

1053

1054

## THE BOTTLE

The following illustrations are based on the series by George Cruikshank, dating from 1847, the year in which he became a total abstainer and resolved 'to give his example as well as his art' to the cause [Blanchard Jerrold, *The Life of George Cruikshank*, 1882]. The text was by Dr Charles Mackay and the eight plates were printed by the then new process of glyphography. The series was purposely sold cheaply, at a shilling for a folded sheet or half a crown stitched into a wrapper, so that the working classes could buy it. They did, and *The Bottle* prints were sold in huge numbers. Their use on plates from several different factories gave them an additional circulation.

The fact that Cruikshank is known to have addressed the Middlesbrough Mechanics' Institute in 1851 may be of relevance: the president of the Mechanics' Institute at that time was Isaac Wilson, the director of the

Middlesbrough Pottery; Robert Blore, the potting manager was active on the committee, and many of the Pottery employees were members.

**1055–1062** A complete set of white earthenware flat-rimmed plates with blue-printed borders and blue transfer prints illustrating *The Bottle*.

*SCENE FIRST:* THE BOTTLE IS BROUGHT OUT FOR THE FIRST TIME. THE HUSBAND INDUCES HIS WIFE JUST TO TAKE A DROP.

*SCENE SECOND:* HE IS DISCHARGED FROM HIS EMPLOYMENT FOR DRUNKENNESS. THEY PAWN THEIR CLOTHES TO SUPPLY THE BOTTLE.

*SCENE THIRD:* AN EXECUTION SWEEPS OFF THE GREATER PART OF THEIR FURNITURE. THEY COMFORT THEMSELVES WITH THE BOTTLE.

*SCENE FOURTH:* UNABLE TO OBTAIN EMPLOYMENT THEY ARE DRAWN BY HUNGER INTO THE STREETS TO BEG.

*SCENE FIFTH:* COLD, MISERY AND WANT DESTROY THEIR YOUNGEST CHILD.

*SCENE SIXTH:* FEARFUL QUARRELS AND BRUTAL VIOLENCE ARE THE NATURAL CONSEQUENCES OF THE FREQUENT USE OF THE BOTTLE.

*SCENE SEVENTH:* THE HUSBAND KILLS HIS WIFE WITH THE INSTRUMENT OF ALL THEIR MISERY.

1055

1056

1057

1058

1059

1060

1061

1062

265

*SCENE LAST:* THE BOTTLE HAS DONE ITS WORK – IT HAS DESTROYED THE INFANT AND THE MOTHER, IT HAS BROUGHT THE SON AND DAUGHTER TO VICE AND TO THE STREETS, AND HAS LEFT THE FATHER A HOPELESS MANIAC.
• Marks: 1055 and 1062 are marked 1 in underglaze blue; 1056, 1057, 1058 and 1060 are marked 2 in underglaze blue; 1059 and 1061 are unmarked • 6¼ ins. diam.

**1063** Rococo edge and pointed-petalled daisy border, with a sepia print (painted) of Plate 1 from *The Bottle*. • Mark: Middlesbro' Pottery impressed in half circle above an anchor; others in the same set may have an impressed circular blob • 8 ins. diam.
Middlesbrough Pottery, Yorkshire, 1834–1844.

**1064** Bevelled edge and border of brick patterns and shamrock sprigs in alternating segments, with a sepia print of Plate 1 from *The Bottle*. • No mark • 6½ ins. diam.

**1065** Rococo edge and unmoulded border decorated with black-printed patterns. The black central print is Plate III from *The Bottle*. • Mark: Moore & Co, impressed, and Moore & Co The Bottle, printed • 6½ ins. diam.
Moore & Co., Wear Pottery, Southwick, Sunderland, 1803–1874.
*The Bottle* series was also produced by Moore & Co. on plates with vine and grape borders.

**1066** Wavy edge and round-petalled blobbed daisy border, and a sepia print (painted) of Plate VIII from *The Bottle*. • No mark • 7¾ ins. diam.

## THE EFFECTS OF THE BOTTLE

These four 7½ ins. plates are part of a series obviously inspired by George Cruikshank's *The Bottle*, in which the action takes place in a printer's composing room. Printers have always been notoriously bibulous. The artist has not been identified, but each engraving is dated Jany 1849. The plates have moulded borders of pointed-petalled blobbed daisies and the prints are in sepia with sparse overpainting. All are marked Middlesbro' Pottery in a half circle above an anchor (impressed).

**1067** *PLATE 1st.* THE LIQUOR IS BROUGHT OUT FOR THE FIRST TIME./ THE JOURNEYMAN URGES THE APPRENTICE 'JUST TO TAKE A DROP'.

**1068** *PLATE 3rd.* HAVING GAMBLED AWAY HIS MONEY AT THE CARD TABLE/ HE IS TURNED OUT WITH EMPTY POCKETS.

**1069** *PLATE 4th.* DRUNK AND DISORDERLY IN THE STREET/HE BECOMES ACQUAINTED WITH THE POLICE STATION.

**1070** *PLATE 6th.* DISCHARGED FROM HIS WORK IN WANT AND IN DEBT/THE PARTNER OF HIS VICE BECOMES THE SHARER OF HIS MISERY.

## THE BAND OF HOPE

Temperance work among children had been growing since the 1830s, but the first official Band of Hope, so named by an Irish Presbyterian minister's widow, Anne Carlile, was formed at a Leeds Sunday School in 1847 by Jabez Tunnicliff. The Band of Hope movement became, effectively, a temperance offshoot of the Sunday school system. Children probably had a less developed sense of self-sacrifice when they signed the pledge; more difficult may have been their obligation to influence their parents towards abstention. The movement gained momentum from its beginning: in 1852 6,000 children came to a Band of Hope mass-meeting in Exeter Hall, London, and by 1860 there were 120 Bands of Hope in London. A periodical, the *Band of Hope Review*, was already flourishing with a circulation of over 250,000 in 1861, and another magazine, *Onward*, was started in 1865.

Band of Hope meetings characteristically began with a temperance hymn and prayers. These would be followed by the chairman's address, music, readings, recitations and speeches, then pledge-signing and a final prayer. As well as such religious gatherings there were picnics, tea-meetings, singing classes and 'exhibitions of dissolving views' [*Onward*, Aug 1870, quoted by Brian Harrison P 193]. Children were encouraged to take an active role in the organisation: evidence for this is shown in the children's plate 'How to form Bands of Hope'.

The Band of Hope still exists: today it is particularly concerned with drug-taking and other contemporary problems.

**1071** Rococo edge with rose, tulip and aster border and a green print of a boy beside a tripod table resisting a drink and a pipe. The encircling inscription reads: 'BAND OF HOPE BROTHERHOOD/ FORTITUDE/PERSEVERANCE/NEVER NO NEVER'. • No mark • 6 ins. diam.

**1072** Octagonal with rope-twist edge and indistinctly moulded daisy border with a central sepia transfer of a boy and girl holding a scroll inscribed 'BAND OF HOPE'. • No mark • 5¾ ins. diam.

**1073** Straight edge and border of posies in feathery sections, and a sepia print illustrating 'THE DRUNKEN MOTHER' with shocked onlookers. • No mark • 6¼ ins. diam.

**1074** Straight edge and primrose border with a black print illustrating 'BAND OF HOPE/THE MOUNTAIN RILL – HOW PLEASANT, ON A SUNNY DAY, TO REST BESIDE THE BROOK,/AND WATCH THE RIPPLES, AS THEY PLAY, DOWN IN SOME SHADY NOOK'. • Mark: a strap encircling indecipherable letters, impressed • 6½ ins. diam.

This print, signed Dalziel, appeared in *The Children's Friend* in September 1861 (S. W. Partridge) with the acknowledgement 'From *Illustrated Songs and Hymns for the Little Ones.*'
A version of The Mountain Rill has been noted in manganese on a plate with a blue sponged border like 1076.

**1075** Wavy edge and blobbed daisy border with a black print of 'BAND OF HOPE – MAKE THE TEMPERANCE ARMY STRONG AND ON TO VICTORY'. • Mark: impressed asterisk • 7 ins. diam.

**1076** Straight edge with a blue sponged border and a black print of 'BAND OF HOPE/THE SABBATH KEEPERS/RISE EARLY AND THANKFULLY PUT UP YOUR PRAYER: BE AT SCHOOL IN GOOD TIME, AND BE DILIGENT THERE'. • No mark • 6¼ ins. diam.

**1077** Wavy edge and blobbed daisy border, with a black print illustrating 'BAND OF HOPE/THE SABBATH BREAKERS: THE SABBATH IS A HOLY DAY/TO HIM WHO BREAKES [sic] IT DARKSOME FEARS ARE GIVEN/TO HIM WHO KEEPS IT BRIGHTER HOPES OF HEAVEN'. • No mark • 5¾ ins. diam.
This print appeared in Partridge's magazine *The Children's Friend*, October 1868, as an illustration for The Story of the Cross.

The print has been noted on a similar daisy-bordered plate in a larger size with an impressed asterisk mark, and on a larger plate with a straight edge and narrow border of blobbed line-petalled daisies.

**1078** Straight edge and green sponged border with a black print showing a meeting: 'BAND OF HOPE/HOW TO FORM BANDS OF HOPE'. • Mark: rounded Maltese cross, impressed • 7¼ ins. diam.

**1079** Wavy edge with blobbed daisy border and a black print, slightly painted, of a Band of Hope meeting as 1078. • No mark • 6 ins. diam.
The same print has been noted on an 8 ins. plate with a similar border.

# Chapter 16 BENJAMIN FRANKLIN'S MAXIMS

Benjamin Franklin (1706–1790), philosopher, scientist, printer, publisher, philanthropist and architect of American independence, was the youngest son of a Boston candlemaker, and his successful ascent of the ladder of life through personal effort and determination became celebrated on both sides of the Atlantic through publications from his own printing press. These ranged from periodicals such as the *Pennsylvania Gazette*, *The General Magazine* and *Poor Richard's Almanack* to tracts on politics, legal theory, education, language, anti-slavery and population control.

The maxims purveyed in *Poor Richard's Almanack* (1732–1758) included rephrased versions of sayings culled from earlier sources such as Bacon, Rochefoucauld and Rabelais as well as his own inventions, but their common theme was one of self-help through sobriety, frugality and industry. His (unfinished) autobiography promoted similar ideals, and was included in the working man's favourite reading matter for generations.

Franklin's ideas and maxims were enthusiastically adopted by the temperance reformers, especially Joseph Livesey, the early Preston evangelist and Malt lecturer, and illustrations of them constitute one of the most numerous subject groups among children's wares.

**1080** Straight edge and unmoulded border with manganese transfer-printed alphabet and patterns and a green print illustrating 'Dr FRANKLIN'S MAXIM'S [sic]/ He who saves not as he gets may keep his nose all his life to the grindstone & die not worth a groat./A fat kitchen makes a lean wi[ll Would you be rich: thi]nk of saving.' • No mark: double footrim • 6 ins. diam. Probably Godwin, Burslem.
This plate is to be found in different colours; the same print has been noted on plates with rope-twist edges and moulded alphabet borders and, in slightly varied form, on a small plate with a moulded border of garlands and flower sprays blobbed in green, red and yellow.
The illustration is derived from a picture sheet/jigsaw puzzle comprising 24 scenes of town and country life illustrating Franklin's 'LESSONS for the YOUNG and the OLD, on INDUSTRY, TEMPERANCE, FRUGALITY &c' by Robert Dighton, published by Bowles and Carver, London, 1795, see page 309.

**1081** Rococo edge with rose, tulip and aster border, and a red print of cobblers at work: 'He that hath a trade hath an estate./ Industry pays debts while despair increases them.' • No mark • 5¾ ins. diam.

**1082** As 1080 with green border and a manganese print illustrating 'Dr FRANKLIN'S MAXIMS/Keep thy shop and thy shop will keep thee./If you would have your business done, go, if not, send.' • No mark; double footrim • 6 ins. diam. Probably Godwin, Burslem.
This plate is to be found in different colours.
The print is from the Bowles & Carver picture sheet (see note to 1080).

**1083** Octagonal with rope-twist edge and round-petalled blobbed daisy border, with a sepia print of five men in a tavern: 'Dost thou love life? then do not squander time, for that is the stuff life is made of./The sleeping fox catches no poultry – there will be sleeping enough in the grave.' • No mark • 6½ ins. diam.
A similarly bordered plate has a black print of a cottage interior with a view of a harbour beyond, and the maxims: 'Employ time well if thou meanest to gain leisure. One to day is worth two to morrows,/Since thou art not sure of a minute throw not away an hour.' This print is from the Bowles & Carver picture sheet (noted above).

1080

1081

1082

1083

1084

1085

1086

1087

1088

**1084** Octagonal with rope-twist edge and line-petalled daisy border, and a black print of a woman preparing an elaborate hairdo while her children play: 'SILKS AND SATINS SCARLET AND VELVETS PUT OUT THE KITCHEN FIRE ... FRANKLIN'S PROVERBS ...' • No mark • 5½ ins. diam.

**1085** As 1083 with a sepia print of a fishery scene: 'Industry needs not wish, and he that lives upon hope will die fasting:/There are no gains without pains, then help hands for I have no lands.' • No mark • 6½ ins. diam.
Others in this series include the cobbler print as 1081 and the house removal scene (as 1125).

**1086** Straight edge with dark green line to rim and tulip, bluebell and wheatear border, and a black print (crudely painted) of a man with a cow and sheep and another doffing his hat over a wall: 'NOW I HAVE A SHEEP AND A COW. EVERY BODY BIDS ME GOOD MORROW. FRANKLIN'S PROVERBS.' • Mark: J & G MEAKIN impressed • 7¼ ins. diam.
J. & G. Meakin, Eagle Pottery and Eastwood Works, Hanley, 1851 onwards.

**1087** Rococo edge with moulded border of roses and buds painted red and green, and a black print of a fat man with a cow and a sheep and man on horseback riding by and doffing his hat: 'POOR RICHARD'S WAY TO WEALTH./DILIGENCE IS THE MOTHER OF GOOD LUCK/NOW I HAVE A SHEEP AND A COW/EVERYBODY BIDS ME GOOD-MORROW.' • Mark: blob, ?10, impressed • 6½ ins. diam.
A version of this print was used on wares from Maling, Newcastle.

**1088** As 1086 with a print of a woman doing her hair, similar to 1084 but with the image reversed: 'SILKS AND SATINS SCARLET AND VELVETS PUT OUT THE KITCHEN FIRE. FRANKLIN'S PROVERBS.'

• Mark: J & G MEAKIN impressed • 7¼ ins. diam. J. & G. Meakin, Hanley.

**1089** Rococo edge with border of flowers and leaves in compartments, painted dark green and red, and a sepia-printed decorative vignette of two men conversing in a landscape: 'If you would know the value of money,/Try to borrow some.' • No mark • 7½ ins. diam.
Possibly Goodwins & Harris, Lane End, circa 1831–1838.
This is derived from part of one of the vignettes on the Bowles & Carver picture sheet (see note to 1080).

**1090** As 1089 with a vignette of a man in front of the village lockup and stocks: 'Experience keeps a dear school,/But fools will learn in no other'. • Mark: 6 impressed • 6½ ins. diam.
Possibly Goodwins & Harris.
The illustration is from the Bowles & Carver picture sheet.

**1091** As 1089 etc with an agriculturally decorated vignette showing a man driving a plough and another leading three horses: 'He that by the plough would thrive./Himself must either hold or drive.' • No mark • 7½ ins. diam.
Possibly Goodwins & Harris.

**1092** Straight edge with indistinctly moulded blobbed daisy border and a blue print of paupers outside the workhouse: 'FRANKLIN'S MAXIMS/FOR AGE AND WANT SAVE WHILE YOU MAY/NO MORNING SUN LASTS THE WHOLE DAY'. • No mark • 7½ ins. diam.

**1093** Reeded and feathered edge and vertical sprig border, with a version of the print in 1090 in black, slightly painted, with the same inscription. • Mark: TAYLOR BROS HANLEY impressed • 6¼ ins. diam.
Taylor Bros., Market Street, Hanley, circa 1859–1870.
Illustration from Bowles & Carver picture sheet.

**1094** Rococo edge with continuous daisy garland border painted green, red, blue and yellow, and a blue print of blacksmiths working: 'He that hath a trade hath an estate. At the working man's house hunger looks in but dare not enter./Industry pays debts, while despair increaseth them.' • No mark; double footrim • 7¼ ins. diam.
Illustration from Bowles & Carver picture sheet.

1089

1090

1091

1092

1093

1094

1095

1096

1097

**1095** Indented and grooved edge with a moulded border of rose sprays alternating with rococo curlicues, and a black print of an elderly beggar with a man and a woman: 'FOR AGE AND WANT SAVE WHILE YOU MAY/NO MORNING SUN LASTS ALL THE DAY'. • No mark • 7¼ ins. diam.
This plate may be found with a blue print, crudely painted.

**1096** Hexagonal lobed edge with border of dotted patterns and feathery fronds painted red, blue, green and yellow, and a blue print of a beggar with a lady and gentleman: 'Benevolence is commendable in all persons./Begin to be good in time it cannot be too soon.' • No mark • 6 ins. diam.

**1097** Alphabet-bordered bowl with a dark blue print of blacksmiths working: 'HE THAT HATH A TRADE HATH AN ESTATE/INDUSTRY PAYS DEBTS WHILE DESPAIR INCREASETH THEM' (cf. 1094). • No mark • 7¼ ins. diam.

**1098** Slightly rococo edge with border of tendrilled flower sprigs, and a green print, crudely painted, of gardeners working: 'Industry needs not wish and he that lives upon hope will die fasting/There are no gains without pains: then help hands for I have no lands.' • Mark: L impressed • 7½ ins. diam.
This plate is also be be found with the print in brown.

The print is from the Bowles & Carver picture sheet (see note to 1080).

**1099** Octagonal with rope-twist edge painted yellow and indistinctly moulded border of blobbed daisies, and a green print (crudely painted) of a man outside a building and a donkey being driven across a bridge in the background: 'Sloth like rust consumes faster than labor [sic] wears: while the used key is always bright/God helps them that help themselves: lost time is never [found again].' • No mark • 7 ins. diam.
Illustration from Bowles & Carver picture sheet.

**1100** Edge and border as 1098 with an unpainted green print similar to 1099: 'Sloth like rust consumes faster than labour wears/While the used Key is always bright/God helps them that help themselves. Lost time is never found again.' • Mark: 11 impressed • 7½ ins. diam.
This print, in blue, is to be found on plates with borders like 1104.
Illustration from Bowles & Carver picture sheet.

**1101** Vitruvian scroll and alphabet border with a black print, clumsily painted, of a man leaning on his axe by a felled tree: 'Little strokes fell great Oaks'. • No mark • 6¼ ins. diam.
Probably Staffordshire.

**1102** Vitruvian scroll and alphabet border, and a red print of men felling trees

and working at a well: 'POOR RICHARD'S MAXIM'S [sic]/Handle your tools without mittens: remember the cat in gloves catches no mice./Constant dropping wears away stones: & little strokes fell great Oaks.' • No mark; double footrim • 6¼ ins. diam.
Probably Godwin, Burslem.
A similar print (in green) occurs on plates with borders (and impressed marks) like 1100 and on a plate with a moulded border of dots, flowers and curlicues. The illustration is from the Bowles & Carver picture sheet.

**1103** Indented grooved edge and border of rose sprigs alternating with rococo curlicues, and a black print of men felling trees, with a mill in the background: 'CONSTANT DROPPING WEARS AWAY STONES/AND LITTLE STROKES FALL [sic] GREAT OAKS'. • No mark • 7¼ ins. diam.
A similar print is to be found on alphabet-bordered bowls like 1097; a version of it was used by George Jones, Burslem, circa 1854.

**1104** Rococo edge with continuous daisy garland border painted green, red and blue, and a blue print of gardeners as 1098, and the same circular inscription. • No mark; double footrim • 6¼ ins. diam.
This plate is to be found in a larger size, sometimes with pink lustre to the edge and border.
Illustration from Bowles & Carver picture sheet.

1098

1099

1100

1101

1102

POOR RICHARD'S MAXIMS

1103

CONSTANT DROPPING WEARS AWAY STONES

AND LITTLE STROKES FALL GREAT OAKS

1104

1105

When the well is dry they know the want of water.

Continual dropping wears away stones.

1106

Many a little makes a mickle.

A word to the wise is enough.

**1105** Erratic edge and moulded border of flower sprigs painted red, green and yellow, with a black print (painted) of a woman at a well, within a circle: 'When the well is dry they know the want of water./ Continual dropping wears away stones.' • No mark; double footrim • 7 ins. diam. The same print is to be found in blue on a plate with a rose and curlicue border as 1103.

**1106** Edge and border as 1104, slightly painted red, green and yellow, with a central black print (painted) of a man talking to another holding a sheaf of corn, within a circle: 'Many a little makes a mickle./A word to the wise is enough.' • No mark; double footrim • 6¼ ins. diam. The same print, in black, has been noted on a plate with a rose and curlicue border as 1103 with a painted black line to the edge.

**1107** Wavy edge with blobbed round-petalled daisy border and inner row of sprigs. The sepia print (slightly painted) illustrates 'POOR RICHARD'S MAXIM'S [sic]/He that by the plow would thrive himself must either hold or drive./The eye of the master will do more work than both his hands.' • Mark: a blob impressed; double footrim • 6¾ ins. diam. The illustration is from the Bowles & Carver picture sheet (see note for 1080).

**1108** Octagonal with rope-twist edge and blobbed daisy border, and a blue print of a

man with a whip watching harvesters: 'NOT TO OVERSEE WORKMEN/IS TO LEAVE YOUR PURSE OPEN'. • No mark • 6½ ins. diam.

**1109** Vitruvian scroll and alphabet border, with a black print (clumsily painted) of a scene outside a tavern: 'DOST THOU LOVE LIFE THEN DO NOT SQUANDER TIME/THERE WILL BE SLEEPING ENOUGH IN THE GRAVE' (cf. 1083). • No mark • 7¼ ins. diam. Staffordshire. Illustration from Bowles & Carver picture sheet.

**1110** Slightly wavy edge and round-petalled blobbed daisy border, with a green print of a man and a gaoler in a debtors' prison: 'PRIDE THAT DINES ON VANITY SUPS ON CONTEMPT'. • Mark: 1883 impressed – probably the date • 5¾ ins. diam.

**1111** Rococo edge with blue line and border of flowers, leaves and tendrils, and a blue print of people at a meal with surrounding inscriptions and triangular motifs: 'FRANKLIN's MAXIMS/Who dainties love shall beggars prove/Fools lay out money and buy repentance/Foolish men make feasts/and wise men eat them.' • No mark • 7 ins. diam. The companion plate to this is 1130.

**1112** Straight edge with green line and tulip, bluebell and wheatear border, and a black print (clumsily painted) of a woman

beekeeping: 'INDUSTRY/A DEAD BEE MAKETH NO HONEY'. • Mark: J & G MEAKIN impressed • 5½ ins. diam. J. & G. Meakin, Hanley. Larger examples of this plate, also marked Meakin, are to be found.

**1113** Slightly indented edge and border of rose sprigs alternating with rococo curlicues, and a blue print within a circle of a woman looking at two beehives: 'Diligence is the mother of good luck/And GOD giveth all things to industry'. • No mark • 5½ ins. diam.

**1114*** Erratic edge and continuous daisy garland border blobbed in green, red and yellow, with a sepia print (painted) within a circle, of a woman and child begging from another: 'Those who dainties love shall beggers [sic] prove./Pride is as loud a begger as Want.' • No mark; double footrim • 5¼ ins. diam. This plate is to be found in a larger size.

**1115** Straight edge with border of florets blobbed in red, green and yellow, and a sepia print within a circle of a man beside two beehives: 'Dr. FRANKLIN./Keep within compafs, and you shall be sure to avoid many troubles which others endure.' • No mark; double footrim • 5¼ ins. diam.

1107

1108

1109

1110

1111

1112

1113

1114

1115

**1116** Indented edge and moulded border of feathery fronds with posies of roses, pansies and leaves in sections, and a blue print of gardeners working: 'THERE ARE NO GAINS WITHOUT PAINS/THEN HELP HANDS FOR I HAVE NO LANDS'. • No mark; quadruple footrim • 7¼ ins. diam.
This border was used by Samuel Barker & Son, Don Pottery, Swinton, Yorkshire, 1834–1893.
The illustration is loosely based on a vignette from the Bowles & Carver picture sheet (see source picture for 1098).

**1117** Straight edge painted green with fern and vertical sprig border and a black-printed farming scene: 'Dr. FRANKLIN'S MAXIM'S [sic]/Plow deep while sluggards sleep; and you shall have corn to sell and to keep./Work to day for you know not how much you may be hindered to morrow.' • Mark. BW & Co printed within a scroll • 5¾ ins. diam.
Bates Walker & Co., Dale Hall Works, Burslem, 1875–1878, or Buckley Wood & Co., High Street Pottery, Burslem, 1875–1885.
The illustration is derived from the Bowles & Carver picture sheet (see note to 1080).

**1118** Reeded and feathered edge painted green with vertical sprig border and a red (slightly painted) version of the print and inscription in 1117. • No mark • 6½ ins. diam.
The same print appears on a straight-edged, unmoulded bordered plate with two black lines, marked Pountney & Allies (Bristol Pottery, Temple Backs, Bristol, circa 1816–1835).
The illustration is derived from the Bowles & Carver picture sheet.

**1119** Vitruvian scroll and alphabet border and a black (slightly painted) print of four men in a rowing boat, with a paddle steamer in the distance: 'POOR RICHARDS WAY TO WEALTH/LOST TIME IS NEVER FOUND AGAIN./WHAT WE CALL TIME ENOUGH ALWAYS PROVES LITTLE ENOUGH.' • No mark • 6¼ ins. diam.
Probably Staffordshire.
This print was also used by Maling, Newcastle.

**1120** Edge and border as 1118, crudely painted in green, red and blue, with a black print of two men in conversation and a woman spinning outside a house in the background: 'Dr. FRANKLIN'S MAXIM'S. [sic]/Fly Pleafure and it will follow you. The diligent spinner as [sic] a large garment./Now I have a sheep and a cow every body bids me good morrow.' • No mark • 7¼ ins. diam. Illustration from the Bowles & Carver picture sheet.

**1121** Straight edge with garland and medallion border and a clumsily painted sepia variant of the print in 1120. • No mark • 6 ins. diam.
Illustration from the Bowles & Carver picture sheet.

**1122** Slightly indented edge with border of rose sprays alternating with rococo curlicues, and a black print (slightly painted) of a ploughing scene, within a circle: 'He that by the plough would thrive,/Himself must either hold or drive.' • No mark • 7½ ins. diam.

**1123** As 1122 with a print of two children with a kite: 'Employ thy time well/If thou meanest to gain leisure.' • No mark • 7½ ins. diam.

**1124** As 1122 etc with a print of a man outside a cottage handing a drink to a traveller: 'At the working man's house/Hunger looks in but dares not enter.' • No mark • 7¼ ins. diam.

1116

1117

1118

1119

1120

1121

1122

1123

1124

**1125** Rococo edge with border of roses, fuchsia and vertical columnar sprays painted dark green, red and yellow, and a sepia print of a family moving house: 'I never saw an oft removed tree, nor yet an oft removed family that did so well as those that settled be./Three removes are as bad as a fire and a rolling stone gathers no moss. • Mark: four blobs impressed • 7 ins. diam.
Llanelly Pottery (the four blobs signify SWP for South Wales Pottery), 1839–1858.

**1126** Vitruvian scroll and alphabet border, and a sepia print (slightly painted) of a horse-drawn cart loaded with furniture: 'POOR RICHARD'S MAXIM'S [sic]/I NEVER SAW AN OFT REMOVED TREE NOR YET AN OFT REMOVED FAMILY THAT DID SO WELL AS THOSE THAT SETTLED BE/THREE REMOVES ARE AS BAD AS A FIRE & A ROLLING STONE GATHERS NO MOSS.'
• No mark; double footrim • 6¼ ins. diam.
Probably Godwin, Burslem.
The same plate is found in smaller sizes and with different colouring.
The illustration is derived from the Bowles & Carver picture sheet (see note to 1080).

**1127** Straight edge with moulded alphabet border interspersed with trilobate sprigs, and a black print (painted) of a horse-drawn cart piled with furniture outside a house: 'THREE REMOVES ARE AS BAD AS A FIRE A ROLLING STONE GATHERS NO MOSS FRANKLIN'S PROVbs'. • Mark: J & G

MEAKIN and 20 impressed • 7¼ ins. diam. J. & G. Meakin, Hanley.

**1128** Wavy-edged octagonal with a deep border of moulded patterns and a single green line. The sepia print shows a horse and wagon falling off a bridge into a river, illustrating 'Dr. FRANKLIN'S MAXIM'S [sic]/Want of care does us more damage than want of knowledge/For want of a nail the shoe was lost, and for want of a shoe the horse was lost.' • No mark • 7½ ins. diam.
Bailey & Ball, Longton, circa 1843–1850.
Illustration from Bowles & Carver picture sheet.

**1129** Octagonal with rope-twist edge painted in pink lustre and dimpled floret border, and a black print (painted) of an upset horse and wagon in front of the Beggars Arms public house: 'Want of care does us more damage than want of knowledge.' • No mark • 6¼ ins. diam.

**1130** Rococo edge with green line and border of flowers, leaves and tendrils, and a blue print of a coaching accident, with a woman run over, with surrounding inscriptions and triangular motifs: 'FRANKLINS MAXIMS/Want of care does us more/damage than want of knowledge/For want of a nail the shoe was lost/& for want of a shoe the Horse was lost.' • No mark • 7 ins. diam.
This is the companion plate to 1111.

**1131*** Straight edge with border of florets blobbed in red, green and yellow, and a sepia print (painted) of a man carrying a small barrel and a rake, within a circle: 'Early to bed and early to rise,/Makes a man healthy wealthy and wise.' (See 1115).
• No mark; double footrim • 5¼ ins. diam.
The same print occurs on plates with star and dot borders, or rose sprays and rococo curlicues (the latter may be marked with a Maltese cross, impressed).

**1132** Slightly indented edge and crisply moulded border of floral sprigs alternating

with vertical C-scroll motifs painted in green, blue and red, with a black print within a decorated circle of a boy fallen from his horse, within a decorated circle: 'A LITTLE NEGLECT MAY BREED GREAT MISCHIEF.' • No mark • 8 ins. diam.
This print is similar, but not identical, to an illustration in the *First Chapter of Accidents and Remarkable Events: containing caution and instruction for children* published by Darton & Harvey, London, 1801.

**1133*** As 1131 with a version of the print in 1132 in sepia (painted) within a circle. • No mark; double footrim • 5¼ ins. diam.

1125

1126 POOR RICHARD'S MAXIMS

1127

1128 Dr FRANKLIN'S MAXIMS

1129

1130

1131

1132 A LITTLE NEGLECT MAY BREED GREAT MISCHIEF

1133

**1134** Shaped base and reeded loop handle, with black-printed lozenge patterns and central print of figures in a room: 'Lying rides upon Debts back It is hard for an empty bag to stand upright/ Creditors have better memories than debtors.' • No mark • 2¾ ins. ht.; 2⅝ ins. diam.
Illustration from the Bowles & Carver picture sheet (see note for 1080).

**1135** Cylindrical with loop handle and a red print of farming trophies and figures surrounding a vignette of a ploughing scene: 'He that by the plough would thrive/Himself must either hold or drive' (cf. 1091). • No mark • 2½ ins. ht.; 2¾ ins. diam.
Another print in this series, in sepia, illustrates the maxim: 'Experience keeps a dear school/But fools learn in no other.'

**1136** Cylindrical with loop handle and sepia-printed lozenge patterns and central print (slightly painted) of a family outside the workhouse: 'For age & want save while you may no morning sun lasts all the day/ Experience keeps a dear School but Fools will learn in no other.' • No mark • 2½ ins. ht.; 2½ ins. diam.

**1137** Shaped base and reeded loop handle, and red-printed lozenge patterns and inscriptions and a central print of a weeping woman and two men: 'He then who would avoid a sorrow/This useful maxim he must borrow/That haste makes waste and waste is wont/To make wilful waste the cause of want.' • No mark • 2⅜ ins. ht.; 2½ ins. diam.

**1138** Shaped base with loop handle and black-printed patterns inside rim and on handle; black-printed lozenge patterns and central print of three men in a room: 'If you would know the value of money to try to borrow some/When the well is dry they know the worth of water.' • No mark • 2¾ ins. ht.; 2⅝ ins. diam.

**1139** Shaped base and loop handle, and black prints (slightly painted) of farming scenes – ploughing on one side and sowing on the other: 'Plough deep while Slug/gards sleep & you shall/have corn to sell & to keep/Work to day for you know/ not how much you may be/hindered to morrow' (cf. 1117, 1118 and 1122). • No mark • 2⅝ ins. ht.; 2⅝ ins. diam.
This print is from the Bowles & Carter picture sheet (see note to 1080).

**1140** Cylindrical with loop handle and brown prints of gardeners – planting on one side and rolling on the other: 'Dr FRANKLINS MAXIMS/Industry needs not wish/And he that lives upon/hope will die fasting/There are no gains without/pains then help hands for I have no lands.' (cf. 1098 and 1104). • No mark • 3 ins. ht.; 2⅝ ins. diam.
Illustration from Bowles & Carver picture sheet.

**1141** Cylindrical with loop handle and green prints – working at the well on one side and tree-felling on the other: 'Dr FRANKLINS' [sic] MAXIMS/Handle your tools without/mittens remember the cat/ in gloves catches no mice/Constant dropping wears/away stones & little strokes fell great Oaks' (cf. 1102). • No mark • 2½ ins. ht.; 2⅜ ins. diam.
Illustration from Bowles & Carver picture sheet.

**1142** Cylindrical with loop handle and black prints of a woman spinning and (on the opposite side) two men conversing in a field: 'Dr. FRANKLIN'S MAXIMS/Fly Pleasure and it will fol/low you the diligent [sic] spin/ner has a large shift/ Now I have a Sheep and/a cow every body bids/me good morrow'. • No mark • 2⅝ ins. ht.; 2⅜ ins. diam.
Illustration from Bowles & Carver picture sheet.

**1139** The opposite side.

**1140** The opposite side.

**1141** The opposite side.

**1142** The opposite side.

1134         1135         1136         1137         1138

1139         1140         1141         1142

1139         1140         1141         1142

# Chapter 17 SOLDIERS AND WARRIORS

Most of the plates on this page depict Rifle Volunteers, a movement which started in 1859 as a response to the threat of a French invasion by Napoleon III. The prints illustrate training and drill movements and are probably based on those in one of the many illustrated drill books produced in the 1860s, such as the *Hythe School of Musketry Manual*.

**1143** Octagonal with red line to edge and garland and medallion border, and a manganese print (painted) of two soldiers engaged in combat exercise. • No mark • 8 ins. diam.

**1144** As 1143 with a manganese print (painted) of a cavalryman and a foot soldier engaged in combat exercise. • No mark • 7¼ ins. diam.

**1145** As 1143 with a manganese print (painted) of two cavalrymen with spears in an exotic landscape, with two dogs. • No mark • 8 ins. diam.

**1146** Straight edge with beaded and alphabet border on a granular background and a black print of 'SWORD EXERCISE'. • No mark • 7¼ ins. diam.

**1147** Indented edge and well-moulded border of rose sprays alternating with rococo curlicues, and a red print of drilling soldiers: 'FIRE KNEELING/ENGLAND'S DEFENDER'S' [sic]. • No mark • 7½ ins. diam.

**1148** As 1146 with a red line to edge, and a black print of 'TARGET EXERCISE.' • No mark • 6½ ins. diam.

**1149** Toy plate with straight edge and plain border with a sepia print of soldiers 'ON DRILL'. • No mark • 3½ ins. diam. The soldiers' uniforms shown here are pre-1855.

**1150** Wavy edge and blobbed daisy border with a black print of a soldier guarding a camp: 'WHOM ARE YOU FOR.' • No mark • 8 ins. diam.

**1151** Indistinctly moulded alphabet border with two blue lines and a red print of 'THE BAND./RIFLEMEN.' • No mark • 6¼ ins. diam.

**1152** Straight edge and plain border with two black lines and a black print of soldiers drilling with 'ROYAL STANDARD.' • No mark • 6½ ins. diam.
This print has also been found on an 8 ins. rococo-edged plate with a plain border.
Another print in this series has a print entitled 'AWKWARD SQUAD'.

1143

1144

1145

1146

1147

1148

1149

1150

1151

1152

**1153** Octagonal with rope-twist edge and blobbed daisy border, with a green print of a Nubian horseman. • No mark • 7 ins. diam.

This print has been noted on a plate with a grooved border from Dawson's Low Ford Pottery, Sunderland.

**1154** Wavy-edged octagonal with wide border of patterns, and green painted lines, with a black print of children playing on a gun carriage while a Tartar warrior looks on: 'NORMADE TARTARS'. • No mark • 7¾ ins. diam.

Bailey & Ball, Longton, design registered 1847.

**1155** As 1153, with a green print of exotic horsemen. • No mark • 6¾ ins. diam.

**1156** Rococo edge with moulded border of feathered fronds and florets painted in pink lustre, iron red, blue, yellow and pale green, and a black print of 'The Cossack.' • Mark: two lustre lines • 7½ ins. diam.

**1157** Indistinctly moulded alphabet border with a red print of a mounted Sioux Indian. • Mark: STAFFORDSHIRE ENGLAND printed • 7½ ins. diam.

Probably Allerton, Longton, made for the American and Canadian export market, circa 1890.

**1158** Rococo edge with border of roses, fuchsia and vertical columnar sprays, and a green print of oriental horsemen. • No mark • 7 ins. diam.

Another plate in this series shows an Arabic horseman with a lance, galloping at full tilt.

**1159** Edge and border as 1158 with a green print of a mounted lancer. • No mark • 6 ins. diam.

This is probably a trooper of the yeomanry (an auxiliary cavalry force), circa 1860. The same plate may be found in a smaller size, with a sepia print.

**1160** Octagonal with rope-twist edge and indistinctly moulded dimpled daisy border

blobbed in red and green, and a green print of a hussar on the 'BATTLEFIELD'. • No mark; double footrim • 4¾ ins. diam.

**1161** As 1160 with a sepia print of a 'FIELDMARSHAL'. • No mark; double footrim • 4¾ ins. diam.

The uniform shown here is not that of a field marshal, but more like that of a light dragoon.

**1162** Rococo edge and moulded border of flowers and leaves in compartments, and a green print of 'RECRUITS'. • No mark; double footrim • 5½ ins. diam.

Probably Goodwins & Harris, Crown Works, Lane End, Staffordshire, circa 1831–1838.

Recruiting was a popular print subject, and recruiting parties were almost invariably accompanied by a drummer, as here.

1153

1154

1155

156

1157

1158

159

1160

1161

1162

# Chapter 18 PEOPLE, PLACES AND CAMPAIGNS

This is mainly a commemorative section, and one where the question of what were considered suitable presents for children arises most insistently. One would hardly regard 'Wellington as Prime Minister' as a childish subject, but when it appears on an alphabet-bordered plate one must assume that it was intended for a child. Most of the subjects shown here occur on the types of moulded bordered plates that were just as often decorated with unmistakably child-oriented prints, and we have come to the conclusion that commemoratives then, as now, were distributed among children as often as adults. Our range of 19th century commemoratives is necessarily limited. The subject has been covered in depth by John May (see bibliography).

**1163** Rococo edge and continuous daisy garland border painted iron red, green, blue and yellow, with a manganese-printed portrait of Queen Adelaide. • Mark: C impressed • 7 ins. diam.
*Private Collection.*

**1164** Straight edge with moulded border of leaves and florets painted without regard for the moulding in iron red and green, with a portrait of Queen Caroline. • Mark: D impressed; B painted in iron red • 5¾ ins. diam.

**1165** Straight edge with border of curling fronds and a blue-printed portrait of George III. • No mark • 6½ ins. diam.
*Private Collection.*

**1166** Straight edge with dog, fox and monkey border painted with two black lines, and a black-printed portrait of

William IV. • No mark • 5¾ ins. diam. Possibly Fell, Newcastle.
*Private Collection.*

**1167** Wavy edge with well-moulded basket-weave and rope border and painted crown cartouches, and a central moulded and painted portrait of 'KING GEORGE IIII' with laurel wreath and red military tunic. • No mark • 8¾ ins. diam.
Attributed to Gordons Pottery, Prestonpans, 18th century – 1832.

**1168** Straight edge and rose garland border with a blue print of 'QUEEN CAROLINE'. • Mark: L painted • 5¼ ins. diam.
*Private Collection.*

**1169** Erratic edge and moulded border of royal busts and crowns alternating with sprigs painted in bright multicolours, with printed motifs (similarly painted) commemorating the coronation of William IV and Queen Adelaide. • Mark: I impressed; Z painted • 6¼ ins. diam.
*Private Collection.*

**1170** Straight edge and basket-weave border with flower sprays painted pink and green, with a black-printed portrait of Queen Caroline. • No mark; triple footrim • 6½ ins. diam.
*Private Collection.*

**1171** Indented edge with moulded border of royal motifs and flowers painted in blue, green, apricot and brown, and a central moulded (and painted) portrait of Queen Caroline. • No mark • 6½ ins. diam.
*Private Collection.*

**1172** Vitruvian scroll and alphabet border with a painted blue line, and a black-printed double portrait of Queen Victoria & Prince Albert. • No mark; double footrim • 5 ins. diam.
*Private Collection.*

**1173** Straight edge with border of moulded pendant three-leaf motif alternating with pink lustred spots, blue painted lines, and a central moulded vignette of Queen Victoria's marriage. • No mark • 4½ ins. diam.
*Private Collection.*

**1174** Rococo edge with a border of florets and leaves in compartments and a black print of 'VICTORIA REGINA/Born 25 of May 1819, Proclaimed 20 of June 1837'. • No mark; double footrim • 4½ ins. diam.
*Private Collection.*

**1175** Octagonal with pink lustre line to edge and blobbed daisy border, and a sepia print (painted) of 'VICTORIA REGINA'/Crowned 28th of June 1838/Born 24th of May 1819. Proclaimed 20th of June 1837'. • No mark; double footrim • 6 ins. diam.
*Private Collection.*

**1176** Wavy-edged octagonal with wide border of moulded patterns and two red lines, and a black print of Queen Victoria. • No mark • 7½ ins. diam.
Bailey & Ball, Longton.
*Private Collection.*

**1177** Straight edge with moulded and orange lustre lozenge pattern border with a black-printed portrait of Queen Victoria commemorating the jubilee of 1897. • Mark: printed but indecipherable • 6½ ins. diam.

**1178** Octagonal with dimpled floret border and a black print (painted) of Queen Victoria in a garden. • No mark • 6¼ ins. diam.
*Private Collection.*

**1179** Wavy edge and blobbed daisy border, with a black print of Queen Victoria and the initials 'VR'. • No mark; double footrim • 7¼ ins. diam.
*Private Collection.*

**1180** Rococo edge with rose, tulip and aster border painted in bright colours, and a black print of Queen Victoria. • Mark: a star impressed and VICTORIA printed • 8 ins. diam.
*Private Collection.*

**1181** Unpainted border as 1180 with a manganese-printed portrait of Queen Victoria and the inscription as 1175.
*Private Collection.*

**1182** Straight edge painted black, with well-moulded garland border and painted black lines, and one red. The black print is of 'LORD JOHN RUSSEL' [sic]. • Mark: O impressed • 6½ ins. diam.
This plate commemorates Lord John Russell, one of the leading campaigners for parliamentary reform and architect of the 1832 Reform Bill. Later, as Earl Russell, he became Prime Minister.

**1183** Wavy-edged octagonal, with wide border of patterns and two green lines, with a sepia print (painted) of 'THE QUEEN' with Windsor Castle in the background. • Mark: printed diamond registration mark for Bailey & Ball, April 1847. • 6¾ ins. diam.
The source for this print is the portrait by Sir Francis Grant, painted for the United Service Club in 1843 for a fee of £315, and described in the inventory as 'H.M. Queen Victoria, full length in evening dress with the Order of the Garter and Crown; a vase of flowers on the table to her right.' The picture was exhibited at the Royal Academy in 1843.
This plate may be found in larger sizes.

Child's plate with vitruvian scroll and alphabet border and a black-printed portrait of Queen Victoria. • No mark • 5¼ ins. diam. (Compare with 1176).

1172  1173  1174  1175

1176  1177  1178

1179  1180  1181

**1184** Reeded and feathered edge with vertical sprig border, spotted in pale green, red, pale blue and yellow, with a sepia print of 'THE LATE SIR ROBERT PEEL BART'. • No mark • 6½ ins. diam.
Peel died in 1850 at the age of 62 after being thrown from his horse in Hyde Park; this is a commemorative of the time.

**1185** Vitruvian scroll and alphabet border, with black line to the edge and a sepia print of 'WELLINGTON AS PRIME MINISTER'. • No mark • 7¼ ins. diam.
Probably Godwin, Burslem.
Wellington was prime minister from 1828–1830; this plate may commemorate his death in 1852.

**1186** Slight rococo edge with border of feathered fronds and florets painted in pink lustre, pale green, yellow, blue and iron red, with a print of 'Queen Victoria' beside a tomb. • No mark • 6¾ ins. diam.

**1187** Wavy edge with indistinctly moulded border of blobbed daisies and a sepia print of the 'DUKE OF WELLINGTON/ Born 30 April 1769/Died 14 Sep. 1852./ ASSAYE WATERLOO./"up, guards, and at them!"'. • No mark • 7¼ ins. diam.
The inscription contains an error: Wellington was baptised on 30 April 1769 but his actual date of birth is in doubt. The quotation 'Up Guards and at them' is apocryphal; the Duke's order was 'Now Maitland [the commander of the Guards] . . . Now's your time!' The battle of Assaye was fought in India in 1803 and was one of Wellington's hardest-fought victories.
This print is based on a painting (and later engraving) by Thomas Jones Barker (1815–1882) of Wellington on the field of Waterloo.

**1188** Octagonal with pink lustred ropetwist edge and dimpled floret border, with a sepia print (painted) of 'LORD BYRON.' • No mark • 6¼ ins. diam.
This print is based on a portrait by George Sanders (1774–1846), now in the Royal Collection, and engraved by William Finden in 1830; it was used as the frontispiece to Vol I of Byron's *Works* and was adapted for a Victorian song sheet cover.

**1189** Wavy edge and blobbed daisy border with inner row of florets, and a black print of 'SHAKSPERE' [sic]. • No mark; triple footrim • 8¼ ins. diam.
Probably Moore & Co., Wear Pottery, Southwick, Sunderland, 1803–1874.
This print was used on the cover of a school copy book, dated 1856.

SHAKSPERE.

**1190** As 1188 with a black print (painted) of 'THE ROYAL CHRISTENING' watched by an all-seeing eye. • No mark • 6¼ ins. diam.
The christening was that of Princess Victoria, daughter of Queen Victoria, in 1841. The same print is sometimes titled 'THE BISHOP OF HELIOPOLIS' for reasons as yet undiscovered. For a note on this subject, see *Victoria Remembered* by John May (Heinemann, 1983).

1182     1183     1184

1185     1186     1187

1188     1189     1190

**1191** Straight edge and blobbed daisy border with a black print of a boy on a pony: 'ENGLAND'S HOPE/PRINCE OF WALES' as 738. • Mark: an asterisk impressed • 8 ins. diam.
Another Prince of Wales commemorative, an octagonal plate with blobbed daisy border, shows a boy on a pony with two accompanying children and the inscription 'England's future King.'
*Private Collection.*

**1192** Straight edge with moulded garland border and a manganese print of 'LOUIS KOSSUTH/THE HUNGARIAN PATRIOT' (see note to 1207). • Mark: a crescent impressed • 8¾ ins. diam.
The same print was used (in blue) for a plate commemorating the 'DUKE OF CAMBRIDGE/COMMANDER IN CHIEF'. A more convincing image of Kossuth shows him, three-quarter length in an overcoat, with a romantically decorated top hat.
*Private Collection.*

**1193** Rococo edge and moulded border of birds and butterflies painted in iron red, blue, yellow, green and purple, with a sepia print (painted) of the 'MARQUIS OF ANGLESEA K. G.'. • No mark • 7½ ins. diam.
*Private Collection.*

**1194** Slightly wavy edge with rose garland border painted pale blue, yellow and green, with a moulded (and painted) portrait of 'H BROUGHAM Esqr MP'. • No mark • 5¼ ins. diam.
Henry Brougham was Attorney General and defender of Queen Caroline during her trial in 1820. A companion plate commemorates another of her champions, Thomas Denman.
*Private Collection.*

**1195** Straight edge with dog, fox and monkey border and a mauve print advocating 'REFORM' within a decorative garland incorporating a small portrait of 'RUSSELL'. • No mark; double footrim • 6¾ ins. diam.
*Private Collection.*

**1196** Octagonal with rope-twist edge and dimpled floret border with a black print (painted) of 'THE BISHOP OF HELIOPOLIS' (see 1190). • No mark • 6¼ ins. diam.
*Private Collection.*

**1197** Octagonal with herringbone edge and border of florets painted in blue and red, and a black-printed portrait of 'LORD ALTHORPE'. • No mark • 7½ ins. diam.
John Charles Spencer, Viscount Althorpe (1782–1845) was Chancellor of the Exchequer in the Whig parliament of 1830.
*Private Collection.*

**1198** Erratic edge and moulded garland border painted in bright colours, and a printed portrait of Daniel O'Connell. • No mark; double footrim • 6½ ins. diam.
This was O'Connell (1775–1847), the Irish patriot, charismatic anti-unionist and campaigner for Catholic emancipation.
*Private Collection.*

**1199** As 1197 with a parody of verse 2 of the National Anthem within a decorated border: 'Confound the Bishoprics/Frustrate their knavish tricks/On BILL our hopes we fix/God save the King!' • No mark; double footrim • 7½ ins. diam.
*Private Collection.*
Octagonal plate with dimpled floret border and a black print (painted) of 'England's Future King.' (Edward VII). • No marks • 6¾ ins. diam.

Octagonal plate with dimpled floret border and a black print (painted) of 'England's future King.' (Edward VII). • No marks • 6¾ ins. diam.

1191

1192

1193

1194

1195

1196

1197

1198

1199

**1200\*** Slight rococo edge with border of feathered fronds and florets, painted in pink lustre, green, blue, yellow and iron red, with a green print of 'HAMBURG, ANSICHTEN/RATHAUS' (Views of Hamburg – Town Hall). ● Mark: lustre circle ● 6½ ins. diam.

**1201** As 1200 without lustre, and a black print, 'HAMBURG, ANSICHTEN/HAMBURG'S BURGERMILITAIR' (Views of Hamburg – Hamburg People's Army). ● No mark ● 6½ ins. diam.

**1202** As 1200 etc with a red print, 'HAMBURG, ANSICHTEN/DAS DAMMTHOR' (Views of Hamburg – The Dam Gate). ● No mark ● 6½ ins. diam.

**1203** Octagonal with blue rope-twist edge and blobbed floret border, and a black print of 'HAMBURG ANSICHTEN/AUSSICHT VON STINTFANG AUS' (Views of Hamburg – View from the Stintfang). ● No mark ● 7 ins. diam.

**1204** As 1203 with unpainted edge, and a sepia print of 'HAMBURG ANSICHTEN/NEUER JUNGFERNSTIEG' (Views of Hamburg – The New Jungfernstieg). ● No mark ● 7 ins. diam.

**1205** As 1203 etc with a black print of 'HAMBURG ANSICHTEN./DIE ESPLANADE' (Views of Hamburg – The Esplanade). ● No mark ● 7 ins. diam.

**1206** Wavy edge and sectioned border with a blue print of a harbour scene with sailing ships and a paddle steamer: 'COUNTRIES OF EUROPE/GREAT BRITAIN AND IRELAND'. ● Mark: an indecipherable name around a small anchor, impressed, and a printed 2 ● 6½ ins. diam.
Possibly John Carr, Low Lights Pottery, North Shields, Northumberland, circa 1845–1900.

**1207** Twelve-sided, with a black line to the edge and a slightly sectioned border, and a black print of MADAME KOSSUTH AND HER CHILDREN'. ● No mark ● 6¼ ins. diam.
Possibly William Smith, Stafford Pottery, Stockton-on-Tees, 1825–1855.
Madame Kossuth was the wife of the beleaguered Hungarian patriot, Louis Kossuth, who came to England in 1851. This family portrait is based on a daguerreotype by Claudet which was published in the *Illustrated London News* during that year.

MADAME KOSSUTH AND HER CHILDREN.—FROM A DAGUERREOTYPE BY CLAUDET.

**1208** As 1206 with a blue print of a bull-fighting scene: 'COUNTRIES OF EUROPE/FRANCE SPAIN AND PORTUGAL'. ● Mark: indecipherable name around a small anchor, impressed ● 7½ ins. diam.
Possibly John Carr, North Shields.

1200

1201

1202

1203

1204

1205

1206

1207

1208

**1209** Vitruvian scroll and alphabet border with a pale blue edge and a black print of the 'THAMES TUNNEL'. • No mark; double footrim • 5¼ ins. diam.
Probably Thomas Godwin, Canal Works, Navigation Road, Burslem, 1834–1854.
The Thames Tunnel, from Wapping to Rotherhithe, was the first sub-aqueous tunnel ever built, and was the work of Marc Isambard Brunel who invented the tunnel shield (still used for such work) for the project. The tunnel is now in use as part of the Metropolitan Line of the London Underground.

**1210** Octagonal with pink-painted rope-twist edge and dimpled floret border, with a black print (painted) of 'WINDSOR CASTLE.' • No mark • 6½ ins. diam.

**1211** Rococo edge and border of roses, tulips and asters, with a black print of 'THAMES TUNNEL./1200 feet long, 76 feet below high water mark, was 8 years building and cost £446,000. Opened the 25th day of March 1843.' • No mark • 6¼ ins. diam.
Probably Scott, Southwick Pottery, Sunderland.
See note on 1209.
This view of the opening of the Rotherhithe entrance of the Thames Tunnel for foot passengers in 1843 (the carriage-way came later) is taken from a souvenir print of the time – a card printed in coppered ink on glazed paper, issued by 'Brandon, 28 Monkwell St. City'. Such souvenirs as these, and Staffordshire figures inscribed

'Present from the Thames Tunnel' were probably sold from booths near the entrance.

**1212** Rococo edge and border of roses, tulips and asters with two black lines, and a green print of the 'CHURCH OF ST. AUSTELL CORNWALL'. • Mark: EVANS & GLASSON SWANSEA impressed in a triangle (indistinct) • 6¼ ins. diam.
Evans & Glasson, Cambrian Pottery, Swansea, 1850–1862.
This is one of a series of views which included places in Jersey and Guernsey as well as mainland Britain.

**1213** Straight edge with a sepia-printed alphabet and two views of 'FAMOUS PLACES' – Westminster Abbey and the Albert Memorial, London. • Mark: Rd No 26734 B. P. Co • 6½ ins. diam.
Brownhills Pottery, Tunstall, 1872–1896.

**1214** Vitruvian scroll and alphabet border with black edge, and a black print of 'Salisbury Cathedral/A PRESENT FROM SALISBURY'. • No mark; double footrim • 7¼ ins. diam.
Probably Godwin, Burslem.

**1215** Straight edge painted green and tulip, bluebell and wheatear border, and a black print (painted) of 'THE BUILDING FOR THE GREAT EXHIBITION IN LONDON 1851/PROPOSED BY H.R.H. PRINCE ALBERT/DESIGNED BY JOSEPH PAXTON ESQ F.L.S./ERECTED BY FOX, HENDERSON & Co/DIMENSIONS/LENGTH 1848 FEET. WIDTH 456 FEET/HEIGHT OF PRINCIPAL ROOF 66 FEET/HEIGHT OF TRANSEPT 108 FEET/GLAZED SURFACE 900,000 FEET/OCCUPIES 18 ACRES/OF GROUND'. • Mark: J & G MEAKIN impressed • 7½ ins. diam.
J. & G. Meakin, Eagle Pottery and Eastwood Works, Hanley, 1851 onwards.

**1216** Reeded and feathered edge with vertical sprig border crudely painted in dark green, red and blue, with a man-ganese print of 'THE GREAT EXHIBITION OF 1862'. • No mark • 5½ ins. diam.

Possibly Moore & Co., Wear Pottery, Southwick, Sunderland, 1803–1874.
The print shows a view of the exhibition building by Captain Francis Fowke who was later to be one of the designers of the South Kensington Museum (subsequently the V&A) Museum.

**1217** Nearly straight edge with border of pointed-petalled blobbed daisies, and a black print of 'CRYSTAL PALACE 1851.' • Mark: MIDDLESBRO POTTERY in a semi-circle around an anchor, impressed • 6½ ins. diam.
Middlesbrough Pottery Co., Yorkshire, 1834–1844.
The same plate may be found in a larger size.

1209

1210

1211

1212

1213

1214

1215

1216

1217

## THE GREAT EXHIBITION

The plates on this page were souvenirs of the 1851 Exhibition at Crystal Palace, and illustrate some of the sculptures on view. Most are of poor quality and were probably sold very cheaply, in sets or at least pairs.

**1218** Wavy edge painted blue and blobbed daisy border, with a blue print of 'THE HAPPY CHILD'. • No mark • 7 ins. diam.

This figure and its sequel *The Unhappy Child* (1222) were originally executed in marble, life-size, by the Belgian sculptor Simonis.

**1219** Indented and grooved edge with a moulded border with the words 'HONOUR THY FATHER AND MOTHER IN ALL THY DAYS', and a sepia print of Britannia's statue and figures representing different parts of the world, with trophies of industry and the Crystal Palace in the background. • No mark; double footrim • 7½ ins. diam.

**1220** As 1218 with an uncoloured edge, and a blue print of the statue 'INNOCENCE AND FIDELITY'. • Mark: a circle divided into three parts, impressed • 7¼ ins. diam.
This sculpture, and *Gratitude* (1226) and a third, not shown here, of *Cupid and Psyche*, were by G. M. Benzoni. They were modelled in parian as well as being sold in engraved form and in such ceramic translations as this.

**1221** Wavy edge with blobbed daisy border and a sepia print of a sculpture depicting the 'MASSACRE OF THE INNOCENTS/1851 EXHIBITION.' • Mark: impressed crown • 7¾ ins. diam.
Possibly Middlesbrough.
The sculptor was Henry Wiles.

**1222** Straight grooved edge with moulded border of leaves and flower sprays, clumsily painted in dark green, blue, red and black, with a black print of the sculpture 'Boy with broken Drum.' • No mark • 8½ ins. diam.

This figure, sometimes called *The Unhappy Child*, is the sequel to *The Happy Child* (1218): 'The boy has broken his drum, and, in a violent fit of temper has kicked his clothing about his feet till they have become entangled, and add to his ebullition of rage. The work is most truthful.' [*Art Journal Catalogue of the Great Exhibition, 1851*].

**1223** As 1221 with a sepia print of 'Boy with broken Drum/1851 EXHIBITION.' • Mark: impressed crown • 7¾ ins. diam. See note for 1222.
Versions of this print are to be found on plates with moulded wheatear borders and on daisy-bordered plates as 1224; the latter may have an impressed asterisk mark.

**1224** Nearly straight edge with indistinctly moulded blobbed daisy border and a sepia print of a child with a large dog and a snake: 'THE DEFENDER'. • Mark: a circle divided into three parts, impressed • 6 ins. diam.

This group, also called *The Attack*, and its sequel *The Deliverer* were by the French sculptor, Lechesne. The *Art Journal Catalogue* of the exhibition praised the 'vigour with which the story is told by the sculptor. A boy is accompanied by his dog, both are attacked by a serpent, but the faithful animal is on the defensive, and destroys the reptile.' In *The Deliverer* 'The dog has destroyed the aggressive serpent, and is receiving the caresses of the boy who has been saved by his prowess.'
*The Defender* and *The Deliverer* were also reproduced as Staffordshire figures.

**1225** Rococo edge and border of strap-work and cartouches enclosing posies of flowers, and a sepia print of 'THE DELIVERER/1851 EXHIBITION.' • Mark: NORTH SHORE POTTERY and initials, in a semicircle, impressed indistinctly • 8 ins. diam.
William Smith junior, North Shore Pottery, Stockton-on-Tees, 1845–1884.
See note on 1224.

1218      1219      1220

1221      1222      1223

1224      1225      1226

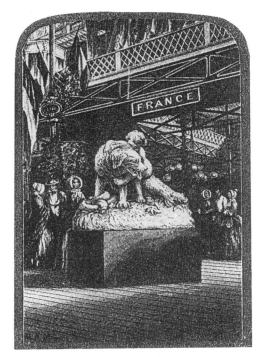

**1226** Edge and border as 1224 with a black print of 'GRATITUDE'. • No mark; double footrim • 5½ ins. diam.
See note for 1220.

**1227** Rococo edge and border of florets and leaves in compartments painted green, red and yellow, with a green print of 'THE KING OF PERSIA'. • No mark • 7¼ ins. diam.
*Private Collection.*

**1228** Octagonal with rope-twist edge and blobbed round-petalled daisy border, with a sepia print of 'WOMEN ON CAMELS'. • No mark • 5¾ ins. diam.
Another version of this image, entitled 'MOUNTED CAMELS' occurs on a wavy-edged octagonal plate with a wide patterned border by Bailey & Ball.

**1229** Straight edge and plain border painted with two blue lines, and a black print of 'A TURKISH POULTRY SELLER'. • Mark: TURNBULL impressed • 7½ ins. diam.

Turnbull, Stepney Pottery, Newcastle, 1863–1875.

**1230** Indistinctly moulded alphabet border with a sepia print (painted) of the 'MARINE RAILWAY STATION. MANHATTON [sic] BEACH HOTEL.' • No mark • 7 ins. diam.
Probably Allerton, Longton, 1859–1942.
This plate is one of a series showing great American hotels and other views, for the export trade.

**1231** Octagonal with pink rope-twist edge and border of line-petalled blobbed daisies, and a sepia print (painted) showing 'MARRIAGE DRESS/RUSSIANS'. • No mark • 7 ins. diam.

**1232** Rococo edge with border of pendant lambrequins and birds painted red, green and yellow, and a blue print showing 'MARRIAGE DRESS/ILLYRIANS'. • No mark • 7¼ ins. diam.

**1233** Erratic edge with red line and border of moulded flower sprigs, with a sepia print (painted) showing 'MARRIAGE DRESS/TURKS'. • No mark • 5¾ ins. diam.
*Private Collection.*

**1234** As 1233 with a sepia print (painted) of 'MARRIAGE DRESS/SCOTCH'. • No mark • 5¾ ins. diam.
*Private Collection.*

**1235** As 1233 etc with a sepia print (painted) of 'MARRIAGE DRESS/SPANIARDS'. • No mark • 5¾ ins. diam.
*Private Collection.*

1227     THE KING OF PERSIA.

1228

1229     A TURKISH POULTRY SELLER

1230

1231     MARRIAGE DRESS    RUSSIANS

1232     MARRIAGE DRESS    ILLYRIANS

1233     MARRIAGE DRESS    TURKS

1234     MARRIAGE DRESS    SCOTCH

1235     MARRIAGE DRESS    SPANIARDS

**1236** Finely potted octagonal, with rope-twist edge and border of dimpled florets painted in dark green, blue and mauve, and a black print of a statue of 'WILLIAM III/NO SURRENDER 1690'. • Mark 11/32 impressed, probably for the date (November 1832); double footrim • 5½ ins. diam.

A version of this print was used by E. C. Challinor, Tunstall, 1842–1867.

This plate commemorates the Battle of the Boyne and was probably made for the Orange Society of Northern Ireland, first established in 1794. In 1826 political societies were banned in Ireland, but they were revived in 1828. The Duke of Cumberland became Grand Master of the Orange Society, which had 175,000 members in Ireland and 140,000 in England, Wales and Scotland.

**1237** Straight edge with indistinctly moulded border of swagged garlands, roses and honeysuckle, painted without regard for the moulding with tulips and leaves in iron red, green and brown. The sepia print (painted) shows a couple marrying before a blacksmith, outside the smithy: 'THE NEW MARRIAGE ACT'. • No mark • 6¼ ins. diam.

This print illustrates a marriage at Gretna Green, just over the Scottish border from Carlisle. In Scotland the marriage contract (until 1856) merely required that a couple declared their willingness to marry before a witness. Elopers reaching Gretna Green, and traditionally the blacksmith's forge there, were thus able legally to marry without licence, banns, or priest. An Act was passed in 1856 requiring that at least one of the couple should be resident in Scotland for 21 days or more before a marriage could take place, so Gretna Green became obsolete as a place for shotgun weddings.

**1238** Rococo edge with border of birds and pendant lambrequins, the birds painted in pale green, yellow and blue, and a sepia print of a statue: 'WILLIAM III/No surrender'. • No mark • 5½ ins. diam. See note for 1236.

THE ANTI-CORN LAW LEAGUE

The following three plates represent the Anti-Corn-Law campaign of the 1830s and 40s. The Anti-Corn-Law League, formed in 1838 and headed by Richard Cobden and John Bright, focused working-class agitation against the high price of (taxed) corn and campaigned for free trade in every commodity – the freedom to buy in the cheapest market and to sell in the dearest, without restriction. The League gathered many supporters, through its travelling orators, pamphlets and even such means as children's plates, but the Irish potato famine of the 1840s eventually provided the most cogent reason to suspend the Corn Laws and abolish the duties on imported foodstuffs.

Like the temperance movement, the Anti-Corn-Law League attacked fundamental aspects of the 19th century establishment. It was a largely Liberal campaign, motivated by ideals of free trade: many members of the anti-spirits movement in the 1830s were also free traders and members of the Anti-Corn-Law League.

**1239** Octagonal with pink lustred rope-twist edge and dimpled floret border with a black print (painted) of a harbour scene, with pennons inscribed 'NO MONOPOLY' and 'Free Trade'; a sack labelled 'CHEAP CORN', and 'CORN LAW' written on a torn sheet of paper. • No mark • 6¼ ins. diam.

**1240** Straight edge and blobbed daisy border with a sepia print (crudely painted) of a sailing ship with a barrel and crates in the foreground: 'COMMERCE./The Staffordshire Potteries/And free trade with all the world.' • No mark • 5½ ins. diam.

**1241** As 1239 with a black print (painted) of farming implements within and around a flower-decked cartouche with the super-scription, 'OUR BREAD UNTAXED OUR COMMERCE FREE'. • No mark • 6¼ ins. diam.

This print may be found on larger octagonal plates with blobbed daisy borders.

**1242** Wavy edge and border of blobbed, round-petalled daisies, with a manganese print (painted) of a row of shops, one titled 'TEA WAREHOUSE WARD'. • Mark: G 5 impressed, and J. WARDLE, CHINA MANUFACTURER. MIDDLESBRO in a printed garter mark.

An earthenware dealer named John Wardle is recorded as having premises in the Market-place, Middlesbrough in 1871; he may be the same John Wardle who ran the Denaby Pottery, near Mexborough, Yorkshire, during the 1860s, subsequently moving to Middlesbrough and producing wares transfer-printed with scenes of local interest.

**1243** Slight rococo edge with border of feathered fronds and florets, painted in pink lustre, iron red, blue, yellow and green, with a blue print of the 'GREAT WESTERN STEAM SHIP./Length 236 Feet Breadth 58⅓ Feet'. • Mark: a pink lustre line and two dots • 6½ ins. diam.

**1244** Wavy edge and blobbed daisy border, with a black print of the English and French flags surmounting clasped hands and 'CRIMEA', with the inscription, 'GOD SAVE THE QUEEN/MAY THEY EVER BE UNITED/VIVE L'EMPEREUR/ALMA/INKERMAN/BALACLAVA.' • No mark • 5¾ ins. diam.

A plate commemorating the alliance between England and France during the Crimean War of 1854–1856.

1236

1237

1238

1239

1240

1241

1242

1243

1244

**1245** Cylindrical with spurred ear-shaped handle and a blue-printed tablet with the inscription: 'Should the Corsican Tyrant/Set foot on our Shore/We'll play him such a Hornpipe/He ne'r danc'd before.' • No mark • 2⅜ ins. diam. ht.; 2⅜ ins. diam.
This is a defiant reference to Napoleon's promised invasion of Britain in 1804.

**1246** Cylindrical with loop handle and leaf terminals, and a blue-printed rectangular inscription, 'May British thunder/On her foes be hurld/And ENGLAND prove the market of the World'. • No mark • 2½ ins. ht.; 2⅜ ins. diam.
This is an anti-Napoleon slogan with Free Trade propaganda thrown in.

**1247** Cylindrical with loop handle and leaf terminals, and a sepia print (painted) of a portrait of 'WASHINGTON' in a medallion with flanking flags and the dates '1776' and '187(?)6'. • No mark • 2¾ ins. ht.; 2¾ ins. diam.
This commemorates the Washington centennial of 1876.

**1248** Shaped base and top rim, with loop handle and black prints (washed with

blue) of the mounted Duke of Wellington, 'THE DUKE AT WATERLOO' on one side and a view of 'WALMER CASTLE KENT' on the other. • No mark • 2¾ ins. ht.; 3 ins. diam.
The Duke of Wellington died at Walmer Castle in 1852. He was Lord Warden of the Cinque Ports and Walmer Castle was his favourite residence. This mug probably commemorates his death.
The print on the front of the mug, showing the Duke on horseback carrying a telescope, is reminiscent of the statue of Wellington by Matthew Cotes Wyatt and his son James, originally placed on top of Decimus Burton's arch at Hyde Park Corner, but later removed to Aldershot.

**1249** Porcelain with shaped base and spurred, ear-shaped handle, with purple lustre decoration and manganese prints (painted) of a coronetted boy flying a kite in front of a castle (possibly Windsor) on one side, and a girl with a dog in a bower on the other. • No mark • 2½ ins. ht.; 2¼ ins. diam.

**1248** The opposite side.

**1249** The opposite side.

**1250** Pearlware plate, border moulded with continuous garland of leaves and flowers, and a grey print of 'PRINCE LEOPOLD' (husband of Princess Charlotte, the daughter of George IV). He was the first King of the Belgians and Queen Victoria's uncle. • No mark • 5½ ins. diam.
*Private Collection.*

**1251** Straight edge with a moulded border of doves in flight bearing branches of olive between foliate scroll work, and a brown print of Louis Napoleon on horse back: 'LOUIS NAPOLEON/MY UNCLE'S NEPHEW/LIBERTY EQUALITY FRATERNITY'. • No mark • 7½ ins. diam.

Should the CorsicanTyrant
Set foot on our Shore
We'll play him such a Horn
He ne'r danc'd before

1245

May British thun der
On her foes be hurld
And ENGLAND prove
The market of the World

1246

WASHINGTON

1247

THE DUKE AT WATERLOO

1248

1249

WALMER CASTLE KENT

1248

1249

PRINCE LEOPOLD.

1250

LOUIS NAPOLEON
MY UNCLE'S NEPHEW

LIBERTY EQUALITY FRATERNITY

1251

# SELECT BIBLIOGRAPHY

Baker, John C., *Sunderland Pottery* (Tyne & Wear County Council Museums 1984).

Bell, R. C., *Tyneside Pottery (Studio Vista, 1971)*.

*Chalala, M. & J. A Collector's Guide to ABC Plates, Mugs and Things* (Pridemark Press, Lancaster, Pennsylvania, 1980).

Clarke, H. G., *The Pictorial Pot Lid Book* (Courier Press, London, 1955).

Cox, Alwyn & Angela, *Rockingham Pottery and Porcelain* (Faber & Faber 1983).

Coysh, A. W. & Henrywood, R. K., *The Dictionary of Blue and White Printed Pottery*, 1780–1880 Vol I (Antique Collectors Club, 1982) and Vol II (Antique Collectors Club, 1989).

Flick, Pauline, *Children's China* (Constable, 1983).

Godden, Geoffrey, *Encyclopaedia of British Pottery and Porcelain Marks* (Barrie & Jenkins, 1964).

Haggar, R. G., Mountford, A. R. and Thomas, J., *The Staffordshire Pottery Industry* (Reprinted from the *Victoria History of the County of Stafford* by Staffordshire County Library, 1981).

Harrison, Brian, *Drink and the Victorians*, (Faber & Faber, 1971).

Hillier, Bevis, *Pottery and Porcelain 1700–1914* (Weidenfeld and Nicolson, 1968).

Hughes, Gareth and Pugh, Robert, *Llanelly Pottery* (Llanelly Borough Council, 1990).

Lawrence, Heather, *Yorkshire Pots and Potters* (David & Charles, 1974).

Lewis, Griselda, *A Collector's History of English Pottery* (Studio Vista, 1969).

Little, W. L., *Staffordshire Blue* (Batsford, 1969).

Lockett, T., & Godden, G., *Davenport* (Barrie & Jenkins, 1989).

May, John, *Commemorative Pottery 1780–1900* (Heinemann, 1972).

May, John, *Victoria Remembered* (Heinemann 1983).

McLean, Ruari, *Victorian Book Design* (Faber & Faber, 1963).

Milbourne, M. & E., *Understanding Miniature British Pottery & Porcelain 1730–Present Day* (Antique Collectors Club, 1983).

Moon, Marjorie, *The Children's Books of Mary (Belson) Elliott – a bibliography* (St Paul's Bibliographies, 1987).

Moore, Steven & Ross, Catharine, *Maling* (Tyne & Wear Museums Service, 1989).

Muir, Percy, *English Children's Books* (Batsford, 1954, fourth impression, 1985).

Nance, E. Morton, *The Pottery and Porcelain of Swansea and Nantgarw* (Batsford, 1942).

Oliver, Anthony, *The Victorian Staffordshire Figure* (Heinemann, 1971).

Opie, Iona & Peter, *The Oxford Dictionary of Nursery Rhymes* (Oxford University Press, 1951 & subs.).

Pugh, P. D. Gordon, *Staffordshire Portrait Figures* (Antique Collectors Club, 1987).

Quayle, Eric, *The Collector's Book of Children's Books* (Studio Vista, 1971).

Ray, Anthony, *English Delftware Tiles* (Faber & Faber, 1973).

Vries, Leonard de, *Flowers of Delight* (Dennis Dobson, 1965).

Vries, Leonard de, *A Treasury of Illustrated Children's Books* (Abbeville Press, New York, 1989).

Whalley, Joyce Irene & Chester, Tessa, *A History of Children's Book Illustration* (John Murray/V & A, 1988).

Williams, Mary, *The Pottery That Began Middlesbrough* (C Books, Redcar, 1985).

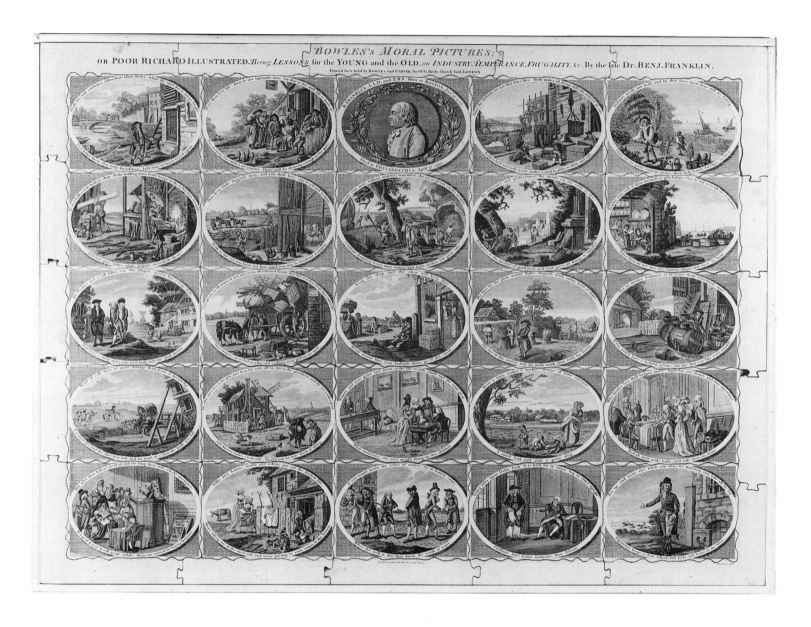

A picture sheet/jigsaw puzzle comprising 24 scenes of town and country life, illustrating Benjamin Franklin's 'LESSONS for the YOUNG and the OLD, on INDUSTRY, TEMPERANCE, FRUGALITY &c' by the artist Robert Dighton, published by Bowles and Carver, London 1795.